HIJRAH

THE ESTABLISHMENT OF THE FIRST ISLAMIC STATE

MEDINA PERIOD (623-632)

THE QURAN: IN EASY-TO-UNDERSTAND FORMAT SERIES

VOLUME 4

FAROOQ MIRZA

The first-ever rendition of the Quran

According to specific topics and the subject matter

A new paradigm in understanding the Quran

From

The Quran Foundation

Copyright © 2024 Farooq Mirza

All rights reserved.

No part of this book may be reproduced, stored in a retrieval system, or transmitted, in any form or by any means, electronic, mechanical, photocopying, recording, or otherwise, without prior written permission from the publisher, except for brief quotations embodied in critical reviews and certain other noncommercial uses permitted by copyright law.

Printed in the United States of America

DEDICATION

The seven-volume book series about the Quran is dedicated to the memory of Muhammad Asad, whose work, *"The Message of the Qur'an,"* was the first-ever attempt at an idiomatic, explanatory rendition of the Quranic message in English. In my opinion, it is the best translation and commentary on the Holy Quran.

Muhammad Asad was born Leopold Weiss in July 1900 in Lviv, now Ukraine. He was the descendant of a long line of rabbis, a line broken by his father, who became a barrister. Asad himself received a thorough religious education that would qualify him to keep alive the family's religious tradition. He left Europe for the Middle East in 1922 for what was supposed to be a short visit to an uncle in Jerusalem. There, he came to know the Arabs and was struck by how Islam infused their everyday lives with existential meaning, spiritual strength, and inner peace. Weiss then became, at the remarkably young age of twenty-two, a correspondent for *The Frankfurter Zeitung*, one of the most prestigious newspapers in Germany and across Europe. As a journalist, he traveled extensively, mingled with ordinary people, held discussions with Muslim intellectuals, and met heads of state in Palestine, Egypt, Transjordan, Syria, Iraq, Iran, and Afghanistan.

Back in Berlin from the Middle East, a few years later, Weiss underwent an electrifying spiritual epiphany—reminiscent of the experiences of some of the earliest Muslims—that changed his mind and his life. "Out of the Quran spoke a voice greater than the voice of Muhammad," Weiss said. Thus, it was that Weiss became a Muslim. He converted in Berlin before the head of a small Muslim community in the city. He took the name Muhammad to honor the Prophet and Asad—meaning "lion"—a reminder of his given name, Leopold, which is derived from the Latin word for lion. Asad spent some six years in the holy cities of Mecca and Medina, where he studied Arabic, the Quran, and the "Hadith"—the traditions of the

Prophet and Islamic history. He mastered the Arabic language not only through academic study but also by living with a tribe that spoke the Arabic dialect of the Holy Quran. At the age of eighty, after seventeen years of effort, he completed his life's dream, for which he felt all his life had been an apprenticeship: a translation and exegesis, or "tafsir," of the Quran in English: *The Message of the Qur'an*.

TABLE OF CONTENTS

Part 1 The Formation Of Secular Ummah

Chapter 1 Hijrah (Migration To Medina) 2
Chapter 2 The Constitution Of Medina 10
Chapter 3 Impacts Of The Constitution Of Medina 20

The True Believers And The Hypocrites

Chapter 4 The True Believers (Among Emigrants, Ansars, And Bedouins) 26
Chapter 5 The Definition And Origin Of Hypocrisy In Islam 34
Chapter 6 The Characteristics Of Hypocrites 40
Chapter 7 Dealing With The Hypocrites 47
Chapter 8 The Punishment For The Hypocrites 52

The Jews Of Medina

Chapter 9 The Arabian Jews 58
Chapter 10 The Jewish Opposition 64

The Quranic Rebuttal To Jewish Polemics

Chapter 11 God's Chosen People: Spirtual Versus Inherited? 70
Chapter 12 The Quranic Rebuttal Of The Racially Based Chosenness . 79
Chapter 13 The Errors Of The Jews (Continued) 87
Chapter 14 The Consequences Of Breaking The Covenant 94
Chapter 15 Islam Is A False Religion? 99
Chapter 16 Why Rejection Of Muhammad's Prophethood? 104
Chapter 17 The Quran Is Not God's Speech 115
Chapter 18 Demand For Supernatural Proofs 124
Chapter 19 The Errors Of Rabbis, Monks, And Islamic Clerks 126
Chapter 20 Greed, Arrogance, And False Pride 128

Chapter 21 The Denial Of Afterlife 134

Forging Unity Among Monotheists

Chapter 22 The Divine Law Of Diversity 139

Chapter 23 The Common Beliefs Among Jews, Christians, And Muslims 145

Chapter 24 Evil Of Sectarianism 157

Chapter 25 Anti-Semitism 163

Chapter 26 Sectarianism Among Muslims 168

Chapter 27 The Rightly Guided Caliphs 179

Chapter 28 The Karabla Tragedy And Ideological Differences Between Shiah And Sunni 194

Chapter 27 Doctrine Of Salvation And Call For Unity 201

Part 2 The Prophet's Marriages And The Tribute To The Prophet

Chapter 28 The Prophet Pattern Of Marriages 207

Chapter 29 The Marriage To Aishah 213

Chapter 30 Marriage To Zaynab Bint Jahsh 222

Chapter 31 The Marital Laws Exclusive To The Prophet 231

Chapter 32 Why Muhammad, The Greatest Man Ever Lived 241

Chapter 33 The Final Sermon 248

Chapter 34 Famous Non-Muslims Tribute To The Prophet 253

References 259

PART 1
THE FORMATION OF SECULAR UMMAH

(TRUE BELIEVERS, HYPOCRITES, JEWS, AND PAGANS)

CHAPTER 1
HIJRAH (MIGRATION TO MEDINA)

The major historical events during the lifetime of the Prophet Muhammad are well documented in the Quran. The battles fought by Muslims against the pagan Arabs are described in volume five of the Quran series. This chapter provides background information and context to properly understand these events.

The period just before he moved to Medina, the Prophet faced the severest career crisis and had to hide in caves, escape in disguise, and fly hither and thither, homeless, in continual peril of his life. More than once, it seemed all over with him. More than once, it turned on a straw. Whether Prophet Muhammad and his doctrine had not ended or heard, it was not to end.

ESCAPE FROM MECCA

And [remember, O Prophet] how those bent on denying the truth were scheming against thee, restraining thee [from preaching], slaying thee or driving thee away. Thus, they [always] conspired. God brought their scheming to failure—for God is above all schemers. (8:30)

Those who deny the truth of divine revelation are always intent on rendering their preachers powerless. They destroy them, either physically or figuratively, through ridicule. The Prophet encouraged his followers to immigrate in small numbers, unnoticed by the leaders of Quraysh. Most of his disciples had left, and the Prophet, Ali, and Abu Bakr remained behind.

PLOT TO KILL THE PROPHET

Fearing the escape of the Prophet, an assembly of the Quraysh chiefs met to decide upon further action. It was proposed to assassinate the Prophet, but the assassin would be exposed to the vengeance of blood by the Hashim clan. Abu Jahl suggested that several men, chosen from different families, should attack the Prophet simultaneously to solve the difficulty. The responsibility of the deed would rest upon all, and the relatives of Muhammad would be unable to avenge it. The assassins were posted around the Prophet's dwelling. They watched through a hole in the door all night, waiting to murder him when he should leave his house in the early dawn. The Prophet confided his plan to Ali ibn Abu Talib and asked him to cover himself with the Prophet's green mantle and sleep in his bed. The killers outside felt reassured whenever they peered through the hole in the door and saw somebody in the bed. Just before dawn, the Prophet slipped away without being noticed. The verse (47:13) below was revealed on the first night of the Prophet's Hijrah from Mecca to Medina.

How many a community of greater power than your community, which has driven you out, [O Muhammad], We have destroyed, with none to succor them! Can he who takes his stand on clear evidence from his Sustainer be likened to one whom the evil of his doings [always] seems goodly, and unto such as would follow but their lusts? (47:13-14)

JABAL THAWR

After fleeing from his home, the Prophet picked up Abu Bakr at his house and traveled southward towards the cave of Thawr, where they hid. They were expected to go northward towards Yathrib, and the southerly direction of their flight was meant to confuse their enemies. For three days, Abu Bakr's son and daughter visited the cave under the cover of night to bring food and water.

The **Cave of Thawr** is very popular with tourists, Hajj and Umrah pilgrims, as it is a symbol of hope and God's mercy for the oppressed. Jabal Thawr is a mountain in Saudi Arabia located about 12 km south of Mecca. It houses the well-known **Cave of Thawr,** also known as Ghar Thawr or Ghar e Soor. The cave had a very narrow entrance, and one can only enter it by crawling. There are several legendary stories associated with this cave:

The snake bite: In this cave, Abu Bakr was bitten by a poisonous snake to his leg, causing excruciating pain. The Prophet applied his saliva, and the wound healed miraculously.

Spider web and a bird nest: It is believed a spider wove a web at the cave entrance and a bird laid her eggs close by as if the cave is empty for a long time. The legend has it that the spider web and a bird nest convinced the pagan Meccans not to investigate any further. Thus, the Prophet and Abu Bakr were saved from getting caught.

MASSIVE MANHUNT

When the Meccan leaders got wind of the exodus, they started a massive manhunt. The horsemen scouring the countryside came so close to discovering them. Abu Bakr was moved to despair and said, "We are but two." The Prophet answered, "No, we are three, for God is with us." The verse 9:40 below alludes to this incident.

FLIGHT TO MEDINA

If you do not succor the Apostle, [Muhammad], then [God will do so. [Just as] God succored him at the time when those bent on denying the truth drove him away, [and he was but] one of two. When these two were [hiding] in the cave, [and], the Apostle said to his companion, "Grieve not God is with us." And thereupon God bestowed upon him from on high His [gift of] inner peace and aided him with forces which you could not see and brought utterly low the cause of those bent on denying the truth, whereas God's cause remained supreme for God is almighty, wise. (9:40)

The Prophet and Abu Bakr procured two camels. Their servant brought the third camel for himself. And three men made their hazardous journey on untrodden paths to the city of their destination. Their servant and guide, Abdullah ibn Urayqit, headed south of Mecca and then to the mountain range of Tihamat, close to the Red Sea's shore. He took an unknown path northward parallel to the coast but far removed from it. His purpose was to remain off the beaten track and reduce the chances of being caught. For seven days, they traveled, lying low during the day's heat and moving with haste under the cover of night until they reached their destination.

CHOICE OF RESIDENCE AND THE MOSQUE

After about nine days of traveling, the Prophet and Abu Bakr reached the outskirts of Medina's oasis on September 24th, 622. When the Prophet arrived in Medina on his camel, he decided not to choose the site of his house. The spot where his camel stopped was chosen for his future home. The purpose was to avoid the appearance of siding with one faction or another. It was a plot of land that belonged to two orphans. The Prophet obtained lodging in a neighboring house, paid the orphans, and built his home. He assisted in the building process with his own hands. The Prophet and his wives lived in small huts around the courtyard's edge. A simple building, the mosque expressed the austerity of early Islamic ideals. A portion of the mosque was set aside as a shelter for the homeless.

THE SIGNIFICANCE OF HIJRAH

Physical and Spiritual Hijrah: The term Hijrah (lit., "exodus"), derived from the verb *hajara* ("he migrated"), is used in the Quran in two senses: the historical sense, which denotes the departure of the Prophet and his Companions from Mecca to Medina, while the other has a moral connotation—namely, man's "Exodus" from evil towards God, which does not necessarily imply the leaving of one's homeland in the physical sense.

O you servants of Mine who have attained faith! Wide is My earth: worship Me, then, Me alone! (29:56) O, you who have attained faith! Remember the blessings God bestowed upon you when [hostile] people were about to lay hands on you, and He stayed their hands from you. Be conscious of God, and in God, let the believers place their trust. (5:11) And [remember] vast is God's earth [and] they who are patient in adversity will be given their reward in full, beyond all reckoning! (39:10)

When the freedom of religion is denied, the believers must "forsake the domain of evil." Thus, the believers must "migrate toward God" to live by their faith, which is the spiritual connotation of the concept of Hijrah. Since the earth offers multiple facilities to human life, there is no excuse for forgetting God due to the pressure of adverse circumstances.

ISOLATION AND LONELINESS

And he who forsakes the domain of evil for the sake of God shall find on earth many a lonely road, as well as life abundant. And if anyone leaves his home, fleeing from evil unto God and His Apostle, and then death overtakes him—his reward awaits him with God. God is indeed much-forgiving, a dispenser of grace. (4:100)

For those who leave their loved ones behind against their will, the separation from one's familiar environment is described as the "breaking off" or the "cutting off from friendly or living communion." All this can best be rendered as "a lonely road"—a metaphor for the heartbreaking loneliness that accompanies the first steps of one who sets forth on his departure from evil unto God.

REMAINING STEADFAST DURING PERSECUTION

Those who forsake the domain of evil in the cause of God, after having suffered wrong [on account of their faith]—We shall most certainly grant them a station of good fortune in this world. But their reward in the life to come will be far greater yet. If they [who deny the truth] could understand that, but those who attained patience in adversity and placed their trust in their Sustainer!" (16:41-42)

If the truth deniers could understand the believers' spiritual motivation, they would begin to believe.

ISLAMIC CALENDAR

The Hijrah marks the end of the pre-Islamic era of ignorance and the Islamic age of enlightenment. The Hijrah is the basis of Islamic chronology, but the reckoning commences on the first day of the Arab year. Muslims chose to date their history from neither the Prophet's birth date nor his reception of the first revelation in 610 but from the creation of the Islamic community (Ummah). With this migration, the Meccan period ended, and another, the Medinese, began with the advent of a new revolution in the world's history.

TRANSFORMATION OF THE PROPHET'S LEADERSHIP

The migration marked a turning point in the Prophet's fortunes and a defining stage in the Islamic movement's history. The city of Medina lacked the unified leadership exercised in Mecca by the Umayyads, which favored a forthcoming leader. Also, contact with the Jews familiarized the Arabs of Medina with the concept of an inspired religious leader.

THE CITY OF MEDINA

The city of Medina is about two hundred miles north of Mecca. It was not a commercial center like Mecca. Its main livelihood was agriculture, where farmers lived by cultivating date palms. The city of Medina was also in a transition state, passing from a nomadic to an urban culture, with concomitant dislocation in the economic, social, and psychological structures. The city was established by an Amalekite chief, whose name it bore until the Prophet's arrival. Yathrib changed its ancient name and was henceforth styled Medinat an-Nabi, "the city of the Prophet," or, in short, Medina, the city par excellence because it became the pattern of the exemplary Muslim society.

Demographics: Its population structure comprised two mighty Arab tribes—the Al Aws and Al Khazraj. Both tribes were linked to each other through blood but were constantly at odds, occasionally taking up arms. Medina's population also included the three Jewish tribes (Qurayzah, Nadir, and Qaynuqa) and some other minor Jewish clans. During the conflict between two Arab tribes, the Jews regularly shifted their allegiance from one faction to the other.

THE BATTLE OF BUATH

There had been ongoing fighting in the oasis for nearly a hundred years before 620. At first, it had been between single clans; then, clans joined together in larger groups. In 618, there was a great battle at Buath, and nearly all the clans of Oasis were involved. There had been heavy slaughter in this battle, and though fighting had ceased, there had been no agreement about the resulting claims for blood money or compensation. More moderate men on both sides believed they needed a chief who would unite them as Qusayy had united the Quraysh. One of the most powerful men in the oasis, **Abd Allah bin Ubayy**, had, along with his clan, remained neutral at Buath. He hoped to become such an adjudicator acceptable to all. He belonged to Khazraj, and it was doubtful whether Aws would accept him as a king. The arrival of Muhammad doomed whatever chances Abd Allah bin Ubayy had to become king of Medina.

PROPHET MUHAMMAD TO ADJUDICATE DISPUTES

Medinese needed one impartial man with authority to adjudicate in disputed cases.

Muhammad was invited by a delegation from Yathrib to serve as chief arbitrator or judge in a bitter feud between its two Arab tribes. They must have known that a neutral outsider to Medina, like Muhammad, would be in a better position to act as an impartial arbiter than any Medina resident. Muhammad's conflict resolution skills were known far and wide. Earlier during the Mecca period, while rebuilding the Kabah (destroyed during a flood), a dispute broke out among various clans about who would have the honor of placing the Black Stone, a celestial object, in its place. Muhammad mediated the dispute successfully and averted bloodshed. This incident probably was one of the main reasons Muhammad was selected as a chief arbitrator or judge in a bitter feud between Arab tribes.

CHAPTER 2
THE CONSTITUTION OF MEDINA

TRANSITION FROM TRIBAL TO IDEOLOGICAL SOCIETY

Medina was bitterly divided, with occasional bursts of violence and bloodshed. Forging unity was the need of the hour. The main goal was to create some semblance of harmony in this war-torn community. The initial purpose of the agreement was to mediate the tribal conflicts raging in Medina and to begin the transition from pre-Islamic kinship or family ties, to the ideological institution of Islamic ummah. The intent was to eliminate old intertribal intrigues based on kinship. It began the process of creating a single community among diverse religious and tribal groups.

THE SECULAR NATURE OF THE DOCUMENT

The Medina agreement was a document outlining the formal responsibilities that governed the relationship between Medina inhabitants after the Prophet's arrival. The agreement detailed no religious requirements. The contracting parties did not embrace Islam but agreed to recognize the Prophet's authority as the community leader and abide by his political judgments. Despite the religious tone of the agreement, it established a single, common, political community made up of Muslims, Jews, and idolaters.

Religious Freedom: He incorporated the principle of religious freedom, the first charter of freedom of conscience in human history. It was a breakthrough in political and civil life against exploitation, tyranny, and corruption.

The Constitution of Medina, which the Prophet wrote down fourteen centuries ago, established the inviolability of the city and human life. The agreement outlined political and military responsibilities ranging from blood money payment to mutual defense against outside aggression.

FORMATION OF A SECULAR UMMAH

In the name of God, the Beneficent and the Merciful.

(1-2): This is a prescript of Muhammad (the Prophet and Messenger of God) concerning the Quraysh and the people of Medina and those who follow them, are attached to them, and strive with them. They shall constitute a separate political unit (Ummah) distinguished from all the people (of the world).

The constitution of Medina establishes an alliance or federation between nine different groups: eight clans from Medina and the clan of Emigrants from the Quraysh of Mecca. The Jews were later included in the Ummah.

And, verily, this Ummah of yours is one single Ummah since I am the Sustainer of you all. (23:52)

Ummah in Arabic means "community" formed of common and coherent features.

The centrality of unity, both divine and human, is reflected in the importance of community, or ummah.

TREATING WAR PRISONERS WITH KINDNESS

(3-11) Quraysh emigrants are responsible for owning their ward, and they must pay their blood money in collaboration with each other and pay ransom for their own prisoners. This is so that mutual dealings between believers comply with goodness and justice. And Banu Awf, Banu Al-Harith-ibn-Khazraj, Banu Saida, Banu Jusham, Banu an-Najjar, Banu Amr-ibn-Awf, Banu-al-Nabit, and Banu-al-Aws shall be responsible for their own ward and shall pay their blood money in mutual collaboration, and every group

shall secure the release of its own prisoners by paying their ransom from themselves so that the dealings between the believers will be in accordance with the principles of goodness and justice.

Every clan shall ransom its prisoners with kindness and justice common among believers. The Muhajirun from Quraysh are bound together and ransom their prisoners in kindness and justice as believers do. Following their custom, Banu Awf is bound together as before. (The text here repeats the same prescription concerning every clan of Muslims in Medina.)

CARING FOR THE POOR

***(12) (a)** And the believers shall not leave anyone hard-pressed with debts, without affording him some relief, in order that the dealings between the believers be in accordance with the principles of goodness and justice.*

Neither believers nor their followers should leave any of their members in destitution without giving them what they need.

***(b)** Also, no believer shall enter a contract of clientage with one who is already in such a contract with another believer.*

UNITY AMONG BELIEVERS AGAINST INJUSTICES

***(13)** And the hands of pious believers shall be raised against anyone who rises in rebellion or attempts to acquire anything by force or is guilty of any sin or excess or attempts to spread mischief among the believers; their hands shall be raised all together against such a person, even if he be a son to any one of them.*

***(14)** A Believer will not kill a Believer [in retaliation] for a non-Believer and will not aid a non-Believer against a Believer.*

(15) *Allah's protection is one. The least of them* [i.e., the Believers] *can, by extending his protection to anyone, put the obligation on all; believers are each other's allies to the exclusion of others.*

(16) And those who obey us among the Jews will have help and equality. They will not be oppressed, nor will help be given against them.

All believers shall rise as one man against anyone who rebels or seeks to commit injustice, aggression, sin, or spread mutual enmity between the believers. This is even though he is one of their sons. Article 14 refers to revenge killings, so much part of pre-Islamic life continued during the Islamic period. The major difference was that kinship was no longer the determinant factor. This article is meant to establish a new mode of relationship based on believer versus non-believer. No believer shall slay a believer in retaliation for an unbeliever; neither shall he assist an unbeliever against a believer. Just as God's bond is one and indivisible, all believers shall stand behind the commitment of the least of them. All believers are bonded to one another to the exclusion of other men. Any Jew who follows us is entitled to our assistance and the same rights as anyone else of us, without injustice or partisanship. This Pax Islamica is one and indivisible.

WAR IN GOD'S WAY

(17) And the peace of believers shall be one. If there be any war in God's way, no believer shall be under any peace (with the enemy) apart from other believers unless it (this peace) be the same and equally binding on all.

(18) And all those detachments that will fight on our side will be relieved periodically.

(19) And the believers as a body shall take blood vengeance in God's way.

The state of peace shall be common to all Muslims; no individual shall have the right to conclude peace with their enemies. When fighting for God's cause, no believer shall enter a separate peace apart from those sharing the same faith. However, they will do so only based on equality and justice for all. The idiom "in the path of God" is a qualifying phrase and it makes a distinction between fighting in the path of God for which there must be absolute solidarity between believers. Unbelievers who sign the document are exempt from fighting "in the path of God". However, in defending Medina, both believers and non-believers must be equally responsible. Those dedicated to the same objective must accompany our members on every military expedition. In the fight for God's cause, all believers must avenge one another's blood whenever someone falls.

(20) (a) And pious believers are the best and in the right course. (b) And that no associator shall protect the life and property of a Qurayshite, nor shall he come in the way of any believer in this matter.

No unbeliever shall be allowed to place under his protection against a believer's interest in any wealth or person belonging to Quraysh.

UNJUST KILLINGS

(21) And if someone intentionally murders a believer, and it is proved, he shall be killed in retaliation, unless the murdered person's heirs be satisfied with blood money. And all believers must stand for this ordinance, and nothing else is proper.

(22) And it shall not be lawful for anyone, who has agreed to carry out the provisions laid down in this code and has affixed his faith in God and the Day of Judgment, to give help or protection to any murderer, and if he gives any help or protection to such a person, God's curse and wrath shall be on him on the Day of Resurrection,

and no money or compensation shall be accepted from such a person.

"Whoever is convicted of killing a believer deliberately but without a righteous cause shall be liable to the relatives of the killed. The killer shall be retaliated against by every believer until the aggrieved party is satisfied. The killer shall have no rights until this believers' right is satisfied. Whoever has entered this covenant and believed in God and the last day shall never protect or shelter a convict or a criminal. Anyone who does so shall be cursed by God, and divine wrath will fall on the Day of Judgment. Neither repentance nor ransom shall be accepted from him.

MUHAMMAD AS THE CHIEF MAGISTRATE

(23) And that whenever you disagree about anything, you refer to God and Muhammad.

The Prophet had no special power or authority except disputes endangering the oasis' peace must be referred to him. It constituted the Prophet as the chief magistrate of this rudimentary state and established the rule of law. Reference to God and Muhammad in case of disagreement allowed the tribes participating in this pact to retain most of their independent autonomy while resolving disputes peaceably.

RELIGIOUS FREEDOM

(24) And the Jews shall share with the believers the expenses of war so long as they battle together.

This article defines the network of relationships by which community members support each other in war. Here, very specifically, Jews who are considered believers and are party to the agreement must contribute to the cause of ummah with Muslims.

(25) And the Jews of Banu Awf shall be considered as one community (Ummah) along with the believers—for the Jews their religion, and for the Muslims theirs, be one client or patron. But whoever does wrong or commits treachery brings evil only to himself and his household. (26-31) And the Jews of Banu-an-Najjar, Banu-al-Harith, Banu Saida, Banu Jusham, Banu al-Aws, and Banu Thalaba, shall have the same rights as the Jews of Banu Awf.

(32) And Jafna, who are a branch of the Thalaba tribe, shall have the same rights as the mother tribes.

(33) And Banu-ash-Shutaiba shall have the same rights as the Jews of Banu Awf; they shall be faithful to, and not violators of, the treaty.

(34) And the mawlas (clients) of Thalaba shall have the same rights as the original members of it.

(35) And the sub-branches of the Jewish tribes shall have the same rights as the mother tribes.

Article 25 allows Jews and pagans to practice their faith without restrictions. The Covenant of Medina was the first political document to establish religious freedom as a fundamental constitutional right. He incorporated the principle of religious freedom, the first charter of freedom of conscience in human history. It was a breakthrough in political and civil life against exploitation, tyranny, and corruption.

(36) (a) And that none of them shall go out to fight as a soldier of the Muslim army, without Muhammad's permission. (b) And no obstruction shall be placed in the way of anyone's retaliation for beating or injuries; and whoever sheds blood brings it upon himself and his household, except he who has been wronged, and Allah demands the most righteous fulfillment of this [treaty].

(37) (a) And the Jews shall bear their expenses and the Muslims theirs. (b) And if anyone fights against the people of this code, their (i.e., Jews and Muslims) mutual help shall come into operation, and there shall be friendly counsel and sincere behavior between them, and faithfulness and no breach of covenant.

This article establishes a wider definition of expenses for which there is no mutual responsibility between Jews and Muslims except for shared protection at war. It reinforces the mutual responsibility between two groups of believers in Ummah's defense.

(38) And the Jews shall bear their own expenses so long as they fight with the believers.

Article 38 repeats the first part of Article 24.

MEDINA DESIGNATED AS A SACRED PLACE

(39) And the Valley of Yathrib (Medina) shall be a Haram (sacred place) for the people of this code.

Thus, Medina and all the territories surrounding it became inviolate to their peoples, who were now bound to defend and protect themselves together. These people were now bound to guarantee one another the implementation of the covenant. They were to establish the rights arising therefrom and provide the freedom it called for. They could not attack one another and vowed to protect one another. An old anarchic custom was discarded, which obliged the aggrieved and the injured to rely upon his or his kinsmen's power to exact vengeance or satisfy justice.

(40) The clients (mawla) shall have the same treatment as the original persons (i.e., persons accepting clientage). He shall neither be harmed nor break the covenant.

(41) And no refuge shall be given to anyone without the permission of the people of the place (i.e., the refugee shall have no right to give refuge to others).

(42) And that if any murder or quarrel takes place among the people of this code, from which any trouble may be feared, it shall be referred to God and God's Messenger, Muhammad. God will be with him who will be most particular about what is written in this code and act on it most faithfully.

(43) The Quraysh shall not be protected, nor shall they who assist them in any way.

(44) And they (i.e., Jews and Muslims) shall help each other in the Yathrib invasion.

(45) (a) And if they (i.e., the Jews) are invited to any peace, they also shall offer peace and be a party to it. If they invite the believers to some such affairs, it shall be their (Muslims) duty to reciprocate the dealings, except that anyone makes a religious war. (b) On every group shall rest the responsibility of (repulsing) the enemy from the place which faces its part of the city.

(46) And the Jews of the tribe of al-Aws, clients, and original members, shall have the same rights as the people of this code: and shall behave sincerely and faithfully towards the latter, not perpetrating any breach of covenant. As one sows, so shall he reap. And God is with him who will most faithfully implement this code.

(47) And this covenant shall not benefit oppressors or covenant breakers. And one shall have security whether one sets out on a campaign or remains in Medina, or else it will be oppression and breach of covenant. And God is the Protector of him who performs his obligations faithfully and with care, as also His Messenger Muhammad (peace be upon him).

At the Prophet Muhammad's insistence, Muslims and Jewish clans signed a pact to protect each other. This document contains the following terms:

Equal Rights for Jews: "The Jews who attach themselves to our commonwealth shall be protected from all insults and vexations. They shall have equal rights to assistance and good offices among our people. The Jews of various branches and all others domiciled in Yathrib shall form with the Muslims **one composite nation.** They shall **practice their religion as freely as the Muslims** and the clients and allies of the Jews shall enjoy the same security and freedom."

Chapter 3
IMPACTS OF THE CONSTITUTION OF MEDINA

FROM DESPISED PREACHER TO BRILLIANT STATESMAN

When the Prophet arrived in Medina, its inhabitants greeted him warmly, and from that point on, he assumed a different role. The despised preacher became a masterful politician and statesman. We see him not only as the leader of a handful of devotees but as the collective life of the city. He is its judge and general and its teacher. Even his enemies concede that he played his expanded role brilliantly. Despite the complexity of the problems, he appears to be an exceptional statesman. With the constitution, the Prophet became the supreme authority and leader of all Medinese. Tradition depicts his administration as a balanced blend of justice and mercy. As chief of state and trustee of his people's life and liberty, he exercised the judgment necessary for order, unflinchingly punishing those guilty. He was gentle and merciful towards his enemies when injury was directed toward him. For the remaining ten years of his life, his personal history merged with that of the Medinese commonwealth, of which he was the center. The Medinese found the Prophet to be a master whom it was difficult not to love or obey. He had, as one biographer wrote, "the gift of influencing men, and he had the nobility only to influence them for good."

FORMATION OF A SUPER-TRIBE

From Kinship to Ummah: This document began the transition from pre-Islamic kinship or family ties to the ideological institution of the Ummah. Kinship, a system of social organization based on real or putative family ties, is a powerful universal human phenomenon.

Deep kinship attachment was transferred to religion, and kinship ties had less divisive effects. Such a radical change cannot be abruptly implemented. In the past, kinship responsibility for paying blood commitments was not completely abandoned. Later, believers must undertake a blood commitment, blurring kinship lines, as outlined in article 19 (See previous chapter). The eventual goal of the agreement was to form a "super tribe" to eliminate conflicts. Kinship and blood ties were replaced with another relationship determinant. The super tribe consisted of Muslims (the true believers), nominal Muslims (the hypocrites), pagans, and Jews. Bringing unity among the heterogeneous population was a breakthrough in political and civil life against exploitation, tyranny, and corruption.

From the Medinan Ummah to the Muslim Ummah: Despite the political nature of the Medina agreement and the secular tone of the early Ummah, with time, more and more Medinans became believers. The nature of the Ummah evolved from a political association designed to mediate tribal conflicts to a religiously defined community.

From the Unified City to United Arabia: Exercising superb statecraft, the Prophet welded the heterogeneous and conflicting tribes of the city into an orderly confederation. Now, he had become the head of a super tribe, bound not by blood but by a shared ideology—an incredible innovation in any society. The task was not easy; however, in the end, he succeeded in awakening a spirit of union unknown to the city's history.

Medina's unity later transformed into a united Arabia. It eventually unified a diverse Arabian population into an extremely effective and powerful religious, political, and military force. This evolution from the Medinan Ummah to the Muslim Ummah was critical in creating a large, cohesive population from which fighters could be recruited for future battles. The major outcome of the agreement was the eventual conquest of the two major superpowers, the Roman and Persian empires. This was shortly after the Prophet's death.

PLURALISTIC ISLAMIC SOCIETY

Prophet Muhammad's Medina charter/covenant governed a multi-tribal, pluralistic society with multiple religious beliefs, allowing freedom for all. The first Islamic state was founded on this social contract. Islam took on a political form with the establishment of an Islamic community-state at Medina to realize God's will on earth. The Prophet had the opportunity to implement God's governance and message, for he was now the prophet-head of a religio-political entity. The community of Medina served as the nucleus of the emerging Arab nation, and its government developed into a prototype of a Muslim empire. The Prophet's example offers a paradigm shift in the fusion of religion and state in the Muslim experience. Medina's Islam was the basis from which world Islam grew.

THE FUSION OF RELIGION AND STATE

In the newly built courtyard of the Mosque, Muslims routinely met to discuss all the ummah's social, political, military, and religious concerns. The Prophet's example offers a paradigm for an ideology for the fusion of religion and state in the Muslim experience. Islam became a religion and a state in one. In the Quranic vision, there is no dichotomy between the sacred and the secular. The aim was to integrate the whole of life into a unified community, which would give Muslims a sense of God's unity.

FUSION OF RELIGION AND POLITICS IN THE WESTERN EXPERIENCE

In the Western experience, the fusion of religion and politics was a total disaster. Religious wars between Catholics and Protestants in Europe lasted 30 years. About 4.5 to 8 million soldiers and civilians died of battle, famine, and disease, while some areas of modern Germany experienced a population decline of over 50%. From the seventeenth century onwards, Western civilization exempted religion from state affairs. It is a lesson for all Muslims that religious fanaticism will eventually lead to religion's death and be replaced by atheism and secularism. The Western civilization reached its pinnacle with peace and looted wealth from the so-called "third world" countries.

Secularism has left Europe's churches empty, and some are converted into mosques. Marriage and family life have taken a severe toll. Some men have stopped taking responsibility for their children, many born outside the traditional marital system. Abortions are common, and women have stopped bearing enough children to maintain the population. Europe is dying. The population vacuum thus created is filled by immigrants, most of whom are nonwhite Muslims. Rather than blaming themselves for moral decline, many ultra-right parties want to ban Muslims from their lands. What Muslims lost at the battle of Tours (732) will be won by Islam's strong moral and family system. The combination of Islamic morals and European intelligentsia's genius has the potential to propel European civilization to new heights.

The inclusion of non-denominational moral or ethical values into the educational system may be the partial answer to moral decline in a society.

WAR AND PEACE

Muslims were allowed to use force to defend the fledgling state since any state's primary duty was to protect its citizens from aggression. The spirit of self-sacrifice through pacifism, a characteristic of the Mecca period, complimented the idea of sacrifice through action.

The Prophet's reputation spread, and people flocked from Arabia to see the man who accomplished this feat.

THE TRUE BELIEVERS AND THE HYPOCRITES

CHAPTER 4
THE TRUE BELIEVERS
(AMONG EMIGRANTS, ANSARS, AND BEDOUINS)

THE EMIGRANTS

The term **muhajirun** or emigrants were those who forsook evil. It applies to the Prophet's Meccan followers who migrated from Mecca to Medina. The term muhajirun also has a general spiritual meaning to describe those who morally "forsake the domain of evil."

THE FIRST AND THE FOREMOST AMONG EMIGRANTS?

First and foremost are those who have left the domain of evil and those who have sheltered and helped the faith. They follow them [in the way of] righteousness. God is well-pleased with them. Well-pleased are they with Him. And for them, He has prepared Gardens, through which running waters flow, therein to abide beyond the count of time: this is the triumph supreme! (9:100)

The **"first and foremost"** were the earliest emigrants who left Mecca for Yathrib in or before 622 CE, which marked the beginning of the Islamic Hijri at a time when Mecca was still in the hands of Islam's enemies.

THE ANSARS

The honorable designation of Ansars, or helpers, became a collective title for the Medinese Muslims. They "sheltered and succored" the Meccan emigrants and helped Islam in its hour of great trial. The term 'ansar' also has a general spiritual meaning to describe those who "shelter and succor the Faith," transcending its purely historical connotation and to apply to all believers who aid and comfort those who flee evil unto God. Thus, the exiles and the local helpers formed the kernel of Islam.

THE FIRST AND THE FOREMOST AMONG ANSARS

The **"first and foremost" among the Ansars** were early Muslims who attended the two meetings at Al-Aqabah between the Prophet and the delegations of the Yathrib tribes of Al-Aws and Khazraj. It also includes those Ansars who embraced Islam shortly after the Prophet's and his companions' exodus from Mecca.

THE SAHABAH (COMPANIONS)

Medina's Muslim ranks included those who entered the faith with true conviction to serve God. The emigrants and Ansars, or helpers, became collectively known as the Sahabah (Companions), a distinct group, the true believers, and Islam's vanguards.

TRUE BELIEVERS AMONG THE BEDOUIN

Among the Bedouin, there are [also] who believe in God and the Last Day and regard all they spend [in God's cause] as a means of drawing them nearer to God and of [being remembered in] the Apostle's prayers. Oh, it shall [indeed] be a means of [God's] nearness to them, [for] God will admit them unto His grace: God is much-forgiving, a dispenser of grace! (9:99)

ATTRIBUTES OF THE TRUE BELIEVERS

This Divine writ - let there be no doubt about it - is [meant to be] a guidance for all the God-conscious who believe in [the existence of] which is beyond the reach of human perception, are constant in prayer, spend on others out of what We provide for them as sustenance, who believe in what has been bestowed from on high upon thee, [O Prophet], and bestowed before thy time, for it is they who in their innermost are certain of the life to come! It is they who follow the guidance [which comes] from their Sustainer, and it is they, they who shall attain a happy state! (2:2-5)

Muhammad is God's Apostle, and those who are [indeed] with him are firm and unyielding towards all truth deniers, [yet] full of mercy towards one another. You can see them bowing down, prostrating themselves [in prayer], seeking favor with God and [His] goodly acceptance: their marks are on their faces, traced by prostration. This is their parable in the Torah and the Gospels. [They are] like a seed that brings forth its shoot. Then He strengthens it to grow stout and [in the end] stands firm upon its stem, delighting the sowers. [Thus, will God cause the believers to grow in strength] and He might confound the deniers of the truth through them. [But] unto such of them as may [yet] attain faith and do righteous deeds, God has promised forgiveness and a reward supreme. (48:29)

Prostration is a sign of humility in prayer. For example, when Moses and Aaron "fell upon their faces" (Num. XVI. 22). Jesus fell with his face to the ground and prayed (Matthew 26:39). "Their marks" signifies the spiritual reflection of that faith in the believer's manner of life, even in their outward aspect. God has promised forgiveness and reward supreme to the deniers of the truth spoken of in the preceding sentence: those who might attain faith and thus achieve God's forgiveness. A promise was fulfilled a few years after the revelation of this verse. This is because most of the Prophet's Arabian enemies embraced Islam, and many became its torchbearers. In a broader sense, this divine promise remains open until Resurrection Day, when the truth may arrive.

FAITH IN GOD AND HIS APOSTLE

[Know that true] believers are only those who have attained faith in God, His Apostle, have left all doubt behind and strive hard for God's cause with their possessions and lives. It is they, they, who are true to their word! (49:15)

PAY HEED UNTO GOD AND HIS APOSTLE

The only response of believers, whenever they are summoned unto God and His Apostle so that [the divine writ] might judge between them, can be no other than, "We have heard, and we pay heed!" It is they, they who shall attain to a happy state; for, they who pay heed unto God and His Apostle, and stand in awe of God and are conscious of Him, it is they, they who shall triumph [in the end]! (24:51-52) Say [O Prophet], "If you love God, follow me [and] God will love you and forgive you your sins, for God is much-forgiving, a dispenser of grace. Say: "Pay heed unto God and the Apostle." (3:31-32)

CONSTANT IN PRAYER, GENEROUS IN CHARITY

Believers are only those whose hearts tremble with awe whenever God is mentioned and whose faith is strengthened whenever His messages are conveyed. Those who place their trust in their Sustainer are always praying and spending on others what We provide for them as sustenance. It is they, they, who are true believers! Theirs shall be great dignity in their Sustainer's sight, the forgiveness of sins, and most excellent sustenance. (8:2-4)

FORSAKE THE DOMAIN OF EVIL

And they who have attained faith and forsaken the domain of evil and are striving hard in God's cause, and shelter and succor [them]—it is they, they who are indeed believers! Forgiveness for sins awaits them and most excellent sustenance. (8:74)

The most excellent sustenance may refer to paradise, or it can also be a metonym for the spiritual reward of faith in this world arising from the knowledge of God, the love of Him, and the self-immersion in worshipping Him. The Meccan followers of the Prophet are those who have forsaken the "domain of evil." They migrated from Mecca to Medina when Mecca was still in possession of Islam's enemy. The band of faithful Quraysh, who had left their birthplace and every tie of home.

JUDGING A PERSON'S FAITH

The following dialogue between Noah and his community emphasizes believers' equality:

They [people of Noah] said: "Shall we place our faith in you, even though [only] the most abject [of people] follow you?" Said he [Noah], "What knowledge could I have as to what they were doing [before they came to me]? Their reckoning rests with none but my Sustainer: if you could understand [this]! Hence, I shall not drive away [any of] those [who profess to be] believers; I am nothing but a plain warner." (26:111-115) Those who attained faith [know they] are destined to meet their Sustainer, whereas, in you, I see people without any awareness [of right and wrong]! And O my people, who would shield me from God, was I to repulse them? Will you not, then, keep this in mind? (11:29-31)

The unbelievers' contemptuous statement that Noah's "abject" followers had declared their faith in him not out of conviction but to gain material advantages. They might listen to Noah (implied here) if he rid himself of those low-class people. Noah's answer (11:29) embodies the cardinal elements of Quranic ethics and Islamic law. No human being has the right to judge another person's faith or hidden motives, whereas God knows what is in men's hearts. Society may judge only by external evidence, which comprises words and deeds.

Thus, if anyone says, "I am a believer" and does not act or speak contradicting his professed faith, the community must consider him a believer. The Prophet had a similar experience in the early years of his mission with the leaders of the pagan Quran. Most of his early followers belonged to society's poorer classes. The divine message promised an equitable social order on earth and the hope of happiness in the hereafter. This revolutionary character of every Prophet's mission has always made it so distasteful to the upholders of the established order and the privileged classes of society.

REWARDS FOR GOOD DEEDS

The Apostle, however, and all who share his faith strive hard [in God's cause] with their possessions and lives. It is they whom the most excellent things await [in the life to come], and it is they, they who shall attain a happy state! God has prepared for them gardens through which running waters flow, therein to abide, and this is the triumph supreme! (9:88-89)

It is not befitting for the people of the Prophet's City and the Bedouin [who live] around them to hold back from following God's Apostle. They should also care more about him than for themselves. When they suffer from thirst, weariness, or hunger in God's cause, take any step that confounds the deniers of the truth and whatever is destined by the enemy for them— [either victory, injury, or death] *a virtuous deed is recorded in their favor. God does not fail to requite the doers of good! And whenever they spend anything [for God's sake], be it little or much. Whenever they move on earth [in God's cause]— it is recorded in their favor, and God will grant them the best reward for all that they have done. (9:120-121)*

These verses relate to the people of the Prophet's City and the Bedouins who live around them; it applies to all believers. The specific reference to "the Prophet's City" relates to where the Quran's revelation was completed, and Islam came to full fruition under the Prophet's guidance.

SPIRITUAL SECURITY

God will never allow those who deny the truth to harm believers. (4:141)

The above announcement has a purely spiritual meaning and does not necessarily apply to life's changing fortunes. As this verse points out, those who deny the truth may, on occasion, be in luck; that is to say, they may gain temporal supremacy over believers.

BEWARE OF TRIALS AND TEMPTATIONS

Beware of that temptation to evil, which does not befall only those bent on denying the truth to the exclusion of others. Know that God is severe in retribution. And remember the time when you were few [and] helpless on earth, fearful lest people do away with you—whereupon He sheltered you, strengthened you with His assistance, and provided for you sustenance out of the good things of life so that you might have cause to be grateful. [Hence], O you who have attained faith, do not be false to God and the Apostle and do not knowingly be false to the trust reposed in you. Know that worldly goods and your children are but a trial and temptation, and with God, there is a tremendous reward. (8:25-28) God turns in His mercy unto believing men and women, for God is indeed much forgiving, a dispenser of grace! (33:73)

Greed and a desire to confer benefits on one's family often tempt an otherwise righteous person to offend fellow men's rights. The righteous may fall prey to it unless they remain on guard against anything that might lead them astray from the right course. One should not allow worldly attachments to deflect him from pursuing moral truths. "You were few and helpless" refers to the believers' weakness in Islam's early days before their departure from Mecca to Medina. It is a reminder to every community of true believers, always of their initial weakness due to numerical insignificance.

It is also a reminder of their subsequent growth in numbers and influence. Wealth and children are mentioned together because of the material benefits of having more children in tribal society—especially boys, for more protection, more hands to gather food and help in old age.

ANSARS EXTEND FULL HOSPITALITY TO EMIGRANTS

The primary task was forging harmony among diverse groups in this divided city. The Prophet took two essential steps to forge unity in a divided city. He asked each newly converted Medina family (Ansars) to extend full hospitality to an emigrant family. The Emigrants (Muhajir) from Mecca, almost without exception, arrived in Medina in complete deprivation, and the first two years were challenging. They had problems obtaining food, housing, and adjusting to a different environment. Also, the Prophet feared that the old hatred and prejudice might rear their ugly heads despite the strong ties the Islamic religion had bound them to. Every Muhajir, or Emigrant, was now bound to an Ansar member in a bond of mutual assistance. A true, genuine brotherhood arose and put the new religion of fraternal order into practice. Secondly, he drafted the Constitution of Medina, outlining the responsibilities of Meccan emigrants and Medina inhabitants toward each other and the newly established Islamic state.

CHAPTER 5
THE DEFINITION AND ORIGIN OF HYPOCRISY IN ISLAM

CONSCIOUS HYPOCRITES

The English dictionary definition of hypocrite is a person who puts on a false appearance of virtue or religion or acts in contradiction to his or her stated beliefs or feelings. Conscious hypocrites behave sharply different from believers. According to the Prophet, "the signs of a hypocrite are three: (1) Whenever he speaks, he tells a lie. (2) Whenever he promises, he always breaks it, and (3) if you trust him, he proves to be dishonest."

WAVERERS OR DOUBTERS

The Arabic term munafiq—which, for lack of a better word, is rendered as "hypocrite"—has a much broader meaning. It includes the above English definition of conscious hypocrite and applies to nominal Muslims or waverers and doubters,

Hypocrites, both men and women, are alike. They enjoin the doing what is wrong, forbid doing what is right, and withhold their hands [from doing good]. They are oblivious to God, and so He ignores them. Hypocrites—it is they, they, who are truly evil! (9:67)

These verses have general, timeless importance. Due to their faith's weakness and inner uncertainty, they vacillate between belief and unbelief. Not having any real convictions on this score leaves the question of God's existence and Muhammad's prophethood open.

However, for worldly advantage, they would like to be regarded as believers. An ambivalent attitude implies hypocrisy for lying to themselves and others to avoid a spiritual commitment. They would deceive God and the believers while deceiving none but themselves. Since these people usually pretend to be morally better than they are, the epithet munafiq may be rendered as "hypocrite."

ORIGIN OF HYPOCRISY IN ISLAM

And some people say, "We believe in God and the last day," but they do not [truly] believe. They would deceive God and those who have attained faith, while they deceive none but themselves and do not perceive it. In their hearts is a disease, so God allows their disease to grow, and grievous suffering awaits them because of their persistent lying. (2:8-10)

Muslims from Mecca were always sincere. There was nothing to be gained materially and much to lose upon conversion to Islam for Meccan Muslims. Since the Prophet and the Muslim community gained strength in Medina, there were specific worldly reasons for entering the new religion. Islam spread rapidly throughout the Arabian clans of Aws and Khazraj, and an emerging phenomenon raised its ugly head. Some of the residents of Medina adopted Islam in search of material gains and political expediency. The days of hypocrites being totally absent from Muslims' ranks were gone forever. Others claimed to believe in God and the Apostle when they did not. These were the waverers, doubters, and hypocrites of Aws and Khazraj.

ABU AMIR AND ABD ALLAH IBN UBAYY

Islam's chief adversaries were two cousins; each significantly influenced his tribe. **Abu Amir**, or "The Monk" from the Aws tribe, was an ascetic. He claimed to follow Abraham's religion and acquired religious authority among his people. He came to see the Prophet soon after his arrival to ask about the new religion. The Prophet recited Quran verses mentioning Abraham. Amir accused the Prophet of falsifying the Abrahamic faith. He was further embittered when his son became a Prophet follower. Abu Amir entered self-imposed exile.

His cousin **Abd Allah B. Ubayy** led Medina's hypocrites. As a result of the widespread enthusiasm, he and his followers professed nominal Islam. He never forgave the Prophet for overshadowing him, who, previously, had been unquestionably recognized by Medinans as their potential king. The hypocrites and those members of al-Aws and al-Khazraj tribes who never embraced Islam (the pagans) rallied around the Jews once their opposition to Muhammad and Islam crystallized. Many Jews had close ties with Abd Allah B. Ubayy and may have hoped to increase their influence if he became ruler. Ubayy was bitter about seeing his son and daughter won over by the Prophet. Unlike Abu Amir, Ubayy was prepared to wait, hoping for the Islamic movement's failure.

Ibn Ubayy tried to persuade the Ansars - many of whom supported the newcomers with all the means—to withdraw this material support and force the Muhajirun to leave Medina. This was a strategy that, if successful, would have significantly weakened the Prophet's position. As expected, the Ansar rejected the suggestion of the hypocrites' leader.

Abd Allah bin Ubayy and his disaffected party were ready to turn against Muslims at the slightest opportunity. They were a source of considerable danger to the newborn commonwealth and required unceasing watchfulness on the Prophet's part. Muhammad always showed patience and forbearance, hoping, in the end, to win them over to faith. The result fully justified this expectation. With the death of Abd Allah bin Ubayy, his hypocrites party disappeared.

HYPOCRITES OF THE OLDEN DAYS

Hypocrisy was a new phenomenon among Medina's Muslims, but it has existed since time immemorial.

[Say unto them: "You are] like those [hypocrites] who lived before your time. More powerful than you, they were in power, richer in wealth and children, and enjoyed their share [of happiness]. And you have been enjoying your share—just as those who preceded you enjoyed their share, and you have been indulging in a scurrilous talk—just as they indulged in it. They whose works have been wasted in this world and in the life to come—and it is they, they, who are lost!" Have those stories never come within the ken of these [hypocrites and deniers of the truth]? [The stories] of Noah's people, [the tribes of] Ad and Thamud, Abraham's people, the folks of Madyan, and the overthrown cities? [Sodom and Gomorrah] *To [all] them, their apostles had come with all evidence of the truth, [but they rejected them] and so it was not God who wronged them [by His punishment], but it was they who wronged themselves. (9:69-70)*

THE HYPOCRITES AMONG THE BEDOUIN

[The hypocrites among] the Bedouin are more tenacious in [their] refusal to acknowledge the truth and in [their] hypocrisy [than are settled people], and more liable to ignore the ordinances God has bestowed from on high upon His Apostle—but God is all-knowing, wise. And among the Bedouin, there are such as regard all that they might spend [in God's cause] as a loss, and wait for misfortune to encompass you, [O believers, but] it is they whom evil fortune shall encompass—for God is all-hearing, all-knowing. (9:97-98)

Owing to their nomadic way of life and its inherent hardship and crudity, the Bedouins found it more problematic than the settled people to be guided by ethical imperatives unrelated to their immediate tribal interests. Because of their physical distance from religious learning centers, they have considerable ignorance of most religious demands. Hence, their suffering will be first through failure in their worldly concerns, accompanied by pangs of conscience and the resulting spiritual distress, and then through a full realization, at the moment of dying, of the unforgivable nature of their sin. The Prophet often stressed the superiority of a settled mode of life to a nomadic one. He said, "He who dwells in the desert becomes rough in disposition."

CONDEMNATION OF TRIBALISM AMONG BEDOUINS

The Bedouins say, "We have attained faith." Say [unto them, O Muhammad]:

"You haven't attained faith; you ought to say, 'We have [outwardly] surrendered'—for [true] faith has not yet entered your hearts. If you [truly] pay heed unto God and His Apostle, He will not let the least of your deeds come to waste, for God is much-forgiving, a dispenser of grace." (49:14)

This verse alludes to the intense tribalism of the Bedouins, contemporaries of the Prophet, and their "pride of descent." God will not let the least of "your deeds fall to waste" in distinction from the supposed glorious deeds of your ancestors, which count for nothing in His sight. The Prophet's famous saying. "He is not of us who proclaims the cause of tribal partisanship, and he is not of us who fights in the cause of tribal partisanship, and he is not of us who dies for the cause of tribal partisanship." When asked to explain the meaning of "tribal partisanship," the Prophet answered, "It means helping your people in an unjust cause."

THE BROTHERHOOD OF HUMANITY

O men! Behold, We have created you from a male and a female. We have divided you into nations and tribes so you might come to know one another. Verily, the noblest of you in God's sight is the most deeply conscious of Him. Behold, God is all-knowing, all-aware. (49:13) "

We have created everyone from a father and a mother." The equality of biological origin is reflected in the equality of human dignity common to all. We all belong to one global family without inherent superiority over another. The Quranic teachings reject the Jewish notion of "God's chosen people" or the belief that white people constitute a superior race and should, therefore, dominate society, typically to the exclusion or detriment of other racial and ethnic groups. Humanity's evolution into "nations and tribes" is meant to foster rather than diminish their mutual desire to understand and appreciate essential human oneness. Racial, religious, national, or tribal prejudices are condemned implicitly in the Quran and explicitly by the Prophet.

In addition, speaking of people's boasting of their national or tribal past, the Prophet said: "Behold, God has removed from you the arrogance of pagan ignorance (Jahiliyyah) with its boast of ancestral glories. Man is a God-conscious believer or an unfortunate sinner. All people are children of Adam, and Adam was created out of dust."

CHAPTER 6
THE CHARACTERISTICS OF HYPOCRITES

THE FALSE PROFESSION OF FAITH

When the hypocrites come to you, they say, "We bear witness that you are indeed God's Apostle!" But God knows that you are truly His Apostle, and He bears witness that the hypocrites are false [in their declaration of faith]. They used their oaths as a cover [for their falsehood], turning others away from God's path. Indeed, evil is all they wanted to do because [they claim] they have attained faith. While [inwardly] they deny the truth, a seal has been set on their hearts, and they can no longer understand [what is true and false]. (63:1-3)

RELIGIOUS RITUALS FOR SHOW

Behold, the hypocrites seek to deceive God - while it is He who causes them to be deceived (by themselves). And when they rise to pray, they rise reluctantly, only to be seen and praised by men. Seldom remembering God, wavering between this and that, neither true to either. (4:142-143) Say: "Do you, perchance, [want to] inform God of [the nature of] your faith—although God knows all that is in the heavens and all that is on earth? Indeed, God has full knowledge of everything!" (49:16)

The passage above addresses certain Prophet contemporaries, yet its meaning extends to all people at any time. Some people think they are believers by their mere profession of faith and adherence to its formalities.

PARANOIA AND FALSE PRIDE

Now, when you see them (hypocrites), their outward appearance may please you. When they speak, you listen to what they say. [They may seem as sure of themselves] as if timbers were propped up, but they think every shout is [directed] against them. They are the [real] enemies [of all faiths], so beware of them. [They deserve imprecation.] "May God destroy them!" How perverted are their minds? When they are told, "Come, the Apostle of God will pray [unto God] that you be forgiven," they turn their heads away, and you can see how they drawback in their false pride. (63:4-5)

REVERENCE IN PUBLIC AND SCORN IN PRIVATE

Now, among [hapless sinners] are those who pretend to listen to you, [O Muhammad]. As soon as they leave your presence, speak [scornfully] to those who understood [your message]. "What is it that he has said just now?" It is such whose hearts God has sealed because they are [always] followed but their lusts. (47:16)

Hypocrites pretend to revere the Quranic message but are unwilling to admit its truth in their innermost being. Following their lusts, they sealed their hearts.

SATISFIED DURING BLESSINGS AND TURNS AWAY IN HARDSHIP

Even among men, many worship God at the borderline [of their faith]. Thus, if a blessing befalls him; he is satisfied with Him. If a trial assails him, he turns away utterly, losing [thereby both] this world and the life to come: [and] this, indeed, is a loss beyond compare! [By doing so], he invokes, instead of God, something that can neither harm nor benefit him, and that is the utmost one that can go astray. [And sometimes] he invokes [another human being] one that is far more likely to cause harm than benefit. Vile, indeed, is such a patron, and vile are their followers! (22:11-13)

If anyone thinks that God will not succor him in this world and in the life to come, let him reach out unto heaven by any [other] means and [thus try to] make headway and then let him see whether this scheme of his will indeed do away with the cause of his anguish. (22:15)

The "borderline of faith" refers to the state of being uncertain between belief and disbelief without being committed to either one. He attributes extraneous forces with divine qualities by failing to commit unreservedly to faith. He invokes a human being who, by allowing himself to be idolized by those who worship God on the borderline of faith, causes infinite spiritual harm to himself and his followers. If anyone doubts God's power to guide men towards happiness in this world and hereafter, let him reach out to heaven by any other means; he will find himself helpless and abandoned.

FAVOR BESTOWED UPON YOU, O PROPHET?

Many think they have bestowed favor upon you [O Prophet] by surrendering [to you]. [By professing to be your followers] Say you: "Deem not your surrender a favor unto me, but it is God who bestows favor upon you by showing you the way to faith—if you are true to your word. (49:17)

CORRUPTING GOD'S MESSAGE

And they say, "We pay heed unto you," but when they leave your presence, some devise, in the dark of night, [beliefs] other than you are voicing. All the while, God records what they devise in the dark night. Leave them alone and place your trust in God: none is as worthy of trust as God. (4:81)

They try to corrupt God's Apostle's message in secrecy, symbolized by night's darkness.

POLITICAL EXPEDIENCY

[The hypocrites], who wait to see what betides you; thus, if triumph comes to you from God, they say, "Were we not on your side?" While if those who deny the truth are in luck, they say [to them], "Have we not earned your affection by defending you against those believers?" (4:141)

MORAL EXPEDIENCY

For many of them [who] say, "We believe in God and the Apostle, and we pay heed!" But then, some of them turn away after this [assertion], and these are by no means [true] believers. And [so it is that] whenever they are summoned to God and His Apostle so that [the divine writ] might judge between them, some turn away; lo! But if the truth happens to their liking, they are willing to accept it! Is there a disease in their hearts? Or have they begun to doubt [that this is a divine writ]? Or do they fear God and His Apostle might deal unjustly with them? It is [but] they who are doing wrong [to themselves]! (24:47-50)

The expression "God and His Apostle" is a synonym for the divine writ revealed to the Apostle. Some hypocrites turn away whenever they are summoned so that the divine writ determines their ethical values and social behavior. Do they fear that God and His Apostle might deal unjustly by depriving them of legitimate liberties and enjoyments?

SEEKING MAN'S APPROVAL INSTEAD OF GOD'S

[The hypocrites] swear to you by God [that they are acting in good faith], pleasing you [O believers]—all the while, it is God and His Apostle whose pleasure they should seek above all else if indeed they are believers! Do they not know that for him who sets himself against God and His Apostle, there is in the store the fire of hell, there to abide—that most great disgrace? (9:62-63)

The idea is that God's pleasure is the only worthwhile goal of all human endeavors. A believer must surrender to the Prophet's guidance since he bears God's message to mankind. See in this connection, "Whoever pays heed to the Apostle pays heed to God thereby" (4:80), or "Say O Prophet: 'If you love God, follow me, and God will love you.'" (3:31)

CAUSES OF HYPOCRISY

INGRATITUDE

They could find no fault [with faith] save that God had enriched them and [caused] His Apostle [to enrich them] out of His bounty! Hence, if they repent, it will be for their good, but if they turn away, God will cause them grievous suffering in this world and in the life to come, and they will find no helper on earth and none to give [them] succor. (9:74)

They have been enriched by the spiritual guidance in the Quran and the material welfare resulting from adherence to its moral and social principles. The hypocrites' reluctance to pay heed to the Prophet was not due to fault with faith. It is the lack of gratitude they have for the spiritual and material benefits they have received from it. Despite its historical associations, its moral import is timeless.

FEAR AS THE CAUSE OF HYPOCRISY

And they swear by God that they do indeed belong to you; however, they do not belong to you but are [merely] people ridden by fear. They would turn towards it in headlong haste if they could only find a place of refuge, a cave, or crevice [in the earth]. (9:56-57)

Hypocrisy is a result of inner fears and uncertainties for nominal Muslims. Such "two-faced" individuals always try to find an easy way out of any real commitment, spiritual or social. The course of action they take is influenced by what they believe is likely to give them a practical advantage in the situation they find themselves in.

PERSECUTION

Now, there are among men many who say [of themselves and others like them], "We believe in God." But whenever he is made to suffer in God's cause, he thinks that persecution at man's hands is as [much to be feared, or even more than] God's chastisement. If succor from thy Sustainer comes [to those who truly believe], he will surely say, "We have always been with you!" Is not God fully aware of what is in the hearts of all creatures? [Yea] and most certainly will God mark out those who have [truly] attained to faith, and most certainly will He mark out the hypocrites. (29:10-11)

The above quote is the earliest occurrence of the term munafiq in the Quranic revelation chronology. For those who abandon their faith for fear of persecution, suffering is bound to occur. When it is no longer risky, they like to be called believers. However, mere outward renunciation of faith under torture or threat of death is not a sin in Islam. However, martyrdom for one's faith is the highest degree of merit man can attain.

THE FEAR OF BEING EXPOSED

[Some of] the hypocrites dread lest a [new] surah be revealed [in evidence] against them, making them understand what is [really] in their hearts? (9:64) Or do they think that in whose hearts is a disease, perhaps God would never bring their moral failings to light? Now, had We so willed, We could have shown them clearly to you so that you would know them for sure as by a visible mark. However, you will recognize them by their voice tone. And God knows all that you do, [O men]. (47:29-30)

It refers to a particular type of hypocrite, namely, the doubter, who, by not having any real convictions on this score, leaves the question of God's existence and Muhammad's prophethood open. However, for worldly advantage, he would like to be regarded as a believer. An ambivalent attitude implies hypocrisy about the social environment and self. These people are afraid of admitting what's in their hearts, and this ambivalence is a cover to avoid spiritual commitment.

The phrase "We could have shown them clearly to you" implies that God does not grant anyone a clear insight, as by a visible mark, into another human being's heart or mind. However, a true believer recognizes hypocrisy even without a visible mark.

SATAN HAS EMBELLISHED THEIR FANCIES

Those who turn their backs [on this message] after guidance has been vouchsafed to them [do it because] Satan has embellished their fancies and filled them with false hopes. [They turn their backs on it] as they say unto those who loathe all that God has revealed, "We will comply with your views on some points." But God knows their secret thoughts. (47:25-26)

"Those who turn their backs [on this message] after guidance has been vouchsafed to them" are meant for hypocrites and half-hearted followers of Islam at the time of the Prophet who refused to fight in defense of the Faith. "We will comply with your views on some points: although we cannot agree with you [atheists] regarding your denial of God, or resurrection, or the revelation as such, we do agree with you that Muhammad is an impostor and that the Quran is but his invention.

CHAPTER 7
DEALING WITH THE HYPOCRITES

DANGER POSED BY HYPOCRITES

And when they are told, "Do not spread corruption on earth," they answer, "We are but improving things!" Oh, they are spreading corruption, but they do not perceive it! When told, "Believe as other people believe," they respond, "Shall we believe as the weak-minded?" Oh, it is they, the weak-minded ones, but then they don't know! When they meet those who have attained faith, they assert, "We believe [as you believe]," but when they find themselves alone with their evil impulses, they say, "We are with you." We were only mocking!" God will requite them for their mockery and leave them for a while in their overweening arrogance, blindly stumbling to and fro. [For] they have taken error in exchange for guidance, and neither their bargain brought them to gain nor found guidance [elsewhere]. (2:11-16)

"Do not spread corruption" refers to people who oppose any intrusion of moral considerations into practical affairs and often unwittingly think they are "but improving things." Evil impulses describe the human soul's satanic propensities, especially those that run counter to truth and morality.

WITHDRAW FINANCIAL SUPPORT AND DRIVE OUT THE MUSLIMS

It is they who say [to their compatriots], "Do not spend anything on those who are withmn God's Apostle so that they [may be forced to] leave." However, unto God belong the treasures of the heavens and the earth; the hypocrites cannot grasp this truth. They say, "But when we return to the city, indeed we, the ones most worthy of honor, will drive out from there those most contemptible ones!" However, all honor belongs to God, and [thus] to His apostle and all those who believe [in Him]: but the hypocrites are unaware of this. (63:7-8)

"The city" refers to Medina. Abd Allah ibn Ubayy uttered the above saying during the campaign against Banu Mustaliq in 5 H.

AVOID THE COMPANY OF MOCKERS AND BLASPHEMERS

And, indeed, He has enjoined upon you in this divine writ that whenever you hear people deny the truth of God's messages and mock them, you shall avoid their company until they begin to talk of other things—or else, you will become like them. God will gather them in hell with those who deny the truth. (4:140) NOW, whenever thou meet such as indulge in [blasphemous] talk about Our messages, turn thy back upon them until they begin to talk of other things. If Satan should ever cause thee to forget [thyself], remain not, after recollection, in the company of such evildoing folk, for whom those who are conscious of God are in no wise accountable. Theirs, however, is the duty to admonish [the sinners] so that they might become conscious of God. (6:68-69)

DELIVER THE MESSAGE FULLY

O Apostle! Announce all that has been bestowed upon you by thy Sustainer unless you do it thoroughly. You will not have delivered His message [at all]. And God will protect you from [unbelieving] men behold; God does not guide people who refuse to acknowledge the truth. All that has been bestowed from on high upon you [O Prophet] by thy Sustainer is bound to make them much more stubborn in their overweening arrogance and denial of the truth. But do not grieve over those who deny the truth. (5:67-68) O Prophet! Strive hard against the deniers of the truth and the hypocrites and be adamant about them. And [if they do not repent] their goal shall be hell—and how vile a journey's end! (9:73) As for them—God knows all that is in their hearts, so leave them alone, admonish them, and speak unto them in a gravely searching manner: for We have never sent any apostle save by God's leave, he should be heeded. (4:63-64)

"Strive hard" against the deniers of truth and do not compromise with them in principle, regarding the meaning of the verb *jahada* (meaning, "he strove hard for a righteous cause"). The imperative *jahid* is used here in its spiritual connotation. This implies efforts at convincing both the outspoken unbelievers and the waverers, including the various hypocrites in the preceding passages. Although addressed to the Prophet, it is morally binding toward all believers. The expression "by God's leave" is to be understood as "with God's help" or "by God's grace." The sudden change within the same sentence from the pronoun "We" to "God" is meant to impress that God is not a "person" but rather an all-embracing power that cannot be defined or even adequately referred to within the limited range of any human language.

ONLY REASONABLE COMPLIANCE IS REQUIRED

Now [as for those half-hearted ones], they swear by God with their most solemn oaths that if you [O Apostle] ever bid them do so, they would most certainly go forth [and sacrifice themselves]. Say: "Swear not! Reasonable compliance [with God's message is all required of you]. God is aware of all that you do!" Say: "Pay heed unto God and the Apostle." And if you turn away [from the Apostle, know that], he will have to answer only for whatever he has been charged with, and you, for what you have been charged with. If you heed him, you will be on the right path. Withal, the Apostle is not bound to do more than to deliver the message [entrusted to him]. (24:53-54)

The above quotation is about the self-deceiving enthusiasm of the half-hearted and their supposed readiness for self-sacrifice, in contrast to their apparent reluctance to live up to the Quran's message in their day-to-day concerns. "Reasonable compliance is all that is required" so that God does not burden man with more than he can comfortably bear.

DO NOT CONTEND BUT PRAY FOR THEM

Behold, We have bestowed this divine writ upon thee from on high, setting forth the truth, so that thou may judge between people by what God has taught thee. Hence, do not contend with those who are false to their trust but pray to God to forgive [them], for God is indeed much-forgiving, a dispenser of grace. Yet, do not argue on behalf of those who are false to themselves. God does not love those who betray their trust and persist in sinful ways. They would conceal their doings from men, but from God, they cannot hide them—for He is with them whenever they devise all manner of beliefs, He does not approve of in the dark of night. And God encompasses everything they do with His knowledge. Oh, you might argue on their behalf in this life, but who will argue with God on the Day of Resurrection, or who will be their defender? (4:105-109)

Hypocrites and half-hearted Quran followers are accused of betraying the trust placed in them. They pretend to have accepted the Quranic message but are trying to corrupt it. They are already aware of what the Quran demands and are determined to evade all real self-surrender to its guidance. There is no use arguing with them. You may ask God to forgive them but do not find excuses for their behavior. The Quran characterizes a betrayal of trust as being false to oneself—just as it frequently describes a person who deliberately commits a sin or a wrong as one who sins against himself or wrongs himself—since every deliberate act of sinning damages its author spiritually. All manner of belief denotes an opinion, doctrine, or idea God disapproves of.

DO NOT ALLY WITH HYPOCRITES

How could you be of two minds about the hypocrites, seeing that God [Himself] has disowned them because of their guilt? Do you, perhaps, seek to guide those God has let go astray? You can never find any way for him whom God lets go astray. They would love to see you deny the truth as they reject it, so you should be like them. Do not, therefore, take them as your allies until they forsake the domain of evil for the sake of God. (4:88-89)

The above verse speaks of God and stresses His oneness, the truth inherent in His revealed message, and the certainty of judgment on Resurrection Day. How, then, continues the argument, could you be of two minds regarding the moral stature of people who go so far as to pay lip service to the truth of God's message and are, nevertheless, not willing to make a sincere choice between right and wrong?

CHAPTER 8
THE PUNISHMENT FOR THE HYPOCRITES

FORGIVENESS FOR REPENTANT HYPOCRITES

If then, after sinning against themselves, they would turn to you and ask God to forgive them—with the Apostle, too, praying that they are forgiven. They would assuredly find God as an acceptor of repentance, a dispenser of grace. (4:64) They who repent, live righteously, hold fast to God, and grow sincere in their faith in God alone, for they shall be one with the believers, and in time God will grant a mighty reward to all believers. Why would God cause you to suffer [for your past sins] if you are grateful and attain to belief—seeing that God is always responsive to gratitude and all-knowing? (4:146-147)

Gratitude is a feeling of thankfulness for being alive and endowed with a soul. This gratefulness makes a man realize that this gift of life and consciousness leads to belief in God. Therefore, "gratitude" is placed before "belief" in the above sentence structure.

PREDICTION OF HYPOCRITE DEFEAT

Thus, it is if the hypocrites, [Abd Allah b. Ubayy] *whose heart is a disease, and by spreading false rumors, would cause disturbances in the city [of the Prophet] do not desist [from their hostile acts]. We shall indeed give you mastery over them, [O Muhammad]. They will not remain your neighbors in this [city] for more than a while. Bereft of God's grace, they shall be seized wherever they may be found and slain one and all. Such has been God's way with those who [sinned in a like manner and] passed away aforetime - and never wilt thou find any change in God's way! (33:60-62)*

The verses above refer to the opposition the Prophet and his followers faced in their early years in Medina. You will be able to master them. There will be open warfare between you and them, and they will be slain in vast numbers, resulting in their expulsion from Medina.

NO FORGIVENESS FOR UNREPENTANT HYPOCRITES

[And] whether you pray [to God] that they are forgiven or do not pray for them, [It will all be the same. For even] if you were to pray seventy times that they are forgiven, God will not forgive them, seeing that they are bent on denying God and His Apostle. And God does not bestow His guidance upon such iniquitous folk. (9:80) And never shall you pray over any of them that have died, and never shall you stand by his grave: for they were bent on denying God and His Apostle, and they died in their iniquity. And let not their worldly goods and [the happiness they may derive from] their children excite your admiration: God wants to chastise them by these means in [the life of] this world, and [to cause] their souls to depart while they are [still] denying the truth. (9:84-85)

Among the people of the [Prophet's] city [Medina], there are those who have grown insolent in [their] hypocrisy. You do not always know them, [Muhammad], but We do. We shall cause them to suffer doubly [in this world], and then they will be given over to tremendous suffering [in the life to come]. (9:101) When they are told, "Come, the Apostle of God will pray [unto God] that you be forgiven," they turn their heads away, and you can see how they drawback in their false pride. As for them, it is all the same whether you pray or do not pray for their forgiveness. God will not forgive them—for God does not bestow His guidance upon such iniquitous folk. (63:5-6)

In Arabic, the number "seventy" often stands for "many," just as "seven" is a synonym for "several." The Prophet prayed to God to pardon his enemies. The prohibition of never praying over them relates only to those who "were bent on denying God and His Apostle.

They died as unrepentant sinners. They have lost all dispositions for repentance and belief because they are deeply rooted in their iniquity and persistence in evildoing. "Let not their wealth excite your admiration" is meant to stress the psychological importance of this problem, namely, the insignificance of worldly happiness compared with spiritual righteousness or its absence.

SUFFERING FOR HYPOCRITES AND IDOL-WORSHIPPERS

And [God has willed] to impose suffering [in the life to come] on the hypocrites, both men and women and on those who ascribe divinity to others besides Him, both men and women, all who entertain evil thoughts about God. Evil encompasses them from all sides, and God's condemnation rests upon them. He has rejected them [from His grace] and readied hell for them: how evil a journey's end! For, God's are all the forces of the heavens and the earth. God is indeed almighty, truly wise! (48:6-7)

Evil thoughts about God refer to denying His existence or man's responsibility to Him or offending against His oneness.

DEATH OF ABD ALLAH B. UBAYY

When the lifelong opponent of the Prophet and leader of the hypocrites of Medina, Abd Allah b. Ubayy was dying. He sent his son to the Prophet to get his shirt so he might be buried in it. He also asked that the Prophet pray for him after his death. The Prophet took this request as a sign of repentance, gave him his shirt, and later led funeral prayers over his body. It was a practical example of what Jesus said six hundred years ago:

But I tell you, love your enemies and pray for those who persecute you. In that way, you will be acting as the true children of your Father in Heaven. (Matthew 5:43-45)

Umar ibn al-Khattab was furious at this compassion towards the man regarded as God's enemy. The Prophet answered, "God has granted me a choice in this matter (a reference to verse 80 above, "whether you pray that they are forgiven or do not pray...," etc.), and so I shall pray (for him) more than seventy times."

Are you unaware of those who claim they believe what has been bestowed from on high upon thee, [O Prophet], and what was bestowed before? [And yet] they are willing to defer to the rule of evil powers. Although they were bidden to deny it, seeing that Satan wanted to lead them far astray? Whenever they are told, "Come unto what God has bestowed from on high, and unto the Apostle," you can see these hypocrites turn away from you with aversion. How [will they fare on the Day of Judgment] when calamity befalls them because of what they have wrought in this world? (4:60-62)

The hypocrites claimed they had faith in this divine writ and the earlier revelations. However, they are willing to defer to the power of evil that nullifies all the good they could derive from guidance through revelation. This passage touches on faith's psychological problem. When faith has not penetrated one's psyche, such a person outwardly believes in divine writ. Still, he instinctively recoils from that aspect of ethical behavior that contradicts his biases and questionable desires, described as the power of evil. He becomes guilty of hypocrisy in the most profound and religious sense of the word.

God imposes suffering on men and women, the hypocrites, and those who ascribe divinity to aught beside Him. (33:73) God has promised the hypocrites, men, women, and the [outright] deniers of the truth—the fire of hell, to abide: this shall be their allotted portion. For God has rejected them, and long-lasting suffering awaits them. (9:68)

God imposes suffering on those who offend against reason and conscience. Whether in this world or the hereafter, this suffering is a causal consequence of man's moral failure and not an arbitrary act of God.

DIALOGUE BETWEEN THE HYPOCRITES AND THE BELIEVERS ON JUDGMENT DAY

On that Day, the hypocrites, both men and women, shall speak unto those who have attained faith: "Wait for us! Let us have a [ray of] light from your light!" [But] they will be told: "Turn back and seek a light [of your own]!" And a wall will be raised between them [and the believers], with a gate in it. There will be grace and mercy inside and suffering outside thereof. They [who will remain without] will call out to those [within], "Were we not with you?"[To which] the others will answer: "So it was!" But you allowed yourselves to succumb to temptation, were hesitant [in your faith], and doubted resurrection. Your wishful thinking beguiled you until God's command came to pass [until your death] for [indeed, your own] deceptive thoughts about God deluded you. And so, no ransom [or belated repentance] shall be accepted today from you, and neither from those who were [openly] bent on denying the truth. Your goal is fire: your [only] refuge—and how evil a journey's end!" (57:13-15)

The gate in the wall separating true believers and hypocrites points to their possible redemption.

APOSTATES IN DEPTH OF FIRE

As for those who believe, then deny the truth, and again believe and deny the truth and grow stubborn in their denial of the truth, God will not forgive them, nor will He guide them in any way. You announce to such hypocrites that grievous suffering awaits them. (4:137-138) The hypocrites shall be in the lowest depth of the fire, and you will find none who could succor them. (4:145)

The Jews of Medina

CHAPTER 9
THE ARABIAN JEWS

Unfriendly critics of Islam label the Quran anti-Jewish because it is critical of certain Jewish negative practices. A brief presentation of Jacob, Joseph, Moses, and the liberation of the Israelites provides a proper context for understanding the Jews of Medina. See volume two, The Biblical Prophets in the Quran, for complete details. However, the Quran condemned Arabs in a much harsher tone for their polytheistic beliefs.

JACOB

Abraham's grandson, Jacob, was given a second name of **Israel**, and that name has become closely associated with the Israelite homeland. Biblically, Jacob had four wives: Leah, Rachel, and two slave girls. Leah and Rachel were sisters and Jacob's first cousins. Jacob's fathered twelve sons, who became leaders of Israel's twelve tribes. One of them was Joseph, a key figure in the Old Testament and the Quran. Joseph and Benjamin were full brothers, sons of Jacob's wife Rachel, whereas the other ten were half-brothers. Joseph's mother, Rachel, died while giving birth to Benjamin.

JOSEPH

Joseph was Jacob's favorite son, and his half-brothers were jealous of him. They took Joseph out into the wilderness and threw him in a shallow well. According to the Bible (Genesis 37:25), the caravan of "Ishmaelites", or Arabs, "came from Gilead with their camels bearing spice and balm and myrrh, carrying it down to Egypt." Gilead is the Biblical name for the region east of Jordan. They discovered Joseph in the well, took him to Egypt with them and sold him into slavery.

THE ORIGINS OF HEBREW IN EGYPT

Joseph's descendants were fruitful and increased significantly in Egypt. They enjoyed prosperity and an honorable state for a few generations. There arose a king in Egypt, and he said the people of Israel were too many. Egyptians feared Jews might join foreign invaders (Exodus 1:10). Previously, the alien Hyksos dynasty invaded Egypt and allied with the Hebrews. To protect themselves from this danger, they decided to have every male Hebrew child killed, as mentioned in the Quran and the Bible. Then, the Egyptian dynasty dispossessed them of their wealth and reduced them to slavery, from which Moses was to free them. The Hebrew prophet, teacher, leader, lawgiver, and warrior, Moshe, or Moses, delivered his people from Egyptian slavery.

ISRAELITES' STRUGGLE IS INSPIRATION FOR MUSLIMS

Muslims in Mecca were suppressed and disinherited, struggling in an unbelieving society. They were persecuted for their exclusive monotheistic beliefs. Their plight was comparable to that of the Israelites before them (28:4-5), and how a small band of believers under the leadership of a legendary warrior prophet called Moses overcame Pharaoh, the mightiest man alive at that time. Moses is the most frequently mentioned prophet in the Quran. Moses' life story is mentioned in twenty-five chapters, and his name is cited 136 times in the Quran. The story of the Israelites being freed from the bonds of Pharaoh inspired the persecuted Muslims of Mecca.

THE JEWS OF MEDINA

Judaism was well-established in Medina two centuries before Muhammad's birth. Some records indicate more than twenty Jewish clans, including three prominent ones: the Banu **Nadir**, the Banu **Qaynuqa**, and the Banu **Qurayza**. Although influential, Jews did not rule the oasis. Instead, they were clients of two large pagan Arab tribes, the Khazraj and the Aws, who protected them in return for feudal loyalty.

Various traditions uphold different views, and it is unclear whether Medina's Jewish clans were Arabized Jews or Arabs who practiced Jewish monotheism. Indeed, they were Arabic speakers with Arab names. One possibility is that their ancestors settled in Hijaz when they were expelled from Palestine at various times over the ages:

HISTORY OF PERSECUTION OF JEWS

- After the sack of Jerusalem by Nebuchadnezzar
- Pompey's attack upon Judea (64 BC)
- Titus' conquest of Jerusalem (70 CE) and again
- Hadrian's persecution of the Jews in 136 CE

PAGAN MECCANS CONSULT WITH MEDINAN RABBIS

Some Medina rabbis appeared in Muslim sources soon after Prophet Muhammad proclaimed himself a prophet in 610 CE. At that time, the quizzical Meccans, knowing little about monotheism, consulted the Medinan rabbis to test Muhammad. The rabbis posed three theological questions for the Meccans to ask Muhammad. They asserted that they would know, by his answers, whether he spoke the truth. The first question concerned an ancient parable, and the second was a historical riddle. The third question, though, stumped him. It involved the nature of the spirit. The Prophet told them to return the following day, and he would have answers for them. However, he failed to add "Insha Allah," which means "if Allah wills." By the next day, he had not received any revelation to help him answer the questions, and he had to ask the messengers to return the following day. This was repeated for fifteen days while the Meccans laughed at Muhammad's inability to answer three questions. Finally, Gabriel appeared to the Prophet and told him the three answers. The answer to the third question was that humanity lacks the knowledge to understand the spirit fully.

The rabbis were satisfied with all three answers, yet the Meccans remained unconvinced. (For details of this story, see chapter 22 of the third volume).

The Prophet arrived in Medina in 622 to arbitrate a bloody civil war between the Khazraj and the Aws. Jewish clans, their clients, were embroiled on opposite sides. Medina's Jews were divided and killed by each other while fighting for the pagan Arabs.

THE PROPHET'S FRIENDLY OVERTURES TO THE JEWS

Fasting: The Prophet bound himself to the Jews in friendship and respect because they were monotheists. He supported the Jews so fervently that he fasted with them. During the early part of the Medina period, fasting during Ramadan was not yet instituted. (It was 624 CE, and the very first Ramadan was observed in Medina.) Since the Jews were the people of the first scripture, it was logical to follow their example.

Direction of Prayer: The Prophet prayed facing Jerusalem as the Jews did. Even during the Mecca period, whenever the Prophet offered prayers in the Kabah, he faced both the Kabah and Jerusalem. When he moved to Medina, he continued to pray northward toward Jerusalem.

The Prophet incorporated the principle of religious freedom, which became human history's first charter of freedom of conscience. The Medina Constitution guaranteed complete freedom of religion and equality for Jews. There was, however, no express stipulation that Jews should formally recognize Muhammad as the Messenger and Prophet of God. No tax was levied upon the Jews because they were expected to defend Medina.

Such friendly gestures confused Western historians. They opined that when the Apostle left Mecca, he looked forward to his acceptance by the Jews of Yathrib. He tried to win them over by adopting Jewish practices. However, the Apostle was soon disappointed by Jewish rejection, so he broke up with them and crushed them. This picture represents a contorted reflection of events. In two early Meccan surahs (10:93 and 17:4-5), the Prophet was warned about the Jews' contentiousness. Despite this warning, he extended friendship to the Jewish community based on the principle of presumption of innocence, and the Jews were fellow monotheists.

THE JEWS' CONTENTIOUSNESS

We assigned the children of Israel a most good abode and provided sustenance for them from the good things of life. And it was not until knowledge [of God's revelation] was vouchsafed to them that they began to hold divergent views: [but], verily, thy Sustainer will judge between them on Resurrection Day regarding all on which they differ. (10:93) And we made [this] known to the children of Israel through revelation: "Twice, indeed, will you spread corruption on earth and become grossly overbearing!" Hence, when the prediction of the first of those two [iniquity] came true, We sent against you some of Our bondmen of terrible prowess in war. They wrought havoc throughout the land, and the prediction was fulfilled. (17:4-5)

The expression "**twice**" refers to two distinct, extended periods of Jewish history. The phrase "Our bondmen of **terrible prowes**s in war" probably refers to the Assyrians and Babylonians who overran Palestine.

EXPECTATIONS OF THE JEWISH COMMUNITY

There is no evidence that the Apostle ever considered Medina's Jews converting to Islam. Since Jews worshipped One God and their religion was given equal status to Islam, there was no expectation to become Muslims. Like Christianity, Islam is an evangelizing religion, seeking new converts to the faith. It was not surprising that the Medina Jews were invited to Islam by the Prophet and his companions. However, Jews remained faithful to their faith, with some exceptions. Medina's Muslims, at the least, expected understanding from their fellow monotheists. They were suppressed and persecuted in Mecca, struggling in an unbelieving society due to their exclusive monotheistic beliefs. Their plight was comparable to that of the Israelites in Egypt before them. The story of the Israelites escaping Pharaoh's bonds inspired Muslims of Mecca.

Many of the Jews welcomed the end of the civil war in the oasis. With the reconciliation between the two Arab tribes and the addition of the third, the Jewish community, the dawn of peace in the oasis seemed imminent. However, the euphoria did not last long and was replaced by harsh political realities. Relations with several Jewish tribes in Medina became tense. The Muslims and the Prophet Muhammad's position in these early months in Medina was still precarious.

CHAPTER 10
THE JEWISH OPPOSITION

In the early period of Islam, and especially after their departure to Medina, where many Jews lived, Muslims expected Jews to be sympathetic to the Quran's monotheism. Hope was disappointed because the Jews regarded their religion as a national heritage reserved for the children of Israel alone. They did not believe in the necessity or possibility of a new revelation. Cf. Jeremiah 23:26 - "Ye have perverted the words of the living God." As the "chosen people, the prophets rose only from their tribe. Muhammad's prophethood was incompatible with their understanding of Judaism.

You shall most certainly be tried in your possessions and your persons, as well as you shall hear many hurtful things from those to whom revelation was granted before your time and those who have come to ascribe divinity to other beings besides God. But if you remain patient in adversity and conscious of Him—this is something upon to set one's heart. (3:186)

Can you [the Muslims] hope that they will believe in what you are preaching—seeing that many of them listen to the word of God and then, after understanding it, pervert it Knowingly? (2:75)

RELIGIOUS REASONS

Out of their selfish envy, many among the followers of earlier revelation would like to bring you back to denying the truth after you have attained faith - [even] after the truth has become clear to them. Nonetheless, forgive and forbear until God manifests His will: behold, God has the power to will anything. (2:109)

CONVERSION OF LEARNED JEWS

Those who are deeply rooted in knowledge, who believe in what has been bestowed from on high upon you. Those who are [especially] constant in prayer, and spend in charity, and all who believe in God and the Last Day—these it is unto whom We shall grant a mighty reward. (4:162) And [the essence of] this [revelation] is indeed found in the ancient books of divine wisdom [as well]. Is it not evidence enough for them that [so many] learned men from among the children of Israel have recognized this [as true]? (26:196-197)

Those Jews who are deeply rooted in knowledge do not settle for the mere observance of rituals. Instead, they try to penetrate faith's most profound meaning. The reference to "Those who are [especially] constant in prayer" the construction of the sentence stresses the unique, praiseworthy quality attached to prayer and to those who are devoted to it.

The above verse is in complete accord with the oft-repeated Quranic doctrine that the fundamental teachings revealed to Muhammad are, in their purport, identical to those preached by the earlier prophets. Some learned Jews recognized this truth and became Muslims. For instance, Abd Allah ibn Salam, a learned rabbi, approached the Prophet and announced his conversion, including his household. Kab ibn Malik and other learned Jews of Medina also joined the Muslims in the Prophet's lifetime. Kab al-Ahbar, the Yemenite, and several of his compatriots became Muslims during Umar's reign and countless others throughout the world who embraced Islam over the centuries. The conversion of prominent Jewish community members to Islam triggered their suspicions.

POLITICAL AND ECONOMIC REASONS

When the Prophet arrived at Medina, he worked towards unifying all the peoples of the oasis. To this end, agreements were drawn up which provided a framework for political unity. Muhammad had been summoned to Medina to bring order through his authority. The population was thus more or less willing to acknowledge his political authority, but the Jews (and the Arabs who did not convert to Islam) would not recognize his spiritual authority.

ACTIVE HOSTILITIES BY THE JEWS

Having disagreements on religious matters, the Jews began to be hostile to the Prophet. There was verbal abuse of the Prophet, his wives, and the Muslim community. Despite various peace treaties with the Prophet, Jews actively supported Muhammad's enemies, the Pagans of Mecca. They did everything in their power to destroy Islam and Muslims but brought destruction upon themselves.

INCREASED POLITICAL CLOUT

The Prophet's teachings and leadership profoundly affected the people who joined Islam, and their conversion consolidated and increased Muslim power in Medina. The Prophet became the most powerful man in Medina as Islam spread throughout the clans of Aws and Khazraj, and his power seemed likely to increase.

DIVIDE AND RULE

Medina was not so much a city as a fractious agricultural settlement dotted by fortresses and strongholds, and all relations in the oasis were uneasy. The Jews gained power in the oasis in the old days by joining one warring Arab tribe. Some Jewish clans were uncomfortable with the threatened demise of the old alliances. The division between Arabs greatly enhanced the status of non-Arabs, who were in demand as allies.

REGAINING POLITICAL SUPREMACY

The Jews of Medina hoped to recover political supremacy, perhaps in conjunction with Abd Allah b. Ubayy, a hope that was rapidly extinguished by the Prophet Muhammad's successes. The union of the two dominant tribes of Al Aws and Al Khazraj, and with the addition of Muslim immigrants to the new ummah, the Jews felt disenfranchised. They saw their political position in Medina decline.

At this stage, the Jews began to rethink their position vis-à-vis Muhammad. They asked themselves whether they should let his call, spiritual power, and authority spread while remaining satisfied with the security they enjoyed under his protection and the increased trade and wealth that his peace had brought to their city. The Jews and Abd Allah bin Ubayy had close business ties with the Quraysh of Mecca. They allied themselves with the pagan Arabs to destroy the Prophet and the nascent Islamic state.

The quarrel between Muhammad and the Jews started in the realm of ideas. Unfortunately, ideological warfare was initiated by the Jews and not by Muhammad. The Jews used their knowledge of the Old Testament to criticize Muhammad's claim that the Quran was God's speech.

For Muhammad, the idea that he was a prophet receiving messages from God and with a commission from Him was the basis of the whole political and religious movement he was leading. Remove this idea, and the movement would collapse. The ideational conflict between Muhammad and the Jews became very bitter as it threatened the very core of Islam. Once they had decided to reject Muhammad, the Jews had to justify this decision, at least to themselves, and perhaps this was why they indulged in mocking criticism of Muhammad.

POTENTIAL FOR DESTRUCTION OF THE MUSLIM COMMUNITY

The Muslims and Muhammad's position in these early months in Medina was still precarious. If many Muslims thought that what the Jews were saying was true, the community's whole structure would unravel. The Prophet needed the support of men who wholeheartedly believed in the religious aspect of his mission. The Jews were doing their best to deprive him of such support. Therefore, the vigorous Quranic defense of Islam was the need of the hour to counterbalance the anti-Islamic views of Medinese Jews, potentially threatening the very existence of the Muslim community.

In the next section (Part 2: The Quranic Rebuttal to the Jewish Criticism), explain how the Quran counter the virulent Islamophobic Jewish propaganda. With this background information, the Quranic criticism of the Jews must be understood. The Quran gives a balanced view of Jewish history and highlights its positive and negative aspects. Although the Quran is critical of the Jews for deviating from their revealed scripture, it reserved its harsh condemnation for Arab contemporaries of the Prophet. They were idol worshippers and rejected monotheism.

THE LESSON FOR ALL BELIEVERS

It would be a mistake to judge Judaism from the behavior of the Jews of Medina, just as it would be a mistake to consider Islam or Christianity by some Muslims and Christians' conduct. The criticism of Jews in the Quran is a lesson for the Muslims as to how to avoid the errors of the Jews. Some Muslims of today are also guilty of the same mistakes which the Quran accuses the Jews of. By following the Quran's method, the story of Children of Israel is an object lesson for all believers in God of whatever community or time.

THE QURANIC REBUTTAL TO JEWISH POLEMICS

CHAPTER 11
GOD'S CHOSEN PEOPLE: SPIRTUAL VERSUS INHERITED?

Jewish sources say Jews are "chosen people" and have a special relationship with God. However, this relationship is not without complications and controversy. The biblical notion of "chosen people" is both spiritual and inherited.

1. THE SPIRITUAL BASIS OF THE "CHOSEN PEOPLE"

Jews being chosen spiritually has biblical roots. One of the most prominent says: *"You are a people consecrated to the LORD your God: of all the peoples on earth, the LORD your God chose you to be His treasured people." (Deuteronomy 7:6) So do not fear, for I am with you; do not be dismayed, for I am your God. I will strengthen you and help you; I will uphold you with my righteous right hand. (Isaiah 41:10)*

God chose the Israelites to be His "treasured people" and freed them from slavery in Egypt. It is because the Jews were the first monotheists like their ancestors, Abraham, Isaac, and Jacob. Abraham, alone among his contemporaries, established idolatry as falsehood, affirming that only one God ruled the earth.

ISLAMIC VIEW OF CHOSENNESS

Since Jews were the first to adopt monotheism, the Quran recognizes Jews as the "chosen people" **spiritually**. The reference to the children of Israel, as in the Quran, arises from the fact that their religious beliefs represented an earlier phase of the monotheistic concept, which culminated in the revelation of the Quran.

O Children of Israel! Remember those blessings of mine with which I graced you and how I favored you above all other people. (2:47) Indeed, We have already granted revelation, wisdom, and prophethood to the children of Israel. We provided sustenance for them from the good things of life and favored them above all other people [of their time]. And We gave them a clear purpose of their faith. (45:16-17)

The first divinely inspired law, the Torah, inaugurated a new phase in religious history. God chose the children of Israel as "forerunners in faith." At that time, they were the only truly monotheistic community. The innermost purpose of all true faith is a realization of the existence of God and of every human being's responsibility to Him, making man aware that whatever good or evil he does is but done for the benefit, or to the detriment, of his own self. Thus, man attaining a consciousness of his own dignity, achieving freedom from all manner of superstitions and irrational fears.

The Arabs, for the most part, were idol worshippers, and it took millennia to adopt Islamic monotheism. Jews are the older siblings of the Abrahamic family, worshipping one God alone for more than a thousand years before Islam's birth. Partly due to their religion, Jews have suffered persecution, repeated pogroms, and the Holocaust in the last two thousand years of their history, usually in the hands of Christians.

CONDITIONAL UNDERSTANDING OF "CHOSENNESS"

It is assumed that the Jewish people's chosenness (in a spiritual sense) was a result of a covenantal relationship with God. Exodus 19.5 captures this view: *"Now if you will obey Me faithfully and keep My covenant, you shall be My treasured possession among all the peoples."* Similarly, there is a conditional understanding of chosenness in the Quran as well: *And [remember this]: when his Sustainer tried Abraham by [His] commandments, and the latter fulfilled them, Allah said: "I shall make you a leader of men."*

Abraham asked: "And [wilt Thou make leaders] of my offspring as well?" [God] answered: "My covenant does not embrace evildoers. (2:124) Are you unaware of those who consider themselves pure? It is God who causes whomever He wills to grow in purity, and none shall be wronged by a hair's breadth. (4:49)

Abraham's exalted status would not automatically confer equal status on his physical descendants and certainly not on the sinners among them.

2. THE FAMILIAL OR INHERITED FORM OF "CHOSEN PEOPLE"

As time passed, the concept of spiritual chosenness morphed into Jewish ethnic superiority. Most Jews became convinced that they were "God's chosen people" simply because of their physical descent from Prophet Abraham. According to the Bible, Abraham was the first man with whom God entered covenants, promising a special relationship with God and the children of Israel forever. Through a series of covenants, the Jews evolved into a chosen people. This is described in the chapter of Genesis:

THE FIRST COVENANT (THE PROMISED LAND)

The Lord said to Abram, "Go from your country, your people and your father's household to the land [Canaan] I will show you. "I will make you into a mighty nation, and I will bless you; I will make your name great, and you will be a blessing. I will bless those who bless you, and whoever curses you I will curse, and all peoples on earth will be blessed through you." (Gen 12:1-4)

SECOND COVENANT (THE PROMISE OF ISHMAEL)

The Lord spoke to Abram in a vision: "Do not be afraid, Abram. I am your shield, your very great reward." And Abram said, "You have given me no children, so a servant in my household will be my heir." Then the word of the Lord came to him: "This man will not be your heir, but a son who is your own flesh and blood will be your heir." He took him outside and said, "Look up at the sky and count the stars—if indeed you can count them." Then he spoke to him, "So shall your offspring be." (Gen 15:1-5)

Although no name is mentioned in the above verses, after God promised Abraham a son, Ishmael was born.

BIRTH OF ISHMAEL

Sarai, Abram's wife, bore him no children. But she had an Egyptian slave named Hagar. So, Sarai took her Egyptian slave Hagar and gave her to her husband to be his wife. He slept with Hagar, and she conceived (with Ishmael). (Gen 16:1-4)

PROMISE OF DESCENDANTS AND THE LAND OF CANAAN

When Abram was ninety-nine years old, the *Lord* appeared to him and said, "I am God Almighty; walk before me faithfully and be blameless. Then I will make my covenant between me and you and will greatly increase your numbers." Abram fell facedown, and God said to him, "As for me, this is my covenant with you: You will be the father of many nations. No longer will you be called Abram; your name will be Abraham, for I have made you a father of many nations. I will make you very fruitful; I will make nations of you, and kings will come from you. I will establish my covenant as an everlasting covenant between me and you and your descendants after you for the generations to come, to be your God and the God of your descendants after you. The whole land of Canaan, where you now reside as a foreigner, I will give as an everlasting possession to you and your descendants after you, and I will be their God." Then God said to Abraham, "As for you, you must keep my covenant, you and your descendants after you for the generations to come. (Genesis 17:1-9)

THE COVENANT OF CIRCUMCISION

This is my covenant with you and your descendants after you, the covenant you are to keep: Every male among you shall be circumcised. You are to undergo circumcision, and it will be the sign of the covenant between me and you. For the generations to come, every male among you who is eight days old must be circumcised, including those born in your household or bought with money from a foreigner—those who are not your offspring. Whether born in your household or bought with your money, they must be circumcised. My covenant in your flesh is to be an everlasting covenant. Any uncircumcised male, who has not been circumcised in the flesh, will be cut off from his people; he has broken my covenant." (Genesis 17: 10-14)

On that very day, Abraham took his son Ishmael and all those born in his household or bought with his money every male in his household and circumcised them, as God told him. Abraham was ninety-nine years old when he was circumcised, and his son Ishmael was thirteen; Abraham and his son Ishmael were both circumcised on that very day. And every male in Abraham's household, including those born in his household or bought from a foreigner, was circumcised with him. (Genesis 17:23-27)

The seal of God's covenant was circumcision. Abraham and Ishmael were circumcised on the same day. Ishmael was included in the covenant; however, Isaac's birth will change all that.

BIRTH OF ISAAC: THE ONLY SEED OF ABRAHAM

God also said to Abraham, "As for Sarai, your wife, you are no longer to call her Sarai; her name will be Sarah. I will bless her and will surely give you a son by her. I will bless her so that she will be the mother of nations; kings of peoples will come from her." Abraham fell facedown; he laughed and said to himself, "Will a son be born to a man a hundred years old? Will Sarah bear a child at the age of ninety?" And Abraham said to God, "If only Ishmael might live under your blessing!" Then God said, "Yes, but your wife Sarah will bear you a son, and you will call him Isaac. I will establish my covenant with him as an everlasting covenant for his descendants after him. And as for Ishmael, I have heard you: I will surely bless him; I will make him fruitful and will greatly increase his numbers. He will be the father of twelve rulers, and I will make him into a great nation. But my covenant I will establish with Isaac, whom Sarah will bear to you by this time next year." When he had finished speaking with Abraham, God went up from him. (Genesis 17:16-22)

When God promised Abraham that Sarah would have a son, Abraham felt this was almost too much to expect, given his and Sarah's old age. Abraham was perfectly content with Ishmael as an heir to the covenant promise. However, God disagreed with Abraham, and His covenant would be established through Isaac, who was yet to be born. Ishmael would have a notable line of descendants. Thus, Abraham's second son, Isaac, and his descendants were "**chosen**" as "**the only seed of Abraham.**"

WHAT IS THE MEANING OF ABRAHAM'S SEED?

The first obvious question is what Abraham's seed means. Besides Sarah and Hagar, Keturah was Abraham's third wife. Abraham's sons, from oldest to youngest, were Ishmael (son with Hagar), Isaac (son of Sarah), Zimran, Jokshan, and Medan (sons of Keturah). Abraham's daughters are not recorded in the scripture. Simple common sense says all three wives' children constitute Abraham's seed. But by some twisted, perverse logic, Jews and Christians believe that the seed of promise was Isaac, and Ishmael was no longer part of the covenant. Here the Quran and the Bible part company.

ALTERING THE SCRIPTURE

Woe unto those who write down, with their own hands, [something they claim to be] divine writ. They then say, "This is from God," to acquire a trifling gain thereby. Woe unto them for what their hands have written, and woe unto them for all they may have gained! (2:79)

The reference here is to the scholars responsible for corrupting the text of the Bible and thus misleading their ignorant followers. The "trifling gain" is their feeling of pre-eminence as the alleged "chosen people" because of their descent from Abraham. In the gospel, according to St. Luke in the New Testament, chapter 3, verse 8, John the Baptist condemned the concept of chosen people. "Bring forth, therefore, fruits worthy of repentance, and begin not to say within yourselves, we have Abraham to our father: for I say unto you, that God is able of these stones to raise up children unto Abraham."

DID GOD RENEGE FROM HIS PROMISE WITH ISHMAEL?

According to the human author of the Bible, the God of Israel reneged on His promise to Ishmael and declared Isaac Abraham's only seed. As a teenager, Ishmael endured a painful circumcision, symbolically establishing a covenant with God. Muslim boys are circumcised today, following Ishmael and Abraham's tradition.

The birth of Isaac is described in many different surahs of the Quran, and there is no hint of "chosenness" or reference to "the only seed of Abraham."

And after he [Abraham] withdrew from them [his homeland, Iraq] and from all, they worshipped instead of God. We bestowed upon him Isaac and Jacob and made each of them a prophet. We bestowed upon them [manifold] gifts out of Our grace and granted them a lofty power to convey the truth [to others]. (19:49-50) [As for Abraham], We bestowed Isaac and [Isaac's son] Jacob upon him and caused prophethood and revelation to continue among his offspring. And We vouchsafed him his reward in this world, and in the life to come [too] he shall find himself among the righteous. (29:27)

EVICTION OF ISHMAEL AND HAGAR

Not only was Ishmael removed from the covenant, he and his mother were evicted and abandoned in the desert to certain death.

But Sarah saw that the son of Hagar the Egyptian had borne to Abraham was mocking. She said to Abraham, "Get rid of that slave woman and her son, for that woman's son will never share in the inheritance with my son Isaac." (Gen 21:9-10)

Sarah's statement made abundantly clear that the motivation for evicting Ishmael was greed so that Isaac could inherit all of Abraham's estate.

DENIAL OF ISHMAEL'S PATERNITY

In the famous verse of Abraham's son's sacrifice, Isaac was declared the only son, meaning the only seed of Abraham:

"And God said, take now thy son, your only son Isaac, whom thou lovest, and bring thee into the land of Moriah. (Genesis 22:2)

To a casual reader, it may appear as a typographical error that the scribe forgot that Abraham had other sons. This was a clever move to sanctify Isaac as Abraham's only seed. Isaac was entitled to inherit Abraham's entire wealth, excluding his other sons. It established the status of chosen people for Jews, paving their way to inheriting Canaan. Besides material greed, what were the reasons Ishmael was cut off from the covenant? The Bible is silent on this question, and perhaps the answers are uncomfortable.

ISHMAEL BIRACIAL AND ILLEGITIMATE CHILD OF A BLACK CONCUBINE

Ishmael was born out of wedlock to a slave and a black mother. Bible readers often believe Ishmael was an illegitimate child. The Bible references Ishmael as Abraham's son and Hagar as Abraham's wife in many passages. Ishmael's birth is legal under Jewish law. Ishmael was a biracial child born to a black concubine, thus racially inferior to Isaac, who belonged to Abraham and Sarah's superior tribe.

RACIAL PURITY OF ISAAC

Sarah belonged to the same tribe or ethnic group as Abraham. Isaac's racial purity elevates him among his siblings to be worthy of being the "only seed of Abraham," or heir to the entire wealth of Abraham, including the land of Canaan. Isaac's descendants were declared "the chosen people." This gave rise to the Jewish demand that the land of Canaan belonged only to the "seed of Abraham" and that the Ishmaelites had no right to live on this land. The following biblical verses establish Isaac, Jacob, and their descendants' racial superiority:

THE SUPERIORITY OF JACOB'S SONS

When Isaac blessed Jacob, he told him: *"**May nations serve you and peoples bow down to you. Be lord over your brothers and may your mother's sons bow down to you. May those who curse you be cursed and those who bless you be blessed."** (Gen.27:29)*

These nations are the offspring of Ishmael and Keturah (Gen. Rabbah 66:4). The Rabbis stress that the subjugation of Keturah's children to Israel is eternal. The racial superiority of Jews over Arabs is the foundation of modern Israel, described as an apartheid state by human rights organizations.

CHAPTER 12
THE QURANIC REBUTTAL OF THE RACIALLY BASED CHOSENNESS

The Quran categorically rejects hereditary or familial chosenness. Abraham's descent does not confer racial superiority. All communities subscribed to the doctrine of God's oneness and held that man's self-surrender to Him (Islam in its original connotation) is the essence of all true religions. Their subsequent divergences were caused by sectarian pride and mutual exclusiveness. Jewish assertion of being chosen people is another example of supremacist ideology. The key to understanding any conflict between Arabs and Jews is the notion of chosen people and their superiority over Arabs or Gentiles.

DIVERGENT VIEWS ABOUT ABRAHAM

We have inspired thee, [O Muhammad, with this message]: "Follow the creed of Abraham, who turned away from all that is false. He was not one of those who ascribe divinity to anything besides God. [And know that the observance of] the Sabbath was ordained only for those with divergent views about him [Abraham]. Verily, God will judge between them on Resurrection Day regarding all on which they were inclined to differ." (16:123-124)

The implication is that most of the Jews deviated from the true creed of Abraham, which is the meaning of the phrase "those who came to hold divergent views about him." They became convinced that they were "God's chosen people" simply because of their physical descent from that great Prophet, an assumption that runs counter to every truly religious principle. God will judge those who are convinced of their ultimate salvation because of their alleged status as "God's chosen people" and judge those who believe in man's individual responsibility before Him. The Quran reminds the children of Israel that the way to salvation is through righteousness shown to them by explicit social and moral injunctions. One's condition in the afterlife depends exclusively on how one lives in this life.

THE WAY OF RIGHTEOUSNESS

And lo! We accepted this solemn pledge from [you], the children of Israel: "You shall worship none but God, do good unto your parents and kinsfolk, the orphans, and the poor. You shall speak unto all people kindly, be constant in prayer, and spend in charity." And yet, save for a few of you, you turned away. This is because you are stubborn people! (2:83)

The Old Testament contains many allusions to the waywardness and stubborn rebelliousness of the children of Israel—e.g., Exodus 32:9, 33:3, 34:9; Deuteronomy 9:6-8, 23-24, 27.

DIVINE MESSAGE NOT RESTRICTED TO ANY DENOMINATION

Do they envy others for what God has granted them out of His bounty? But then, We granted revelation and wisdom to the House of Abraham, and We bestowed a mighty dominion. Among them are those who truly believe in him (Abraham) and those who have turned away from him. (4:54-55)

Are they jealous of the Quranic revelations? Jews reserve divine revelation for them alone.

"Those who truly believe" in Abraham are faithful to his message. The Prophet Muhammad, too, was a direct-line descendant of Abraham, whose message is confirmed and continued in the Quran.

THE PROMISE LAND

And [remember] when you were told: "Dwell in this land [Palestine] and eat its food as you wish but say, 'Remove Thou from us the burden of our sins,' and enter the gate humbly. (7:161) O children of Israel! Remember those blessings of Mine with which I graced you, and fulfill your promise unto Me, [whereupon] I shall fulfill My promise unto you; and of Me, of Me stand in awe! (2:40)

According to the Quran, Ishmael and Isaac were righteous men and God's prophets. Their descendants, both Jews and Arabs, have equal rights to live together. This is what God promised Abraham when he left for Canaan and before Isaac's birth. The Quran explicitly states that Jews have the right to live in Palestine.

MODERN GENETIC RESEARCH

THE CANAANITES' ANCESTORS OF JEWS AND ARABS

The Canaanites are best known as the people who lived "in a land flowing with milk and honey" until they were vanquished by the ancient Israelites and disappeared from history. Archaeological and genetic data contradict biblical assertions about the Canaanites' disappearance. Instead, scientific data support that Jews and Palestinians came from the ancient Canaanites. These people extensively mixed with Egyptians, Mesopotamian, and Anatolian peoples in ancient times. A scientific report reveals that the genetic heritage of the Canaanites survives in many modern-day Jews and Arabs.

GENETIC STUDIES NEGATE TWO-NATION THEORY

Scientists have also found that the Y chromosome in Middle Eastern Arabs was almost indistinguishable from that of Jews, pointing towards a common paternal line. (The Y-chromosome is inherited unchanged from father to son to grandson, indefinitely.) Palestinians are biologically related to Jews. Modern genetic studies negate the concept of two nations and show that Jews and Palestinians are essentially the same people. Thus, the Palestinian-Jewish conflict is based on cultural rather than genetic differences. There is no scientific basis for Israel to be a "Jewish state" based on race. It can be a religious state founded on Judaism, but most Israelis are non-religious. They claim that God gave them "Judea and Samaria," but in the same breath, they deny the same God.

RACISM

Racism is an ideology that asserts that one group is inherently superior to others. One ethnicity dominates, excludes, or seeks to eliminate another based on a difference it believes is hereditary and unalterable.

There is a racist in every one of us. The only difference is that some consider racism evil to contend with, while racists take pride in it.

Negative traits associated with a sense of superiority:

- Grandiose sense of self-importance, entitlement, and unreasonable expectations.
- Those deemed inferior should be obedient to their wishes, and the rules don't apply to them.
- Display of arrogant and haughty behavior.
- Unwilling or unable to empathize with others' needs, wants, or feelings.
- Being special or unique, they should only be associated with high-status people.

White Racism: Hindu nationalism and white supremacy are two sides of the same coin based upon a common Indo-European supposed superiority of Aryan ancestry. Brahmins in the Hindu religion consider themselves superior to lower castes and non-Hindus.

Christian identity believes that only the Germanic, Anglo-Saxon, Nordic, or Aryan races are descendants of Abraham and Isaac. White supremacists adopted many of these teachings. It is not the official position of any mainstream church. Christian identity holds that all non-whites (people not of wholly European descent) will either be exterminated or enslaved to serve the white race in the upcoming Heavenly Kingdom on Earth under Jesus Christ.

Arab/Muslim Racism: Although racism is a sin in Islam, some Arabs treat non-Arabs as inferior races. Arabs do not have the religious sanction of "chosen people," but their descent from the prophets Ishmael and Muhammad gives them a false sense of superiority over non-Arabs.

Jewish Racism: Gideon Levy, an Israeli award-winning journalist and author, once said in a speech: "And if you scratch under the skin of almost every Israeli, you will find it there. Almost no one will treat the Palestinians as equal human beings like us. I once wrote that we treat Palestinians like animals. I got so many protest letters from animal rights organizations—rightly so. Jewish people are the chosen people, and there can't be equality between Jews and Arabs. Jews have more rights in Palestine than anyone else."

Some enlightened Jewish thinkers, influenced by egalitarianism and universalism, see this position as racist and inherently immoral. Foremost among such thinkers is Mordecai Kaplan (1881-1983), the founder of Reconstructionist Judaism. He did not believe in a supernatural God that could bestow favor on one nation. He believed that it was practically and morally problematic to posit the fundamental superiority of one person. In fact, most forms of contemporary Judaism have not abandoned their belief in being "chosen" and, therefore, superior.

The Jewish population is only 0.2% of the world's population. God rejected 99.8% of His own creation and selected Jews as His "chosen people." The whole idea of racial supremacy is a ridiculous delusion of grandeur. It is the root cause of most relationship problems. As a result, Jews can commit human rights violations without feeling guilty. The "chosen people" can do whatever they want, and God will always be on their side. Those who challenge their hubris will be branded anti-Semitic. Due to their feelings of victimhood brought about by the Holocaust, they justify their atrocities against those "sub-humans" who dare to speak out for equal rights.

There is plenty of land and resources to support both Jews and Palestinians. The Jewish belief that they are "chosen people" and their superiority entitles them to the entire holy land without Arabs is at the root of the conflict. Israel discriminates against black Jews. Many non-white Jews, brown-colored emigrants from Arab lands, still lack equal rights to white Ashkenazi Jews.

The Quran refutes, as in so many other places, the spurious contention of the Jews that they are "the chosen people" by virtue of their descent from Abraham, Isaac, and Jacob. Therefore, they are a priori "assured", as it were, of God's acceptance. The Quran reiterates that God's blessing on a prophet, like Abraham, does not confer special status on his descendants.

ABANDON THE FALSE IDEA OF "CHOSEN PEOPLE"

Believe in what I have [now] bestowed from on high. Confirm the truth already in your possession. Be not foremost among those who deny its truth; and do not barter away My messages for a trifling gain; and of Me, of Me be conscious! (2:41)

The "trifling gain" is their conviction that they are "God's chosen people" and, by implication, superior to Gentiles - a claim that the Quran consistently refutes. This refers to the persistent Jewish belief that they, alone among all nations, have been graced by divine revelation.

RENEW YOUR BOND WITH GOD AND MAN

Overshadowed by ignominy are they wherever they may be, save [when they bind themselves again] in a bond with God and men. This is because they have earned God's condemnation and are overshadowed by humiliation. All this [has befallen them] because they persisted in denying the truth of God's messages and slaying the prophets against all rights. All this because they rebelled [against God] and transgressed what was right. (3:112)

Thus, the Quran warns those who espouse supremacist ideologies to abandon their evil ways and renew their bonds with God. It also urges them to join the human family as equals. They will not be overshadowed by ignominy if they return to the concept of God as the Lord and Sustainer of all mankind. They should also give up the idea of being "Chosen people" (in a hereditary sense). They will be forgiven through God's mercy and grace otherwise they will be overshadowed by ignominy on Judgment Day.

ISLAMIC TEACHINGS

Islam rejects perceived superiority passed on by birth or circumstance rather than merit or work. Racist ideology is completely alien to Islam. No one enjoys a special status. God's blessings are given to people based on merit, not by group or race. Racism is a narcissistic phenomenon in degenerated societies. Any ideology that divides humanity into superior and inferior categories is inherently evil. It contradicts the basic Islamic doctrine that all human beings are equal and only a man's character determines his status in God's sight.

THE PROPHET SAID:

Humanity comes from Adam and Eve. An Arab has no superiority over a non-Arab, nor does a non-Arab have any superiority over an Arab; also, a white has no superiority over a black, nor has a black any superiority over a white except through piety and righteous actions."

The Quran refutes racist thinking and clearly says:

It is not your desires, nor the desires of the People of the Book that shall prevail. Anyone who commits evil will be punished accordingly. He will not find any protectors or patrons besides God. (4:123)

CHAPTER 13
THE ERRORS OF THE JEWS (continued)

NON-COMPLIANCE WITH THE COVENANTS?

Medina's Jews followed the Torah's fundamental precepts. However, scholars question their familiarity with the Talmud and Jewish scholarship. There is a suggestion in the Quran that they may have embraced unorthodox beliefs, such as considering the Prophet Ezra the son of God. However, Medina's Jews were not representatives of mainstream Judaism.

THE KILLING OF FELLOW JEWS

And Lo! We accepted your solemn pledge that you would not shed one another's blood and drive one another out of your homeland. Whereupon you acknowledged it, and to it, you bear witness [even now]. And yet, it is you who slay one another and expel some of your people from their homelands, aiding one another against them in sin and hatred. But if they come to you as captives, you will ransom them, even though driving them away is unlawful for you! Do you believe in some parts of the divine writ and deny the truth of others? The reward for those among you who do these things is still ignominy in this life and, on the Day of Resurrection, the most grievous suffering of all. For God is not unmindful of what you do. All who buy the life of this world at the price of the life to come—their suffering shall not be lightened nor succored! (2:84-86)

The above verses refer to the conditions prevailing in Medina at the time of the Prophet's Hijrah. Medina's two Arab tribes-Al-Aws and Khazraj—were permanently at war. Out of the three Jewish tribes living there Qaynuqa, Banu al-Nadir, and Banu Qurayzah-the first two were allied with Khazraj, and the third was allied with Al-Aws.

In their warfare, Jews killed Jews in alliance with pagans ("aiding one another in sin and hatred"): a heinous crime under the Mosaic Law. However, they ransom their mutual captives in obedience to that very same Law—this glaring inconsistency to which the Quran alludes in the sentence above.

EZRA, AS THE SON OF GOD

And the Jews say, "Ezra is God's son," while the Christians say, "Christ is God's son." Such are the sayings they utter with their mouths, following in spirit the assertions uttered by people who deny the truth!" [They deserve the imprecation:] "May God destroy them!" How perverted are their minds? The rabbis, the monks, and Jesus Christ, son of Mary, have been made Lords beside God. However, they were commanded to worship One God, save whom there is no deity. This is the one who is utterly remote, in His limitless glory, from anything to which they may ascribe a share in His divinity! (9:30–31)

The phrase "son of God" has different meanings for Jews and Christians. In the Hebrew Bible, it is another way to refer to humans with a special relationship with God. It may also refer to angels, humans, or even all humanity. In Christianity, Jesus is God's Son because He is God made manifest in human form. Almost all classical commentators on the Quran agree that only some Arabian Jews believed that Ezra was God's son. Not all Jews have been accused in this way. A tradition quoted on the authority of Ibn Abbas by Tabari in his commentary on this verse - some of the Jews of Medina once said to Muhammad, "How could we follow thee when thou hast forsaken our Qiblah and dost not consider Ezra, a son of God?"

All Jews regarded Ezra as exceptional, and they always lavished him with praise. He restored and codified the Torah after it was lost during the Babylonian Exile and "edited" it into the form it has today. Thus, he promoted the establishment of an exclusive, legalistic religion that became dominant in later Judaism (Encyclopedia Britannica, 1963, vol. IX, p. 15). Ever since then, he has been revered to such a degree that his verdicts on the Law of Moses have been regarded by the Talmudists as practically equivalent to the Law itself. In Quranic ideology, this amounts to the unforgivable sin of shirk. This implies the elevation of a human being to the status of a quasi-divine lawgiver and the blasphemous attribution to him - albeit metaphorically - of the quality of "sonship" in relation to God.

UNCHARITABLE DISPOSITION

Have they, perhaps, a share of [God's] dominion? But [if they had], lo, they would not give to other people as much as [would fill] the groove of a date stone! (4:53) And they should not think - they who miserly cling to all that God has granted them out of His bounty - that this is a blessing for them: nay, it is a curse for them. That to which they [so] stingily cling will, on the Day of Resurrection, be hung about their necks: for unto God [alone] belongs the heritage of the heavens and the earth, and God is aware of all that you do. (3:180)

"Share in [God's] dominion," an allusion to the Jewish belief that they occupy a privileged position in God's sight. Above is an allusion to the way of life characterized by extreme attachment to the material things of this world - materialism based on a lack of belief in anything that transcends practical problems.

EXTREME ATTACHMENT TO THIS WORLD

Say: "O you who follow the Jewish faith! If you claim that you are close to God [alone], to the exclusion of all others, you should long for death—if what you claim is true! But they will never long for it because [they know] what their hands have wrought in this world, and God has full knowledge of evildoers. Say: "The death you are fleeing from is bound to overtake you. Then you will be brought back to Him, who knows all beyond a created being's perception. He also knows all that a creature's senses or mind can witness. After that, He will make you truly understand all you did [in life]." (62:6-8)

FAILURE TO PROPAGATE MONOTHEISM

The parable of those graced with the burden of the Torah and thereafter failed to bear this burden is that of an ass that carries a load of books [but cannot benefit from them]. Calamitous is the parable of people who deliberately deny God's messages. God does not bestow His guidance upon such evildoing folk! (62:5)

The people entrusted with the Torah's knowledge and practice and the responsibility of guiding the world according to it neither understood this responsibility nor discharged it as they should have. It was because they regarded their religion as a national heritage reserved for the children of Israel alone. Their failure to bear this burden is like the ass who carries a load of books but fails to learn from them. They think this revelation is reserved for them alone. The bestowing of the Torah gave the Jews an illusory feeling of superiority as they were the sole recipients of God's revelation. Since they think they occupy a privileged position in God's sight, Jews do not see the need to share revelations.

PAYING LIP SERVICE TO BIBLICAL TRUTHS

Say: "Who has bestowed from on high the divine writ Moses brought to men as light and guidance? [And] which you treat as [mere] leaves of paper, making a show of them while you conceal [so] much. You have been taught [by it] what neither you nor your forefathers knew before? Say: "God [has revealed that divine text]!" And then leave them to play with their vain talk. (6:91)

These passages are addressed to Bible followers who lip service to its sacred character. In their minds, the document is merely a piece of paper that has no impact on their behavior. The killing of fellow Jews and the belief that Ezra was God's son were just two examples of the discrepancy between belief and behavior. They pretend to admire its moral truths, but they conceal their lack of respect for those truths in their personal lives. Afterward, some Bible believers divided it and picked and chose those parts that appealed to their inclinations and social trends. They disregard others not of their liking, denying its validity.

BREAKING THE SABBATH FOR WORLDLY GAINS

You are well aware of those who profaned the Sabbath, whereupon We said unto them, "Be as apes despicable!" And We set them up as a warning example for their time and all times to come and an admonition to all who are God-conscious. (2:65-66)

As for the substance of God's decree, "Be as apes despicable," this is but a metaphor like the metaphor of "the ass carrying books" (62:5). The expression "like an ape" is often used in classical Arabic to describe a person who cannot restrain his gross appetites or passions.

THE STORY OF SABBATH BREAKER

And ask them about that seaside town. How its people would profane the Sabbath whenever their fish came to them, breaking the water's surface, on a day on which they ought to have kept the Sabbath-because they would not come to them on other than Sabbath-days! They were tried for their iniquitous deeds. Some people [who tried to restrain the Sabbath-breakers] *asked, "Why do you preach to people whom God is about to destroy or [at least] to chastise with suffering severe?" The [truly] pious ones would answer, "To be free from blame before your Sustainer, and that these [transgressors, too] might become conscious of Him." And thereupon, when those [sinners] had forgotten all they had been told to take to heart, We saved those who had tried to prevent the doing of evil and overwhelmed those who had been bent on evildoing with dreadful suffering for all their iniquity. When they disdainfully persisted in doing what they had been forbidden to do, We said, "Be as apes despicable!" (7:163-166)*

Under the Mosaic Law, they were obliged to refrain from all work and, therefore, from fishing on Sabbath days. Fish was more plentiful and came closer to the shore on those days. The town's inhabitants took this as an excuse to break the Sabbath law. The Quran does not mention the town's name nor indicates the historical period in which those offenses were committed. It may be assumed that the story of the Sabbath-breakers is a general illustration of the tendency, so often manifested by the children of Israel, to offend against their religious laws in pursuit of their passions or for worldly gain. Those citizens of the town who did not participate in the profanation of the Sabbath, while not actively protesting the impiety within their environment, asked the truly pious one, why do you preach to people whom God has condemned?

LIGHT UNTO THE NATIONS

"I the LORD have called unto you in righteousness, and have taken hold of your hand, and submitted you as the people's covenant, as a light unto the nations" (Isaiah 42:6).

Are Torah followers a light for the world? Many Jews of today are secular Jews. Evidently, they have rejected the Torah, so their light unto nations is irrelevant. Yes, as far as scientific achievements are concerned, Jews produced most Nobel Prize winners. Their love of knowledge, education, science, and technology is inspiring.

Their dismal human rights record has brought death and destruction for other nations. The puzzling question is how Jews of all peoples, who have been persecuted for two thousand years, now collaborate with the same racist antisemitic persecutors. They adopted their former torturers' cruel methods. According to Amnesty

International, one of the most respected human rights organizations, in its statement, it said: "Amnesty International has analyzed Israel's intent to create and maintain a system of oppression and dominance over Palestinians and examined its key components: territorial fragmentation; segregation and control; the dispossession of land and property; and denial of economic and social rights. It has concluded that this system amounts to apartheid. Israel must dismantle this cruel system, and the international community must pressure it. Those with jurisdiction over crimes committed to maintain the system should investigate them."

CHAPTER 14
THE CONSEQUENCES OF BREAKING THE COVENANT

FORBIDDEN FOODS FOR JEWS

And [only] to those who followed the Jewish faith did We forbid all beasts with claws. We forbade them from oxen and sheep fat, except in their backs or entrails [internal organs] or within the bone. Thus, We retributed them for their evil doing-for We are true to Our word!" (6:146)

[Cf. Leviticus vii, 23 (where "all manners" of fat from ox, sheep or goat are forbidden).

DIETARY LAWS FOR QURAN FOLLOWERS

Say [O Prophet]: "In all that has been revealed unto me, I do not find anything forbidden to eat, if one wants to eat thereof, unless it be carrion, or blood poured forth, or swine flesh - for that, behold, is loathsome - or a sinful offering [idolatrous] over which any name other than God's has been invoked. However, if one is driven by necessity-neither coveting it nor exceeding his immediate need-then [know that], behold, thy Sustainer is much-forgiving, a dispenser of grace." (6:145)

The Jews are wrong in their claim as they overlook the fact that the severe Mosaic food laws were a punishment for their past misdeeds (see 3: 93) and, therefore, intended for them alone.

JEWISH OBJECTIONS TO QURANIC DIETARY LAWS

Jewish people were subject to laws concerning dietary restrictions. Jews believed Mosaic food restrictions were eternal laws decreed by God. However, the Quran annuls certain dietary injunctions and prohibitions laid down in the Torah. The dietary laws for Muslims are much simpler than those for Jews. Jews object to the Quranic annulment of certain dietary injunctions and prohibitions laid down in the Torah. The verses below answer Jewish objections to the Quran's infringement of Biblical laws.

WHY DIETARY RESTRICTIONS WERE IMPOSED?

To answer the objection relating to Jewish food laws, the Quran explains that originally all wholesome foods were allowed to the children of Israel. The Quran stresses that no food restrictions existed before Moses. God commanded some special rules imposed only on Jews and intended to punish them. Therefore, they were intended for them alone and not for a community that truly surrendered itself to God.

All foods were lawful for the Children of Israel, save what Israel had made unlawful unto itself [by its sins] before the Torah was bestowed from on high. Say: "Come forward with the Torah and recite it if what you say is true!" (3:93) For the wickedness committed by those who followed the Jewish faith, We denied them certain good things of life which [aforetime] were allowed to them; and [We did so] because they so often turned away from God's path. (4:160)

The punishment spoken of here is the age-long deprivation of the Jewish people of some "good things in life" for so often turning away from God's path. They endured humiliation and suffering throughout their history, especially after Jesus. The refractory nature of the Children of Israel is repeatedly stressed in the Quran. There is abundant evidence of this effect in the Old Testament.

And [only] to those who followed the Jewish faith did We forbid all that We had mentioned to you before. We didn't do them wrong, but they wronged themselves. And once again, Thy Sustainer [shows mercy] to those who do evil out of ignorance and repent and live righteously afterwards. After such [repentance], Thy Sustainer is indeed much-forgiving, a dispenser of grace. (16:118-119) And all who henceforth invent lies about God—it is they, they who are evildoers! (3:94)

To claim that dietary restrictions represent an eternal divine law is called "inventing lies about God."

And if they give you the lie, say: "Limitless is your Sustainer in His grace, but His punishment shall not be averted from people lost in sin." (6:147)

IMPOSITION OF THE SABBATH

[And know that the observance of] the Sabbath was ordained only for those who held divergent views about him [Abraham], but God will judge between them on Resurrection Day about all their differences. (16:124)

The Biblical explanation is that the Sabbath was for man's benefit. He can rest from toil, worldly cares and anxieties. As a result, attention is directed away from earthly concerns and towards eternity instead.

The Quranic version of the Sabbath imposition on the Children of Israel and all manner of other severe restrictions and rituals served as punishments. The various religious laws served as a test of their willingness to obey God. This enables them to grow spiritually and socially according to God's law. Whether in Judaism or Islam, all God-imposed rituals are only a means to achieve spiritual discipline and never a religious goal.

The meaning of the phrase, "those who held divergent views about him:" The implication is that the majority of Jews deviated from the true creed of Abraham as most of them became convinced that they were "God's chosen people" simply because of their physical descent from that great Prophet. An assumption that runs counter to every religious principle. This spiritual arrogance was punished by God's imposition on the children of Israel—and on them alone — of all manner of severe restrictions and rituals. Of these, the obligation to refrain from work and travel on the Sabbath was one. On Resurrection Day, God will literally inform you where you differ. God will judge those who are convinced of their ultimate salvation based on their alleged status as "God's chosen people". He will also judge those who believe in individual responsibility before God.

REBUILDING THE TEMPLE

And after a time, We allowed you to prevail against them again, aided you with wealth and offspring and made you more numerous [than ever]. [And We said]: "If you persevere in doing good, you will do good to yourselves; and if you do evil, it will be [done] to yourselves." (17:6-7)

The Babylonians, who destroyed the First Temple, were vanquished by the rising Persian Empire. "We allowed you to **prevail**" refers to the return of the Jews from Babylonian captivity in the last quarter of the sixth century BC. This resulted in their state's partial establishment. The Persian king, Cyrus the Great, soon authorized the Jews to rebuild the Temple, and later, King Darius ratified their effort. Under Ezra's and Nehemiah's leadership, Judea's community became vibrant and secure. Under the Romans, Herod was considered a cruel ruler and a brilliant builder. Herod's crowning achievement was the Temple reconstruction. Herod's building campaign and Roman technology made Jerusalem a beautiful city.

THE SECOND TEMPLE DESTRUCTION

And so, when the prediction of the second [iniquity] came true, [We raised new enemies against you, and allowed them] to disgrace you utterly and to enter the Temple as [their forerunners] had entered it once before, and to destroy with utter destruction all that they had conquered. Your Sustainer may show mercy to you; however, if you revert [to sinning], We shall revert [to chastising you]. And [remember this]: We have ordained that [in the hereafter] hell shall close upon all who deny the truth. This Quran shows the way to all that is righteous and assures believers who do good deeds of the glad tiding that theirs will be a magnificent reward. It also announces that We have prepared grievous suffering for those who will not believe in the life to come. (17:7-10)

In 66 CE, the Jewish population rebelled against the Roman Empire. Four years later, in 70 CE, Roman legions under Titus retook and destroyed much of Jerusalem, the Second Temple, and massacred the Jewish population. This Quran shows how righteousness benefits individual and social life. Thus, it shows that sin is synonymous with denying the truth. God always offers man guidance through the revelations He bestows upon His prophets.

WANDERING JEWS OF THE DIASPORA

And lo! Thy Sustainer made it known that He would rouse against them, unto Resurrection Day, people who would inflict them with cruel suffering. Thy Sustainer is swift in retribution, but He is also forgiving, a dispenser of grace. And We dispersed them [Jews] *into [separate] communities all over the earth; some were righteous, and some were less than that. The latter We tried with blessings and afflictions so they might mend their ways. (7:167-168)*

Jews comprise a tiny percentage of the world's population - about 0.2 percent (13.75 million), and they are scattered in communities across the planet, even in remote places.

CHAPTER 15
ISLAM IS A FALSE RELIGION?

ISLAM: CONTINUATION OF ABRAHAM'S MONOTHEISM

At the center of Prophet Muhammad's attempt to contain Jews' attacks was the concept of Abraham's religion. The Quran met the intellectual challenge by stressing that Islam is not a newly formed religion. Islam represents Abraham's pristine monotheism and cannot be called a false religion. It was a significant part of the claim previously presented to the pagan Meccan and was asserted or implied in many Quran passages. The following verses argue for Islam as a continuation of Divine revelation since time began.

ISLAM: THE EVER-TRUE FAITH OF ABRAHAM

Say: "My Sustainer has guided me along the straight path through the ever-true faith. The way of Abraham, who turned away from all that is false, and was not of those who ascribe divinity to aught beside Him." (6:161) The people with the right to claim Abraham are surely those who follow him—as does this Prophet and all who believe [in him]—and God is near the believers. (3:68) And if [others] come to believe in the way you believe, they will indeed find themselves on the right path. If they turn away, they will be deeply wrong. God will protect you from them, for He alone is all-hearing, all-knowing. (2:137)

Abraham's religion was the true religion of God preached by all the prophets, including Muhammad. It was altered with time and restored to purity through Islam.

FOLLOW ABRAHAM'S RIGHT PATH

And they say, "Be Jews"—or "Be Christians"— "and you shall be on the right path." Say: "No, but [ours is] the creed of

Abraham, who shunned away from all that is false, and was not of those who ascribe divinity to anything besides God." (2:135)

Abraham was not a Jew or a Christian, for he lived before the Jewish religion. Jewish faith considers the Torah the final Law of God, and Christians consider the Gospel as the final word. There are considerable differences between the Torah and the Gospel and both cannot be true. If Jews and Christians differed from each other, the differences were due to them. Therefore, follow Islam the Abraham's creed. He was also the prototype (and thus, the spiritual forefather) of all who consciously surrendered to God.

ABRAHAM AS FATHER OF ALL MONOTHEISTIC FAITHS

Abraham was an ancestor of the Prophet Muhammad

O followers of earlier revelations! Why do you argue about Abraham, seeing that the Torah and the Gospel were not revealed until long after him? Will you not, then, use your reason? Lo! You are the ones who would argue about what is known to you, but why do you argue about something unknown to you? Yet God knows [it], whereas you do not know. Abraham was neither a "Jew" nor a "Christian," but turned away from all that is false, surrendering himself unto God (kana musliman), *and he was not of those who ascribe divinity to anything besides Him. (3:65-67)*

While Abraham was regarded as the ancestor of both Jews and Arabs, it was also an undeniable fact that he was not a Jew or Christian since the Jews are either followers of Moses or descendants of Abraham's grandson Jacob. At the same time, Abraham stood for God's worship alone. Why do you argue about Abraham's true creed, who followed principles before the Torah and the Gospel were revealed? You argue about something unknown to you.

WHY ABRAHAM LABELED A MUSLIM?

Muslim signifies "one who surrenders himself to God," and **Islam** denotes "self-surrender to God." Both these terms are applied in the Quran to all who believe in the one God and affirm this belief by unequivocally accepting His revealed messages. When the contemporaries heard the words Islam and Muslim from the Prophet, they understood them as denoting man's "self-surrender to God" and "one who surrenders himself to God," without limiting these terms to any specific community or denomination. In 3:67, where Abraham is spoken of as having "surrendered himself unto God." (kana musliman), or in 3:52, where Jesus' disciples say, "Bear thou witness that we have surrendered ourselves unto God (bi-anna muslimun)." In Arabic, this original meaning has remained intact. But not the non-Arab of today, whether he is a believer or not: to him, Islam and Muslims refer solely to those who follow the Prophet Muhammad. The Quran cannot be understood if we read it considering later ideological developments. This will lose sight of its original purpose and meaning.

ABRAHAM WAS NOT A JEW OR A CHRISTIAN

The concept of "Jewry" came into being many centuries after the patriarchs. In contrast, "Christianity" and "Christians" were unknown in Jesus' time and represented a later development.

"Do you claim that Abraham and Ishmael and Isaac and Jacob and their descendants were 'Jews' or 'Christians'?" Say: "Do you know more than God does?" "Now those people have passed away; unto them shall be accounted for what they have earned and unto you, what you have earned, and you will not be judged on the strength of what they did." (2:140-141)

The Jews could not deny the Muslim assertion that Abraham was not a Jew, for they had to admit that he lived before the Jewish religion was revealed. The religion proclaimed by Abraham was the true religion of God in its purity and simplicity. Its core beliefs were identical to the religion preached by all the prophets, including Muhammad. If the Jews and Christians had something different, then the differences were due to them.

CONTINUATION OF DIVINE REVELATION THROUGH THE PROPHETS

Say: "We believe in God, and in that which has been bestowed from on high upon us, and that which has been bestowed upon Abraham and Ishmael and Isaac and Jacob and their descendants, and that which has been vouchsafed by their Sustainer unto Moses and Jesus and all the [other] prophets: we make no distinction between any of them. And unto Him do we surrender ourselves." (3:84)

The Quran consistently insisted that its message was similar to previous prophets, notably Moses and Jesus, the founders of Judaism and Christianity. This idea cannot be removed from Islam. In many passages, it was asserted or implied that it was a significant part of the claim brought before the pagans of Mecca.

IN CONCLUSION

THE ONE GOD OF MOSES, JESUS, AND MUHAMMAD

And do not argue with the followers of earlier revelation otherwise than in a most kindly manner - unless it be such of them as are bent on evildoing - and say: "We believe in what has been bestowed from on high upon us, and what has been bestowed upon you. For our God and your God is one and the same, and it is unto Him that We [all] surrender ourselves." Thus, we have bestowed this divine writ from on high upon you [O Muhammad]. And they to whom we have vouchsafed this divine writ believe in it—just as among those [followers of earlier revelations] some believe in it. (29:46-47)

MY ENTIRE BEING IS DEVOTED TO ONE GOD'S WORSHIP

Say [to Jews and Christians]: "Do you argue with us about God? But He is our Sustainer as well as your Sustainer—and unto us shall be accounted for our deeds, and unto you, your deeds. It is unto Him alone that we devote ourselves." (2:139) Say: "My prayer, and [all] my acts of worship, and my living and my dying are for God [alone], the Sustainer of all the worlds, in whose divinity none has a share. For thus have I been bidden - and I will [always]be foremost among those who surrender themselves unto Him." Say: "Am I, then, to seek a sustainer other than God, when He is the Sustainer of all things?" (6:162-164)

In the verse above, what is meant by this solemn pledge taken by the community as a whole is their acceptance of the messages conveyed through the prophets.

By citing both positive and negative aspects of Jewish religious history, the Quran furthered its argument. It is within this context that the Quran describes Jews' errors and answers their objections regarding Islam.

CHAPTER 16
WHY REJECTION OF MUHAMMAD'S PROPHETHOOD?

For the Prophet Muhammad, the idea that he was a prophet receiving messages from God and with a commission from Him was the basis of the political and religious movement he led. Remove this idea, and the Islamic movement will collapse. The community's whole structure would unravel if many Muslims thought what the Jews said was true. The Prophet needed the support of men deeply committed to his mission. The Jews tried to deny him support.

And such of the Jewish faith enthusiastically listen to any falsehood, eagerly listen to other people without coming to you [for enlightenment]. They distort the meaning of the [revealed] words, taking them out of their context, saying [to themselves], "If such-and-such [teaching] is vouchsafed unto you, accept it, but if it is not vouchsafed unto you, be on your guard!" (5:41)

Because of their scripture knowledge, the criticism of the Jews of Medina had a far more severe theological threat to Islam than the pagan Quraysh could ever inflict upon Prophet Muhammad. They willingly lend an ear to any false statement about its teachings, preferring to listen to unfriendly non-Muslim "experts" rather than to turn to the Quran itself for enlightenment—which is the meaning of the phrase, "**without having come to thee** (O Muhammad)." They are prepared to accept such Quranic teachings as might suit their preconceived notions but are not prepared to accept anything that goes against their views.

MUHAMMAD IN THE OLD TESTAMENT

"The Lord, thy God will raise up a Prophet from the midst of thee, of thy brethren, like unto me; unto him, ye shall hearken"

(Deuteronomy, 18:15). Words attributed to God Himself, "I will raise up a Prophet from among thy brethren, like unto thee, and will put My words in his mouth." (Deuteronomy, 18:18)

The "brethren" of Israel are the Arabs, particularly the Mustaribah ("Arabianized") group among them, which traces its descent to Ishmael and Abraham. The Prophet Muhammad's tribe in Arabia, the Quraysh, belonged to this group. The above Biblical passages must be taken as referring to the advent of Muhammad. The words attributed to God Himself refer to Deuteronomy 18:18.

"**Like unto thee**," or like Moses, a warrior prophet and lawgiver who brought freedom to the Israelites. It could not have referred to Jesus because, unlike Moses, he was not a warrior. He did not add any significant laws to the law books and gave up his life without a fight. It could not have referred to Joshua, a warrior with no significant additions to the law. As a warrior prophet, Muhammad, like Moses, freed the Arabs from idolatry. He commanded all the major battles. He implemented Shariah laws to reform pre-Islamic Arabia's immoral trends.

Some followers of earlier revelations would love to lead you astray. Yet none do they lead astray but themselves and perceive it not. O followers of earlier revelations! Why do you deny the truth of God's messages to which you bear witness? (3:69-70)

"God's messages to which **you bear witness**," an allusion to Biblical prophecies relating to the coming of the Prophet Muhammad.

REJECTION OF TORAH

For clear instructions, We have bestowed upon thee from on high; none denies their truth except the wicked. It is not so that every time they make a promise to the Lord, some cast it aside. No, indeed, most of them do not believe. And [even now], when there comes an apostle from God, confirming the truth already in their possession, some of those who were granted revelation aforetime cast the divine writ behind their backs as though unaware [of what it says]. (2:99-101)

The divine writ is the Torah. By disregarding the prophecies relating to the coming of the Arabian Prophet, contained in Deuteronomy xviii, 15, 18, the Jews rejected, as it were, the whole of Moses' revelation.

CONCEALING MUHAMMAD'S ADVENT

O followers of earlier revelations! Why do you cloak the truth with falsehood and conceal the truth you are fully aware of? (3:71) And lo, God accepted a solemn pledge from those who were granted earlier revelations [when He bade them]: "Make it known unto mankind, and do not conceal it!" But they cast this [pledge] behind their backs and bartered it away for a trifling gain, and how evil was their bargain! (3:187)

"**Cloak the truth with falsehood**" means misinterpreting, misrepresenting, or corrupting the Biblical text, of which the Quran frequently accuses the Jews (which has since been established by objective textual criticism). The Bible followers were commanded to spread the prophecy of Muhammad's coming instead of suppressing it, as they have done. Perhaps it contradicts the Judeo-Christian claim that all true prophets, after the patriarchs, belong to Israel. The patriarchs of the Bible, narrowly defined, are **Abraham, his son Isaac, and Isaac's son Jacob**, also named Israel. This is the ancestor of the Israelites. "**How evil was their bargain**" that they were buying - alluding to the Jewish belief that they are "God's chosen people" and to the Christian belief that Jesus' "vicarious atonement" automatically assures them of salvation. In both cases, the "bargain" represents an illusion of immunity in the next life.

And of Me, be conscious! And do not overlay the truth with falsehood, and do not knowingly suppress the truth. Instead, be constant in prayer, spend in charity, and bow down with all those who bow down. As you wish others to be pious, you forget yourself, yet you recite the divine writ. Will you not, then, use your reason? And seek aid in steadfast patience and prayer. This, indeed, is a challenging thing for all but the humble in spirit. These people know with certainty that they shall meet their Sustainer and that unto Him, they shall return. (2:41-46) And who could be more wicked than he who suppresses a testimony given to him by God? Yet God is not unmindful of what you do. (2:140)

The "**suppression of truth**" refers to their disregard or deliberately false interpretation of the words of Moses in the Biblical passage Deuteronomy 18:15.

When they meet those who have attained faith, they say, "We believe [as you believe]." When they find themselves alone, they ask, "Do you inform them of what God has disclosed to you so that they might use it in an argument against you, quoting your Sustainer's words? Will you not, then, use your reason?" Do they not know that God is aware of all they conceal and bring into the open? And there are among them (Jews) unlettered people who have no real knowledge of the divine writ [the Old Testament], following only wishful beliefs and depending on nothing but conjecture. (2:76-78)

Some Jews of Medina, when talking among themselves, asked each other not to disclose to Muslims Prophet Muhammad's prophecies. This was to prevent Muslims from using scriptural arguments against them. They were asked if God was unaware of their apparent or hidden deeds.

REJECTING PROPHETS NOT OF THEIR LIKING

Indeed, We accepted a solemn pledge from the children of Israel, and We sent apostles unto them; however, every time an apostle came unto them with anything that was not to their liking, [they rebelled]. To some, they gave the lie, while to others, they slayed, thinking no harm would befall them, and so, they became blind and deaf [of heart]. After that, God accepted their repentance; again, many became blind and deaf. But God sees all that they do. (5:70-71)

Nothing is surprising about the Jewish rejection of Muhammad. This is because they rejected prophets not of their liking sent to them from their tribe, as mentioned in their scriptures. The Jews could not deny that there was some truth in this latter matter. Their scripture proves the fallacy of the above argument.

Vile is that [false pride] for which they have sold their selves by denying the truth of what God has bestowed from on high. This is out of envy that God should bestow His favor upon whomsoever He wills of His servants. Thus, they have earned the burden of God's condemnation, over and over. And for those who deny the truth, shameful suffering is in store. (2:90)

Above is a reference to the persistent Jewish belief that they, alone among all nations, have been graced by divine revelation. The Jews denied the possibility of prophethood being bestowed on anyone who did not belong to their tribe, and so they summarily rejected Muhammad's prophethood. They were envious that God should bestow revelation upon anyone but a descendant of Israel - in this instance, upon the Arabian Prophet, Muhammad.

APES AND SWINE

Say: "Shall I tell you who, in God's sight, deserves greater retribution than these? "They whom God has rejected and condemned, and whom He has turned into apes and swine because they worship evil powers. These [hypocrites] are wretched in the station and farther astray from the right path [than the mockers]." When they come to you, they say, "We do believe," whereas they come with the resolve to deny the truth and depart in the same state. All that they conceal is fully known to God. And you can see many of them vie with one another in sin, tyrannical conduct, and swallowing all that is wicked. Why do not their men of God and their rabbis forbid them to make sinful assertions and to swallow all that is evil? Indeed, it is vile what they come up with! And so, We have cast enmity and hatred among the Bible followers, [to last] until Resurrection Day. Every time they light the fires of war, God extinguishes them, and they labor hard to spread corruption on Earth. God does not love corruption spreaders. (5:60-64)

The reference to "**apes and swine**" is a metaphorical description of the moral degradation such sinners undergo. As apes, they become wildly unpredictable and abandon themselves to their lusts, just like swine. They vie with each other in tyrannical behavior and sin. The expression "**evil powers**" denotes anything worshipped instead of God and, thus, all that may turn man away from God and lead him to evil. The sinners who are even more sinister than the mockers are the hypocrites, especially those who claim to be Bible followers. For the obvious reason that having been enlightened through revelation, they have no excuse for their behavior. God does not allow warring parties to resolve their conflicts through a final victory, resulting in continued **enmity** and hatred.

REJECTING AND SLAYING OF PROPHETS

Those who deny the truth of God's messages, and kill prophets against all rights, slay people who advocate equity—announce grievous chastisement. They are the ones whose works shall bring them no good in this world and life to come, and they shall have no one to help them. (3:21-22)

And so, ignominy and humiliation overshadowed them. As a result of their persistence in denying the truth of God's messages and slaying the prophets against all rights, all of this earned them

God's condemnation. This is because they rebelled [against God] and transgressed the bounds of what is right. (2:61) And Lo! We accepted your solemn pledge, raising Mount Sinai high above you, "Hold fast with [all your] strength to what We have vouchsafed you, and bear in mind all that is therein so that you remain conscious of God!" And you turned away after that! And had it not been for God's favor for you and His grace, you would surely have been among the lost. (2:63-64)

These passages refer to persistent and ever-recurring traits in Jewish history of rejecting prophets and even slaying them to which also the New Testament refers. Individuals from Jewish clans in Arabia plotted to take Muhammad's life twice. Once, they came within a bite of poisoning him.

In earlier phases of Jewish history, Jews killed prophets, such as Zachariah and John the Baptist. We raised the mountain (attur) above you: i.e., letting the lofty mountain witness to their solemn pledge. The expression attur is rendered as "Mount Sinai" since it is used in this sense alone.

THE SLAYING OF ZACHARIAH AND JOHN THE BAPTIST

As for those who maintain, "God has bidden us not to believe in any apostle unless he comes to us with burnt offerings." Say [to them, O Prophet]: "Even before there came unto you apostles with all evidence of the truth, and with that of whom you speak: why, then, did you slay them, if what you say is true?" And if they give you the lie—even before your time, have [other] apostles been given the lie when they came with all evidence of the truth with books of divine wisdom and light-giving revelations. (3:183-184)

God has bidden us not to believe in any apostle unless he conforms to the Mosaic Law. This prescribes burnt offerings as an essential part of divine services. However, this aspect of the Law had been left in abeyance since the destruction of the Second Temple in

Jerusalem. Post-Talmudic Jews were convinced that the Messiah promised to them would restore Mosaic rites. So, they refused to accept as a prophet anyone who did not conform to the Torah Law in every detail. At the time of John the Baptist and Zachariah's martyrdom, the Second Temple was still in existence, and burnt offerings were a daily practice. Thus, the refusal of the Jews to accept the prophets alluded to, culminating in their killing, could not be attributed to those prophets' lack of conformity to the Mosaic Law.

HOSTILITY BY THE JEWS AND THE PAGAN ARABS

You will certainly find that, of all people, the most hostile to those who believe [in this divine writ] are the Jews and those who are bent on ascribing divinity to others besides God [Pagans of Arabia]. (5:82) Now whenever such [people] approach you, [O Muhammad] they salute you with a greeting, which God has never countenanced. They ask themselves, "Why does God not chastise us for what we say?" Hell shall be their allotted portion: they shall [indeed] enter it—and how vile a journey's end! (58:8)

It is recorded that instead of pronouncing the traditional greeting "Peace be upon you" when encountering the Prophet, some of the hostile Jews of Medina used to mumble the word salam ("peace") in such a way as to make it indistinguishable from sam ("death"). They employed the same scurrilous play of words about the Prophet's Companions. The "Greeting which God has never countenanced" is an allusion to the hostile attitude of the Medina Jews toward the Prophet.

SUFFERING FOR REJECTING MUHAMMAD'S PROPHETHOOD

How would God bestow His guidance upon people who have resolved to deny the truth after attaining faith and bearing witness that this Apostle is true? [After] all evidence of the truth has come to them? For God does not guide such evildoers. Their punishment shall be rejection by God, the angels, and [the righteous] men. In this state shall they abide; [and] neither will their suffering be relieved, nor will they be granted respite. But excepted shall be those who repent and put things right, for God is a dispenser of grace. (3:86-89)

The phrase "[After] all evidence of the truth has come to them," refers to Jews and Christians. Their acceptance of the Bible, which predicts the coming of the Prophet Muhammad, has made them witnesses to the truth of his prophethood.

Unfortunately, the Jews of Medina could not grasp the bigger picture owing to their narrow, ethnocentric view of religion. This perspective eventually resulted in an alliance between the monotheistic Jews and the pagan Arabs against the monotheistic Muslims.

COVENANT FROM OTHER PROPHETS

And, lo, God accepted, through the prophets, this solemn pledge [from the followers of earlier revelation]: "If, after all the revelations and the wisdom I have vouchsafed unto you, there comes to you an apostle confirming the truth already in your possession; you must believe in him and succor him. Do you—said He—"acknowledge and accept My bond on this condition?" They answered: "We do acknowledge it." Said He: "Then bear witness [to it] and I shall be your witness. And, henceforth, all who turn away [from this pledge]—it is they, they who are truly iniquitous!" Do they seek, perchance, a faith other than in God, [Any other than God's religion] although it is unto Him that whatever is in the heavens and on earth surrenders itself, willingly or unwillingly, since unto Him all must return? (3:81-83)

God made a covenant regarding Prophet Muhammad binding on all prophets. This is the highest honoring of the Messenger since He connected [Muhammad's] name with His own and affirmed his worth just as He affirmed His own. So [Muhammad] is singular in rank among all people, and [God] has made it possible for all to know His majesty through him. In the whole Quran, there is no verse more complete in explaining the excellence of the Prophet Muhammad to whom this verse is devoted. Talmudic sources confirm God assembled all past, present, and future Prophets on Mount Sinai and entered the compact.

WHY THE JEWS REJECTED PROPHETH MUHAMMAD?

Religious Reason: In almost every conflict between Jews and Arabs, the notion of the superiority of Jews was always at the heart of the problem. The Jews of Medina rejected Muhammad's prophethood for religious reasons. Again, it was all about "chosen people." Prophets only come from the Jewish tribe. If prophets could arise among Gentiles, then Jews were not God's "chosen people." This was tantamount to having no religion left. In their view, Muhammad's prophethood was incompatible with Judaism.

Hubris and Contempt: As a lowly Ishmaelite, Muhammad could not be a prophet for the "chosen People." Jews of Medina considered Muhammad not even a false Messiah but an outright usurper, being a gentile. It was difficult for them to see why they should change the idea based on Abraham's superior lineage for an uneducated upstart (as they considered him) like Muhammad.

Political: As a prophet for the Arabs, he could endanger their already declining influence. Medina Jews had close business and political ties with the pagans of Mecca. If Muhammad was not God's Prophet and messenger, he could only be a self-deceiving impostor and his religion a mere figment of his imagination.

If no prophet is supposed to arise except the Jewish tribe, then in today's 7-8 billion world population, only 14 million people will be monotheists, the Jewish population worldwide. Even with the introduction of Christianity and Islam, the monotheistic population of today's world is barely a majority.

CHAPTER 17
THE QURAN IS NOT GOD'S SPEECH

The Jews initiated ideological warfare and used their Old Testament knowledge to criticize Prophet Muhammad's claim that the Quran was God's speech. Medina's Jews used to listen to Muslims' stories and laugh and scoff at their religion. With their scripture knowledge, they picked holes in the Quran's stories. These stories sometimes differ markedly from the biblical version. They could say, for example, that some Quran passages contradict their ancient scriptures. Thus, the Quran was not God's speech, and Muhammad was not a prophet.

The Quran maintains throughout that there is a substantial element of truth in all faiths based on divine revelation. It also states that their subsequent divergence was the result of "wishful beliefs" and a gradual alteration of the original teachings. Altering the scriptures may mean Jews and Christians interpret passages falsely. Some of the alleged revealed scriptures of the Jews were additions they made, especially the Jewish oral law. Therefore, some differences were due to Jewish deviations.

REJECTION OF THE QURAN DUE TO ENVY

Vile is that [false pride] for they have sold their selves by denying the truth of what God has bestowed from on high. This is out of envy that God should bestow His favor upon whomsoever He wills of His servants. Thus, they have earned the burden of God's condemnation. And for those who deny the truth, shameful suffering is in store. (2:90)

The heart of the problem was Jewish belief in their "chosen" status. All their beliefs were centered on themselves and their alleged exceptional status in God's sight. Instead of objectively examining the Quranic message, they rejected this revelation out of envy that

God should bestow revelation upon anyone but a descendant of Israel—in this instance, upon the Arabian Prophet, Muhammad.

And such of the Jewish faith enthusiastically listen to any falsehood, eagerly listen to other people without coming to you [for enlightenment]. They distort the meaning of the [revealed] words, taking them out of their context. They say [to themselves], "If such-and-such [teaching] is vouchsafed unto you, accept it, but if it is not vouchsafed unto you, be on your guard!" (5:41)

They willingly lend an ear to any false statement about its teachings, preferring to listen to unfriendly non-Muslims rather than to turn to the Quran itself for enlightenment—which is the meaning of the phrase, "without having come to thee (O Muhammad)." They are prepared to accept such Quranic teachings as might suit their preconceived notions but are not prepared to accept anything that goes against their views.

The Jews correctly identified some differences between their religious texts and the Quran. There are some logical explanations for these differences.

DIFFERENT LAWS FOR DIFFERENT TIMES

To every one of you We appointed a [different] law and way of life. And if God so willed, He could surely have made you all one single community: but [He willed it otherwise] to test you by what He has vouchsafed unto you. Vie then, with one another in doing righteous works! Unto God, you all must return, and then He will make you truly understand all you disagree with. (5:48)

It explains the succession of divine messages culminating in and ending with the Quran's revelation. The expression "**every one of you**" refers to the human community. All of God's apostles preached the same unchanging spiritual truths. The laws promulgated through them, and the way of life recommended by them varied according to each community's cultural, social, and moral requirements. This unity in diversity is frequently stressed in the Quran (e.g., in 2:148, 21:92-93, and 23:52). The various religious laws imposed on them test their willingness to surrender to God and obey Him, thus enabling them to grow spiritually and socially. In the end, God will literally "inform you of that wherein you used to differ" (2:113). There is a misperception among some Muslims that Islam, being the greatest of all religions, will be widely accepted by all human beings. This is contrary to the Quran's teachings, as the above verses indicate.

Every age has its revelation: God annuls or confirms whatever He wills [of His earlier messages]—for with Him is the source of all revelation. (13:38-39) And upon you [too] have We bestowed from on high this divine writ for no other reason than that you might make clear unto them all [questions of faith] on which they have come to hold divergent views, and [thus offer] guidance and grace unto people who will believe. (16:64)

DELIBERATE DENIAL OF THE TRUTH

And whenever there came to them a [new] revelation from God, confirming the truth already in their possession—and [bear in mind that] aforetime they used to pray for victory over those bent on denying the truth. They would deny it whenever something came to them that they recognized [as true]. And God's rejection is due to all who reject truth. (2:89)

Medina's Jews used to ask God to aid them by sending a Prophet, against their polytheistic enemies in war. They used to say to polytheists, "A Prophet shall be sent just before the end of this world and we, along with him, shall exterminate you." When God sent Muhammad to the Arabs, they rejected him and denied what they used to say about him.

REJECTION OF NON-BIBLICAL TRUTHS

For when they are told, "believe in what God has bestowed from on high," they reply, "we believe [only] in what has been conferred on us." They deny the truth of everything else, even if it confirms the one already in their possession. (2:91)

They say, "We believe [only] in what has been conferred on us." This means it is enough for us to believe in what was revealed to us in the Torah and this is the path we choose. Then they disbelieve what follows.

IS THE QURAN BORROWED FROM THE BIBLE?

Say: "O followers of earlier revelations! Why do you [endeavor to] bar those who believe [in this divine writ] from God's path by making it appear crooked? This is even though you bear witness [to it being straight]. For God is not unaware of what you do." (3:99)

This is an allusion to Jews and Christians' attempts to prove that Muhammad borrowed the Quran's main ideas from the Bible. He twisted them out of context to suit his alleged ambitions. To this day, Islam is accused of plagiarism. From an Islamic perspective, the Torah, the Quran, and the Gospel come from the same source. This explains the presence of familiar stories in these three scriptures.

Biblical figures and stories belong on their pages. Still, their purpose is to buttress an original and different vision of God, human beings, and the world with unquestionable integrity. The suggestion that the Prophet merely copied of those before is historically inaccurate and has never been proven.

Some of these stories differ markedly from the Biblical version, correcting its errors. Moses' story is described in twenty-five chapters of the Quran. Even with such a fragmented subject matter, there are no contradictions. Denial that the Quran is God's word represents critics' belief that prophets can only arise from their people. It is absurd to suggest that an uneducated man isolated in the desert, without a computer, could pick and choose biblical verses or come up with sophisticated concepts on his own.

GOD'S BOUNTY OF REVELATION FOR ALL

The followers of earlier revelation should know that they have no power whatsoever over any of God's bounty, seeing that all bounty is in God's hands [alone]. He grants it to whomever He wills—for God is limitless in His great bounty. (57:29)

Followers of earlier revelations have no exclusive access to God's bounty of revelations. This is addressed to Jews and Christians, who reject Muhammad's revelation, believing prophethood is their sole preserve.

DIVINE RETRIBUTION FOR REJECTING SACRED SCRIPTURE

O you who received revelations beforehand! Believe in what We have [now] bestowed from on high in confirmation of whatever [of the truth] you already possess. This is lest We efface your hopes and bring them to an end—just as We rejected those people who broke the Sabbath, for God's will is always done. (4:47)

IGNOMINY AND AWESOME SUFFERING

O Apostle! Be not grieved by those who vie with one another in denying the truth. This includes those who say with their mouths, "We believe." In contrast, their hearts do not believe. [Be not grieved by them] for, if God wills anyone to be tempted to evil, you cannot prevail with God on his behalf. It is those whose hearts God is not willing to cleanse. Theirs shall be ignominy in this world and awesome suffering in the life to come—those who eagerly listen to any falsehood, greedily swallowing all that is evil! (5:41-42)

Although it mentions only the hypocrites and the Jews, it refers, by implication, to all people prejudiced against Islam. The **"swallowing of evil"** denotes every false statement made about the Quran by its enemies to destroy its impact.

THE PRACTICE OF DECEPTION TO CONFUSE MUSLIMS

And some of the followers of earlier revelation say [to one another]: "Declare your belief in what has been revealed unto those who believe [in Muhammad] at the beginning of the day. And deny the truth of what came later so that they might turn back [on their faith]. But do not [really] believe anyone who does not follow your faith." Say: "All [true] guidance is God's guidance, consisting of being given [revelation] such as you have been granted." Or would they contend against you before your Sustainer? Say: "All bounty is in God's hand; He grants it unto whom He wills. For God is infinite, all-knowing, choosing whom He wills to receive His grace. And God is limitless in His abundance of bounty." (3:72-74)

In the above verses, Judeo-Christians attempt to mislead Muslims by alternately declaring beliefs and disbelief in the Quranic message. This verse may imply that some Jews and Christians have been hoping to confuse Muslims by admitting, however, reluctantly, that there may be some truth in the early Quranic revelations (revealed at the beginning of the day), while they categorically reject its later parts as they clearly contradict certain Biblical teachings. In this context, bounty is synonymous with divine revelation.

WHY DO MOSES' LAWS DIFFER FROM THE QURAN?

And yet, now that the truth has come to them from Us, they say, "Why has he not been vouchsafed the like of what Moses was vouchsafed?" But did they not also deny the truth of what Moses was granted before this? [For] they do say, "Two examples of delusion, [seemingly] supporting each other!" And they add, "Behold; we refuse to accept either of them as true!" "Produce, then, [another] revelation from God that would offer better guidance than either of these two—[and] I shall follow it if you speak the truth!" And since they cannot respond to this challenge, say: they are following only their likes and dislikes and who could be more astray than he who follows [but]his likes and dislikes without guidance from God? People who are given to evildoing are not graced with God's guidance! (28:48-50)

The Quran enunciates ethical truths the same as in earlier revelations. It is this very statement that the opponents of Muhammad question the authenticity of the Quran: "If God had revealed it," they argue, "would so many of its propositions, especially its social laws, differ so radically from the laws promulgated in that earlier divine writ, the Torah?" The different systems of Law were conditioned for varying social and cultural conditions for particular people during human history (see 5:48). However, as is evident from the immediate sequence, the above specious argument is not meant to uphold the Bible's authenticity against that of the Quran. Rather, it aims to discredit both as examples of delusion. The Quran challenges them to produce another revelation from God, which would offer better guidance, implying that they cannot accept this challenge.

THE QURAN SUPERSEDES THE EARLIER REVELATIONS

Neither those followers of earlier revelation who deliberately deny the truth nor those who ascribe divinity to other beings besides God would like to see any good bestowed upon you from on high by your Sustainer. But God selects for His grace whom He wills—for God is limitless in His vast bounty. We replace any message We delete or consign to oblivion with a better or similar one. Do you not know that God has the power to will anything? (2:105-106)

But anyone who denies the existence of truth has already strayed from the right path instead of believing in it. Out of their selfish envy, many early revelation followers want you to return to denying the truth after you have gained faith [even after] the truth has become evident to them. You should forgive and forbear until God manifests His will. (2:108-109)

"Any good ever bestowed upon you" refers to revelation—which is the highest good. Jews and Christians are unwilling to admit that revelation could have been bestowed on any community but their own. The Quran supersedes earlier revelations, which means any message We annul and replace is superseded by it. Whoever takes a denial of the truth in exchange for belief—i.e., whoever refuses to accept the internal evidence of the truth of the Quranic message and demands, instead, an "objective" proof of its divine origin-has already strayed from the right path.

Hence, they unto whom We have vouchsafed this revelation rejoice at all that has been bestowed upon you [O Prophet] from on high. However, some followers of other creeds deny the validity of some of it. Say [unto them, O Prophet]: "I have only been bidden to worship God, and not to ascribe divine powers to anything besides Him: unto Him do I call [all mankind], and He is my goal!" (13:36)

There will be guidance for those who believe in this revelation in this world and the promise of ultimate happiness in the life to come. The followers of other creeds deny its validity while admitting that the Quran contains much that coincides with their religions' spiritual concepts. "I have only been bidden," the particle "only" indicates that in Islam, there is no obligation, no ordinance, and no prohibition not connected with this principle.

THE CONTENT DIFFERENCE

Sexual content: Several stories recorded in the Old Testament are repugnant or distasteful and even erotic such as Lot's incest and David's adultery. Some stories are so graphic and obscene that one cannot discuss them in decent company. However, that does not mean that the God of the Torah approves of what happened. The Quran is a book of ethics, and it presents the Prophets and other holy men as ideals for Muslims to follow in their everyday lives. God's prophets are not expected to do abominable deeds like ordinary men acting upon their evil instincts.

Killings of Biblical Proportion: Genocide, ethnic cleansing, massacres, and ruthless killings of the innocent were sanctioned and described with pride in the Old Testament. Genocide of Midianites, Amorites, People of Bashan, seven nations, Canaanites, Amorites, etc., is well documented in the Old Testament. In some cases, even babies and animals were not spared. A morally twisted argument can be made that murdering the enemy's children is justified because they will take revenge as adults. The Nazis advocated killing children as a measure of preventative security. However, killing animals is pure barbarism. These deeply ingrained religious ideas are manifested to this day when the deaths of innocent women and children are dismissed as "collateral damage." There are some peaceful verses in the Old Testament, but violent verses by far outnumber the verses with the message of peace.

CHAPTER 18
DEMAND FOR SUPERNATURAL PROOFS

DEMAND FOR MIRACLES

They say, "Why have no miraculous signs ever been bestowed upon him from on high by his Sustainer?" Say: "Miracles are in God's power alone, and as for me—I am but a plain warner." Why is it not enough for them that We have bestowed this divine writ on you from on high, to be conveyed [by you] to them? It is a manifestation of grace and a reminder to those who believe. Say [to those who will not believe]: "God is witness enough between you and me! He knows all that is in the heavens and on earth; and they who are bent on believing in what is false and vain, and thus on denying God—it is they, they who shall be the losers!" (29:50-52)

This verse refers to Jews' and Christians' objections to the Quran's message. The people could not perceive the intrinsic truth of the prophets' words. Instead, they insisted on a miraculous demonstration that those messages came from God and thus failed to benefit from them. In other words, "Are the contents of this revelation not enough to grasp its intrinsic truth without supernatural proof of its divine origin?"

DEMAND FOR DIRECT REVELATION

The Old Testament's followers demanded [O Prophet] that you cause a revelation to be sent down to them from heaven. [In proof of your prophethood] *And an even greater thing than this did they demand of Moses when they said, "Make us see God face to face"—whereupon the thunderbolt of punishment overtook them for this their wickedness. (4:153)*

And [only] those who are devoid of knowledge say, "Why does God not speak unto us, nor is a [miralous] sign shown to us?" So said the people before them words of similar import: their hearts are alike. Indeed, We have made all signs manifest for those endowed with inner certainty. (2:118)

CHALLENGE TO HASTEN GOD'S CHASTISEMENT

Now they challenge you to hasten the coming upon them of [God's] chastisement. If God had not set a time for it, that suffering would already have fallen upon them! But indeed, it will most certainly come upon them suddenly, and they will be taken unawares. Hell is bound to encompass all who deny the truth— [encompass them] on the Day when suffering overwhelms them from above them and from beneath their feet, whereupon He shall say: "Taste [now the fruit of] your doings!" (29:53-55)

The EXCLUSIVITY OF JUDAISM AND CHRISTIANITY

Another telling argument of the Quran against the exclusive claims of the Jews was that the Christians made similar claims and that both could not be true. According to the Jewish faith, Torah is the Final Law of God, and Christians consider the Gospel the final word, and both cannot be right. It is only the Quran that represents the final and most universal of these divine revelations. Therefore, believers are called upon to follow the guidance of their Apostle and thus become an example for all mankind. Now, almost fifteen centuries have passed since Islam's advent, and God has not revealed anything new.

CHAPTER 19
THE ERRORS OF RABBIS, MONKS, AND ISLAMIC CLERKS

ONLY GOD CAN DECLARE WHAT IS LAWFUL OR UNLAWFUL

They have taken their rabbis and their monks—and Christ, son of Mary—for their Lords besides God. Although they were bidden to worship none but the One God, save for whom there is no deity. The one who is utterly remote, in His limitless glory, from anything to which they may ascribe a share in His divinity! They want to extinguish God's [guiding] light with their words. But God will not allow [this to pass]. For He has willed to spread His light in all its fullness; how abhorrent this may be to all who deny the truth. He has sent forth His Apostles with the [task of spreading] guidance and the religion of truth, to make it widespread across all [false] religions-despite how loathsome this may be to those who ascribe divinity to anything besides God. (9:31-33) God does not forgive the ascribing of divinity to anything besides Him. However, He forgives any lesser sin to whomever He wills. He who ascribes divinity to others besides God has committed an awesome sin. (4:48)

Only God can declare what is lawful or unlawful through His prophets. When human beings such as monks, rabbis, and Islamic clerks assume lawgiving, they substantially elevate themselves to Lords besides God. Jews ascribe divine or semi-divine qualities to great Talmudic scholars, whose legal verdicts override any ordinance in their scriptures. In the person of the Scribes and Pharisees, they worshipped the Law as idolatry. The Pharisees' interpretation method was legalistic, focusing on the letter of the Law. This condemnation also applies to Muslim believers who have fallen into the sin of worshipping saints instead of giving God the reverence he deserves.

A belief in God's transcendental oneness and uniqueness frees man from all superstitions and dependence on other influences and powers, thus elevating him spiritually. Since this objective is vitiated by the sin of "the ascribing of divine qualities to anything besides God," the Quran describes it as an "unforgivable" sin unless the sinner repents. God brings His light to completion or perfection across all false religions; see 3:19: "The only true religion in God's sight is man's self-surrender unto Him."

WORSHIP OF WEALTH AND POWER BY RABBIS AND MONKS

Many rabbis and monks wrongly devour men's possessions and turn [others] away from God's path. But as for all who amass treasures of gold and silver and do not spend them for the sake of God—give them the tiding of grievous suffering [in the life to come]. On that Day when their [hoarded wealth] shall be heated in hell's fire, their foreheads, sides and backs will be branded. In addition [those sinners shall be told]: "These are the treasures you have laid up! Taste then [the evil of] your hoarded treasures!" (9:34-35)

The above verses allude to the wealth of the Jewish and Christian communities and their misuse of it including Muslims, who hoard their wealth without spending anything on righteous causes.

CHAPTER 20
GREED, ARROGANCE, AND FALSE PRIDE

LISTENING WITHOUT PAYING HEED

Are you not aware of those who, having been granted their share of the divine writ, now barter it away for an error. They want you to lose your way [too]? But God knows best who your enemies are, and none can befriend as God does, and none can give succor as God does. Among those of the Jewish faith, some distort the meaning of the [revealed] words, taking them out of their context by saying, [as it were], "We have heard, but we disobey" and "Hear without heeding." (4:44-46)

The people referred to here are Bible followers (Jews of Medina). The Quran expounded here on its cardinal theme of man's responsibility for his actions. It also explains how he responds to God's guidance. The Quran accused the Jews of tempering and misinterpreting the revealed words and, thereby, distorting the meaning of the revealed words. The figure of speech, "hear without heeding," addressed by Jews to themselves, describes their attitude towards their scriptures and the Quran's message.

REJECTION OF THE QURAN OUT OF HAND

"You hearken unto us, [O Muhammad]." Thus, playing with their tongues suggests that your faith is false. Had they only said, "We have heard, and we pay attention," and "Hear [us], and have patience with us," it would indeed have been for their good and more upright. But God rejected them because they refused to acknowledge the truth—for they only believed in a few things. (4:46) They say, "Our hearts are already full of knowledge." No,

but God rejected them because they refused to acknowledge the truth: for few are the things they believe. (2:88)

The Jews say, "you hearken unto us," to convey that they had nothing to learn from the teaching propounded by the Prophet Muhammad. They also say that he should defer to their religious views. Religious knowledge they already possess means they do not need further preaching.

SIN OF SELF-RIGHTEOUSNESS AMONG JEWS, CHRISTIANS, AND MUSLIMS

Is it not time that the hearts of all who have attained faith should feel humble at the remembrance of God and all the truth bestowed [on them] from on high? Lest they become like those who were granted revelation aforetime and whose hearts have hardened with time so that many of them are [now] depraved? [But] know that God gives life to the earth after it is lifeless! Indeed, we have made Our messages clear so that you may use your reason. (57:16-17)

Remembrance of God and His revelation should make believers humble rather than arrogant. This is lest they become like the spiritually arrogant Jews, who regard themselves as God's chosen people and, therefore, predestined for His acceptance. Christians claim they are already saved, and some misguided Muslims believe Muhammad's intercession will guarantee their salvation. They act contrary to their religion's ethical precepts. True faith makes man humble and God-conscious rather than self-satisfied. A loss of spiritual humility invariably results in moral degeneration. "**God gives life to the earth**" is a parabolic allusion to the effect of a reawakening of God-consciousness in hearts that had become deadened by self-satisfaction and false pride. This passage is an emphatic warning against all smugness, self-righteousness, and false pride in having "attained faith" and considering themselves pious regardless of their religious affiliation.

DIFFERENT RULES FOR NON-JEWS

Among the followers of earlier revelation, there are many who, if you entrust him with a treasure will [faithfully]return it to you. There is among them many who, if you entrust him with a tiny gold coin, will not return it to you unless you keep standing over him. This is an outcome of their assertion, "No blame can attach to us [for anything we may do] concerning these unlettered folks": and [so] they tell a lie about God, being conscious [that it is a lie]? (3:75) And [for] their taking of usury, which was forbidden to them and wrongful devouring of other people's possessions. For those among them who [continue to] deny the truth, We have readied grievous suffering.) (4:161)

Judaism condemns **usury** towards **Jews** but allows it towards **non-Jews** (Deut. 23:19–20), denying equal status to non-Jews. The people referred to are the Jews of Medina. They falsely claim that God Himself has exempted them from all moral responsibility toward non-Jews (contemptuously described as unlettered folk).

BREAKING BONDS WITH GOD

[God is aware of] those who fulfil their duty towards Him: and God loves those who are conscious of Him. Those who barter away their bond with God and their pledges for a trifling gain shall not partake in the blessings of life to come. God will neither speak unto them nor look upon them on the Day of Resurrection nor will He cleanse them of their sins; and grievous suffering awaits them. (3:76-77)

WE ARE RICH, AND YOUR GOD IS POOR

God has indeed heard the saying of those who said, "Behold, God is poor while we are rich!" We shall record what they have said, as well as their slaying of prophets against all right, and We shall say [unto them on Judgment Day]: "Taste suffering through fire in return for what your own hands have wrought - for never does God do the least wrong to His creatures!" (3:181-182) Who will offer God a goodly loan, which He will amply repay, with manifold increase?" (2:245)

"God is poor while we are rich" is the satire of the Jews of Medina in response to verse 2:245 of the Quran. Abu Bakr invited Rabbi Finhas to Islam. He answered, "We do not need your God, but He who needs us. It is not I who pray to Him; it is He who prays to us. We are self-sufficient, and He is not. If God is self-sustaining, He will not borrow our wealth as your prophet claims." It was after this incident that the above verse was revealed.

YOUR GOD'S HANDS ARE SHACKLED

And the Jews say, "God's hand is shackled!" Their own hands are shackled and rejected [by God] because of this assertion. Wide are His hands stretched out: He dispenses [bounty] as He wills. But all that has been bestowed from on high upon you [O Prophet] by thy Sustainer is bound to make many of them even more stubborn in their overweening arrogance and denial of the truth. (5:64)

The phrase "one's hand is shackled" denotes stinginess and lack of power. The Jews of Medina, seeing the Muslims' poverty, derided their conviction that they were struggling for God's cause. The Jews say, "God's hand is shackled," as well as in 3:181, "God is poor while we are rich," is an example of their attitude toward Islam and Muslims. This attitude of sarcasm is paraphrased: "If it were true that you Muslims are doing God's will, He would have bestowed upon you power and riches, but your poverty and your weakness contradict your claim—or else this claim of yours amounts, in effect, to saying that God cannot help you." It illustrates an attitude of mind, which mistakenly identifies worldly riches or power with one's being, spiritually, "on the right way." Those who see in material success alleged evidence of God's approval are blind to spiritual truths and, therefore, morally powerless and utterly self-condemned in the sight of God.

DO NOT TAKE HOSTILE JEWS AS YOUR FRIENDS

O you who have attained faith! Do not take for your friends those who mock at your faith and make a mockery of it - be they who have been vouchsafed revelation before your time, or [from among] those who deny the truth [of revelation as such]. But remain conscious of God, if you are [truly] believers: for, when you call to prayer, they mock at it and make a joke of it - simply because they are people who do not use their reason. Say: "O, followers of earlier revelations! Do you find fault with us because we believe in God [alone]? He has bestowed from on high upon us and that which He has bestowed aforetime? - or [is it only] because most of you are iniquitous?" (5:57-59)

SPIRITUAL BARRENNESS

And yet, after all this, your hearts hardened and became like rocks, or even harder. There are rocks from which streams gush forth. There are some rocks from which they are cleft, water issues, and some fall for God's awe. And God is not unmindful of what you do! (2:74)

The simile of "the rocks from which streams gush forth" or "from which water issues" illustrates its opposite, namely dryness and lack of life. And this is an allusion to the spiritual barrenness with which the Quran charges the children of Israel. Spiritual barrenness in today's world is, however, not limited to Jews alone.

BELIEF IN BASELESS MYSTERIES

They attribute their false inventions to God-then there is no more obvious sin. Are you not aware of those who, having been granted their share of the divine writ, [now] believe in baseless mysteries and in the powers of evil. They maintain that those bent on denying the truth are more guided than those who have attained faith? God has rejected them and whom God rejects shall find none to succor him. (4:50-52)

The word al-jibt rendered as "baseless mysteries," refers to all manners of mythical divination and soothsaying, a combination of confusing ideas, fanciful surmises, and fictitious stories. As regards the expression "the powers of evil," it seems to refer here to superstitious beliefs and practices—like soothsaying, foretelling the future, relying on "good" and "bad" omens, and so forth—all of which are condemned by the Quran. See 2:256.

SEE GOD FACE TO FACE

Are these people [followers of earlier revelations] waiting, perhaps, for God to reveal Himself in the shadows of the clouds, together with the angels? Though all will have been decided and all things have been brought back unto God? Ask the children of Israel how many clear messages We have given them! And if one alters God's blessed message after it reaches him, God is severe in retribution! Those who are bent on denying the truth, the life of this world [alone] seems good; hence, they scoff at those who have attained faith: but they who are conscious of God shall be above them on Resurrection Day. (2:210-212)

God will only reveal Himself on the Day of Judgment, and then it will be too late for repentance. It is possible that this rhetorical question at the beginning of the above passage relates to their refusal, in the time of Moses, to believe in the divine message unless they "see God face to face".

CHAPTER 21
THE DENIAL OF AFTERLIFE

The Children of Israel lost their conviction that life in this world is the first and final stage of human life. As their Biblical history shows, they abandoned themselves entirely to the pursuit of material prosperity and power. Up to the time of the destruction of the Second Temple and their dispersion by Roman Emperor Titus, the priestly aristocracy among the Jews, known as the Sadducees, openly denied the concepts of resurrection, divine judgment, and life in the hereafter. They advocated a materialistic outlook on life and believed that death is final, with nothing beyond it.

We chose them knowingly above all other people and gave them such signs [of Our grace] as would clearly presage a test. [Now] these [people] say indeed: "That [which is ahead of us] is but our first [and only] death, and we shall not be raised to life again. So then, bring forth our forefathers [as witnesses], if what you claim is true!" (44:32-36)

The sign of God's grace refers to the long line of prophets among the Jewish people. It also refers to the freedom and prosperity they enjoyed in the Promised Land. All this presaged a test of their sincerity regarding ethical principles, which raised them "above all other people" and their willingness to act as God's message-bearers to the entire world. The formulation of the above sentence implies that they did not pass that test as they soon forgot the spiritual mission for which they had been elected.

If an afterlife exists, bring our forefathers back to life and let them witness there is a hereafter. Until the Greeks desecrated the Jewish Temple in 167 BC, the Jews had a vague idea of the hereafter. "Sheol" was a dark numbness, not an end or existence. When the Greeks, with their many gods and decadent ways, threatened the

Jewish way of existence, their leaders came up with a powerful incentive to stay faithful and fight back.

"Many of those who sleep in the dust of the earth will awaken, some to everlasting life and some to shame and endless contempt. Those who are wise shall shine like the brightness of the sky and those who lead many to righteousness, like the stars forever and ever." (Daniel 12:2-3).

In a passage in the Book of Daniel, written around 165 BC, this is the first clear reference to the resurrection in the Bible. Over the centuries, the mainstream Jewish concept of an afterlife has evolved into a spiritual journey. Jews also believe that at the end of time, paradise will exist on earth, and souls will be reunited with their bodies. Theologians stress, though, that the here and now is what matters for Jews, not the hereafter.

PREFERRING WORLDLY GAINS OVER AN AFTERLIFE

They have been succeeded by [new] generations who—[despite] having inherited the divine writ-clutch at the transient good of this lower world and say, "We shall be forgiven." They are ready, if another such fleeting good comes their way, to clutch at it [and sin again]. Have they not been solemnly pledged through the divine writ not to attribute to God anything but what is true? [Have they not] read again and again all that is therein? Since life in the hereafter is the better [of the two] for all who are conscious of God, will you not, then, use your reason? For [We shall requite] all those who hold fast to the divine writ and are constant in prayer: We shall not fail to requite those who enjoin the doing of what is right! (7:169-170)

We shall be forgiven for breaking God's commandments in their pursuit of worldly gain: an allusion to their persistent belief that no matter what they do, His forgiveness and grace are assured to them by their being Abraham's descendants. However, God's forgiveness can only be obtained through sincere repentance. The divine writ mentioned twice in this passage is the Bible.

NO EXEMPTION FROM PUNISHMENT

And they say, "The fire will certainly not touch us for more than a few days." Say [unto them]: "Have you received a promise from God - for God never breaks His promise - or do you attribute to God something that you cannot know?" Yea! Those who earn evil and are engulfed by sinfulness; they are destined for fire, where they will remain. While those who attain faith and do righteous deeds are destined for paradise, therein to abide. (2:80-82) Art thou not aware of those who have been granted their share of revelation [aforetime]? They have been called upon to let God's writ be their Law, yet some of them turn away [from it] in their obstinacy simply because they claim, "The fire will most certainly not touch us for more than a limited number of days." Thus, the false beliefs they invented have [in time] caused them to betray their faith. (3:23-24)

Popular Jewish belief holds that even sinners among the Children of Israel will face only very limited punishment in the life to come. They will be quickly reprieved by belonging to "the chosen people," a belief the Quran rejects. Some Muslims also believe that being nominal followers of Muhammad guarantees their salvation.

PARADISE IS NOT FOR JEWS ONLY

Say: "If an afterlife with God is to be for you alone, to the exclusion of all other people, then you should long for death—if what you say is true!" But never will they desire it, because [they are aware] of what their hands have sent ahead in this world: and God has full knowledge of evildoers. And thou wilt most certainly find that they cling to life more eagerly than any other people. This is even more than those bent on ascribing divinity to other beings besides God. Everyone would love to live a thousand years, although the grant of long life could not save him from suffering [in the hereafter]: for God sees all that they do. (2:94-96)

SALVATION IS NOT RESERVED FOR ANY PARTICULAR DENOMINATION

And they claim, "None shall ever enter Paradise unless he is a Jew"—or "a Christian." Such are their wishful beliefs! Say: "Produce a shred of evidence for what you are claiming if what you say is true!" [from your scriptures] *Furthermore, the Jews assert, "The Christians have no well-founded ground for their beliefs, while the Christians assert, "The Jews have no valid ground for their beliefs"—and both quote the divine writ! Thus, like unto what they say, have [always] spoken to those without knowledge. It is God who will judge between them on Resurrection Day about all on which they differ. (2:111-113)*

The claim of exclusive salvation amounts to spiritual arrogance and self-righteousness, which causes many evils. Such narcissism dehumanizes anyone belonging to a different religious group. The process of denigration leads to discrimination and, if taken to the extreme, can result in violence and genocide.

Thus, according to the Quran, salvation is not reserved for any "denomination" but is open to everyone who consciously realizes the oneness of God, surrenders himself to His will, and, by living righteously, gives practical effect to this spiritual attitude. Such are their wishful beliefs, those who assert that only their denomination followers shall partake of God's grace in the hereafter. God will confirm the truth of what was true in their respective beliefs and show the falseness of what was false therein. The Quran maintains throughout that there is a substantial element of truth in all faiths based on divine revelation. It also states that their subsequent divergence was the result of "wishful beliefs" and a gradual alteration of the original teachings.

FORGING UNITY AMONG MONOTHEISTS

CHAPTER 22
THE DIVINE LAW OF DIVERSITY

This chapter argues that God, although the fountainhead or source, His revelations may differ to suit the needs of the time and the people concerned. It answers the objection, often raised by followers of other creeds, that the message of the Quran differs in many respects from the earlier divine revelations. Differences between the Quran and older scriptures do not automatically render false either the Quran or others' scriptures.

DIVERSITY IS THE ESSENCE OF LIFE

Out of billions of human beings, not one is exactly alike. From the many trillions of leaves on all trees, not one is alike. In his infinite wisdom, God created people of all colors and creeds. We live in a world filled with diversity, from biodiversity to racial, religious, cultural and linguistic diversity.

THE ORIGIN OF HUMANITY IS FROM ONE LIVING ENTITY

O mankind! Be conscious of your Sustainer, who created you from one living entity. Out of it created its mate, and out of the two spawned a multitude of men and women. And remain conscious of God, in whose name you demand [your rights] from one another, and of these kinship ties. God is always watching over you! (4:1) It is He who created you [all] out of one living entity and brought into being its mate. This is so that man might incline [with love] towards a woman. (7:189) Now had God so willed, He could surely have made them all one single community. (42:8)

The implication is that God has not willed humanity to be a single community. The above verses stress the common origin and brotherhood of humanity, and any idea that divides humanity is contrary to God's plan. Such manmade divisions based upon race, caste and creed are inherently evil.

The term zawj (a pair, one of a pair, or a mate) applies to both male and female components. He created its mate (i.e., its sexual counterpart) from its kind.

INTELLECTUAL DEVELOPMENT

At the dawn of man's history, people lived in a relatively homogeneous primitive social order. This was based on following the rules of one's peer group and blind respect for authority. Good behavior involves living up to social expectations and roles without right or wrong. As his thinking developed, his life became more complex. With higher intellectual development, abstract principles such as justice and morality form the basis of a personal code. It began to clash with blind respect for authority and society's expectations. His emotional capacity and individual needs, too, became more differentiated, conflicts of views and interests came to the fore, and humanity ceased to be "one single community" in its outlook on life and moral valuations. It was at this point that divine guidance was necessary.

DIVERSITY OF HUMANKIND AND DIVINE GUIDANCE

All humanity was once one single community [then they began to differ]. After that, God raised the prophets as heralds of glad tidings and warners. Through them He bestowed revelation from on high, setting forth the truth. So that it might decide between people who hold divergent views. Yet the same people who granted this [revelation] began, out of mutual jealousy, to disagree about its meaning after all evidence of the truth had come to them. But God guided the believers to the truth about which, by His leave, they disagreed. God guides those who intend to be guided on a straight path. (2:213)

The phrase "out of mutual jealousy" refers to the various religious groups from the followers of the earlier revelations who, over time, consolidated themselves into different denominations. Each of them jealously guarded its own set of tenets, dogma, and rituals and becoming intensely intolerant of all others.

INTELLECTUAL DISSENTION

And if God had so willed, they who succeeded those [apostles] would not have contended after all evidence of the truth had come to them. But [as it was], they took to divergent views, and some gained faith, while others denied the truth. Yet if God had so willed, they would not have contended, but God does whatever He wills. (2:253)

Again, as in verse 213 above, the Quran mentions the inevitability of disagreement among human beings. In other words, it is the will of God that their way to the truth should be through diversity of opinions and by trial and error. Man's proneness to intellectual disagreement is not an accident of history but an integral, God-willed aspect of human nature. Disagreements and critical thinking are the source of human development and progress.

DIVERSITY IN COLORS, LANGUAGES, AND SEXES

His wonders are this: He creates you out of dust, and then, lo! You become a human being that reaches far and wide! And among His wonders is this: He created for you your kind of mate. [From among yourselves] *so that you might incline towards them, and He engenders love and tenderness between you. In this, there are messages indeed for people who think! And among his wonders are the diversity of your tongues and colors. For in this, there are messages for all who possess [innate] knowledge! (30:20-22)*

If God wanted to create a homogenous humanity, he could have done so by being almighty. Besides the world being boring, it would have been detrimental to humanity. Genetic diversity is crucial because it ensures certain groups of individuals or populations adapt to certain environmental factors. Genetic diversity enables them to resist emerging diseases and epidemics.

This is the answer to all racists of this world: their feelings of superiority are the product of narrow and perverse thinking. Muslim societies suffer from many social problems, but racism is not one of them. Hence, discrimination on any basis is a denial of God's creation and a sinful act. People from different cultures, ethnicities, races, countries, or religions are part of the one-world society or secular Ummah originally defined in the Medina Constitution.

DIVERSITY IN LAW AND THE WAY OF LIFE

See 5:48, in the previous chapte , the Quran is not God's speech.

DIVERSITY OF WORSHIP

Unto every community, We have appointed [different] ways of worship, which they ought to observe. Hence, [O believer], do not let those [who follow paths other than yours] draw you into disputes on this score. Instead, summon [them all] unto thy Sustainer, for you are indeed on the right way. And if they [try to] argue with you, say [only]: "God knows best what you are doing." [For, indeed], God will judge between you [all] on Resurrection Day regarding all on which you differ. Do you not realize that God knows all that occurs in heaven and on earth? All this is in [God's] record: [knowing] all this is easy for God. (22:67-70)

COMMON SPIRITUAL TRUTH

And so, [O man], if you are in doubt about [the truth of] what We have [now] bestowed upon you from on high, ask those who read the divine writ [revealed] before your time. [You will find that] surely; the truth has now come unto you from thy Sustainer. Be not, then, among the doubters and neither among those who are bent on giving the lie to God's messages, lest you find yourself among the lost. They against whom thy Sustainer's word [of judgment] has come true will not attain to faith—even though every sign [of the truth] should come within their ken—until they behold the grievous suffering [that awaits them in the life to come]. (10:94-97)

The above verse alludes to man's uninterrupted religious experience. It also alludes to the fact, frequently stressed in the Quran, that all of God's apostles preached the same fundamental truth.

DIVERSITY IN DIVINE REVELATIONS?

Every age has had its revelation: God annuls or confirms whatever He wills [of His earlier messages]—for with Him is the source of all revelation. (13:38-39) And upon you [too] have We bestowed from on high this divine writ for no other reason than that you might make clear unto them all [questions of faith] on which they have come to hold divergent views, and [thus offer] guidance and grace unto people who will believe. (16:64)

See 5:48, in the previous chapter — "Unto everyone have We appointed a different law and way of life," which explains the succession of divine messages culminating in, and ending with, the revelation of the Quran. This interpretation of the above phrase connects it with the preceding mention of the apostles before Muhammad and the subsequent reference to the supersession of the earlier divine messages by that of the Quran.

VALIDITY OF THE QURAN

Hence, they unto whom We have vouchsafed this revelation rejoice at all that has been bestowed upon you [O Prophet] from on high. However, among other creed followers, there are some who deny the validity of some of it. Say [unto them, O Prophet]: "I have only been bidden to worship God, and not to ascribe divine powers to anything beside Him: unto Him do I call [all mankind], and He is my goal!" (13:36)

For those who believe in this revelation, there will be guidance for them in this world and the promise of ultimate happiness in the life to come. Other creed followers deny its validity while admitting that the Quran contains much that coincides with spiritual concepts taught by their religions. The particle "only" at the beginning of the above sentence clearly shows that there is in Islam no obligation, no ordinance and no prohibition that is not connected with this principle.

CHAPTER 23
THE COMMON BELIEFS AMONG JEWS, CHRISTIANS, AND MUSLIMS

THERE IS A LOT MORE COMMON AMONG THE THREE MONOTHEISTIC FAITHS

The Prophet and the Jews of Medina had bitter disagreements, mostly political and some religious in nature. While the Quran criticizes some Jewish and Christian practices, it provides an overwhelmingly positive message to these two monotheistic faiths. There is a great deal more that these three monotheist religions have in common than distinguishing them. Today, the press and social media obsessively highlight the differences between Judaism, Christianity, and Islam just to prove the superiority of one's religion over the other. Sadly, however, such an initial focus on differences produces gross distortion. There are notable similarities in notions of sacrifice, good works, hospitality, peace, justice, pilgrimage, afterlife and loving God with all one's heart and soul. This chapter is dedicated to the commonalities among three monotheistic faiths according to the Quranic perspective.

(1) OUR GOD AND YOUR GOD IS THE SAME

Do not argue with the followers of earlier revelation otherwise than in a most kindly manner—unless it is such of them as are bent on evildoing—and say: "We believe in that which has been bestowed from on high upon us, as well as that which has been bestowed upon you: for our God and your God is one and the same, and it is unto Him that We [all] surrender ourselves." For it is thus that We have bestowed this divine writ from on high upon you [O Muhammad]. And they to whom we have vouchsafed this divine writ believe in it—just as among those [followers of earlier revelation] some who believe in it. (29:46-47) Say [to Jews and Christians]: "Do you argue with us about God? But He is our Sustainer and your Sustainer—and unto us shall be accounted for our deeds, and unto you, your deeds; and it is unto Him alone that we devote ourselves." (2:139) Say: "My prayer, and [all] my acts of worship, and my living and my dying are for God [alone], the Sustainer of all the worlds, in whose divinity none has a share. For thus have I been bidden - and I will always be foremost among those who surrender themselves unto Him." Say: "Am I, then, seeking a sustainer other than God when He is the Sustainer of all things?" (6:162-164)

Not only are these three monotheistic faiths historically linked, but their adherents worship the same God. The God of the Bible and the Quran is the same Deity with different names in different languages. The word "God" is derived from the proto-Germanic pagan word gott. The Latin Deus, the Spanish Dios, and the French Dieu are all descendants of Zeus. The Aramaic (language of Jesus) word for God was Alaha, the Hebrew Eloah, and the Arabic Allah (the God). In Abrahamic monotheism, God, Dios, Alaha, Eloah, and Allah all refer to the same Deity.

SURRENDER UNTO GOD

Thus, [O Prophet] if they argue with you, say, "I have surrendered my whole being unto God, and [so have] all who follow me!" And ask those who have been vouchsafed revelations aforetime, as well as all unlettered people, [who have no revealed scripture of their own], "Have you [too] surrendered yourselves unto Him?" And if they surrender themselves unto Him, they are on the right path; but if they turn away—your duty is no more than to deliver the message: for God sees all that is in [the hearts of] His creatures. (3:20)

WORSHIP OF ONE GOD AS THE ONLY TRUE RELIGION

Say: "O followers of earlier revelation! Come unto that tenet you and we hold in common: that we shall worship none but God, and we shall not ascribe divinity to anything besides Him, and we shall not take human beings for our Lords beside God." And if they turn away, then say: "Bear witness that it is we who have surrendered ourselves unto Him." (3:64) For, if one seeks a religion other than self-surrender unto God, it will never be accepted from him, and in the life to come, he shall be among the lost. (3:85)

Tenets you and we hold in common (lit: an equitable word between you and us). The term kalimah, meaning "word" or "utterance," is often used in the philosophical sense of a proposition or tenet. We shall not take human beings as our Lords lit. "That we shall not take one another for Lords beside God." Since the personal pronoun "we" applies to human beings, the expression "one another" necessarily bears the same connotation. The above call is addressed not only to Christians, who attribute divinity to Jesus and certain aspects of divinity to their saints. It is addressed also to the Jews, who assign quasi-divine authority to Ezra and even some of their leading Talmudic scholars. (See 9:30-31)

DON'T ARGUE ABOUT GOD

Those who [still] argue about God after He has been acknowledged [by them]—all their arguments are null and void in their Sustainer's sight. Upon them will fall [His] condemnation, and for them is severe suffering in store. This is because God [Himself] bestows revelation from on high, setting forth the truth. In addition, [it gives man] a balance [with which to weigh right and wrong]. And for all you know, the Last Hour may well be nearby! Those who do not believe in it [mockingly] call for its speedy advent— whereas those who have attained faith stand in awe of it and know it to be the truth. Oh, those who call the Last Hour in question have indeed gone far astray! (42:16-18)

Arguments about God's attributes and the "how" of His Being are null and void; it is beyond the grasp of the limited human mind. God Himself has given man, through successive revelations, a standard to discern between right and wrong. It is presumptuous and futile to argue about His nature and His ultimate judgment. Hence the reference in the second half of this and the next verse to the Last Hour and the Day of Judgment. There are those who do not believe in the last hour and demand swift punishment as proof that he is God's messenger. The sarcastic demand of Muhammad's opponents (mentioned several times in the Quran) and an oblique allusion to unbelievers of all times who categorically reject the idea of resurrection and judgment without proof either way.

(2) THE SAME PROPHETS

We bestowed upon him [Abraham] Isaac and Jacob, and We guided each of them as We had guided Noah aforetime. And out of his offspring, [We bestowed prophethood upon] David, Solomon, Job, Joseph, Moses, and Aaron. Thus, We reward the doers of good. And [upon] Zachariah, John, Jesus, and Elijah, everyone was righteous, and [upon] Ishmael, Elisha, Jonah, and Lot. We favored each of them over the others. [We exalted] some of their forefathers, offspring, and brethren. We elected them [all] and guided them on the straightway. Such is God's guidance. Additionally, He guides whoever He wills from among His servants. We vouchsafed revelation, sound judgment, and prophethood to them. (6:84-89)

THE PARABLE OF THE THREE PROPHETS

The story below is a parable and not a historical narrative. Here, we have an allegory of the three great monotheistic religions, presented successively by Moses, Jesus, and Muhammad. These religions embody the same spiritual truths. The township mentioned in the parable represents the common cultural environment within which these three religions appeared. The first two apostles were sent together since the teachings of both were—and are—anchored together in the Old and New Testaments of the Bible.

When their impact proved insufficient to mold people's ethical attitudes, God strengthened them with His final message. This was conveyed by the third and last apostle, Muhammad.

And set forth unto them a parable: [the story of how] the people of a township [acted] when [Our] message-bearers came unto them. Lo! We sent two [apostles], and they gave the lie to both, and so We strengthened [the two] with a third; and they said: "We have been sent unto you [by God]!" [The others] answered: "You are nothing, but mortal men like us; moreover, the Most Gracious has never bestowed any [revelation] from on high. You do nothing but lie!" (36:13-15)

See 6:91— "no true understanding of God have they when they say, 'Never has God revealed anything unto man.'" These passages allude to people who like to think of themselves as believing in God without allowing their belief to interfere with their lives' practical concerns. By relegating religion to a vaguely emotional role, they justify their refusal to acknowledge God's objective revelation of moral values. They reject the idea of an individual submitting to them.

Said [the apostles], "Our Sustainer knows that we have indeed been sent unto you, but we are not bound to do more than deliver the message [entrusted to us]." Said [the others], "Truly, we augur evil from you! Indeed, if you desist not, we will surely stone you, and grievous suffering is bound to befall you at our hands!" [The apostles] replied: "Your destiny, good or evil, is [bound up] with yourselves! [Every human being's destiny We have tied to his neck.] [Does it seem evil to you] if you are told to take [the truth] to heart? You are people who have wasted their own selves!" (36:16-19)*

At that, a man came running from the farthest end of the town, exclaiming: "O my people! Follow these message-bearers! You should follow those who ask for no reward from you and who are rightly guided! "[As for me], why should I not worship Him who brought me into being, and to whom you all will be brought back? Should I take to worshipping [other] deities besides Him? [But then], if the Most Gracious should will that harm befall me, their intercession could not in the least avail me, nor could they save me: and so, I would have, most obviously, lost myself in error! I now believe that there is a Sustainer who sustains you all. Listen, then, to me!" [And] he was told, "[You shall] enter paradise!"— [whereupon] he exclaimed: "Would that my people knew how my Sustainer has forgiven me [the sins of my past] and has placed me among the honored ones!" (36:20-27)

The intervention of the man who "came running from the farthest end of the city" is a parable of the truly believing minority in every religion and of their desperate attempts to convince their erring fellowmen that God-consciousness alone can save human life from futility.

(3) THE HOLY BOOKS

THE DIVINE ORIGIN OF THE QURAN, THE GOSPEL, AND THE TORAH

Step by step has He bestowed upon you from on high this divine writ, setting forth the truth which confirms whatever remains [of earlier revelations]: for it is He who has bestowed from on high the Torah and the Gospel aforetime, as a guidance unto humankind. He has bestowed [upon man] the standard to discern the true from the false. As for those bent on denying God's messages, grievous suffering awaits them, for God is almighty, an avenger of evil. (3:3-4)

"Whatever remains of earlier revelations" refers to the Bible subject to alterations over the millennia established by objective scholarship. The Quran's laws differ from Biblical laws. This leads to the conclusion that the "confirmation" of the latter by the Quran can only be applied to the basic truths still discernible in the Bible. In this context, in 5:46 and, 48 and 61:6, Jesus confirms the truth of whatever remained (i.e., in his lifetime) of the Torah. The Gospel frequently mentioned in the Quran is not identical to what is known today as the Four Gospels but refers to an original, bestowed upon Jesus and known to his contemporaries under its Greek name of Evangelion ("Good Tidings"), on which the Arabicized form Injil is based. It was initially preserved as an oral tradition in Aramaic. It was probably the source from which the Synoptic Gospels derived much of their Greek material. In 5:14, the Quran alludes to it being lost and forgotten.

SAME SOURCE OF DIVINE REVELATION

And, indeed [O Muhammad], We did vouchsafe revelations unto Moses [as well]: so be not in doubt of [you] having met with the same [truth in the revelation vouchsafed to you]. And [just as] We caused that [earlier revelation] to be a guidance for the children of Israel, and [as] We raised among them leaders who, so long as they bore themselves with patience and had sure faith in Our messages, guided [their people] in accordance with Our behest— [so, too, shall it be with the divine writ revealed unto you, O Muhammad]. (32:23-24)

The divine origin of Muhammad's revelation proceeds from the same source as Moses. Furthermore, the same fundamental truths in all divine revelations implies an identity of the moral demands made of the followers of those revelations. This is irrespective of the period, race, or social environment.

The Jewish faith raised leaders who guided their people in accordance with the divine ordinances elucidated in and for their time in the Torah. The Quran is also destined to provide guidance and light so long as the community's religious leaders are patient in adversity and steadfast in their faith. It implies that the Quran will cease to benefit people who have lost their moral virtues and faith.

The Quran frequently points out the Mosaic laws and their pivotal role in man's monotheistic history. It stresses, again and again, its importance as a means of enforcing spiritual discipline on the children of Israel. Their repeated, deliberate breaches of the Mosaic Law are evidence of their rebellious attitude toward that discipline and, thus, toward God's commandments in general.

THE QURAN CONFIRMS THE TORAH'S TRUTH

And yet, before this, there was the revelation of Moses, a guide and a [sign of God's] grace; and this [Quran] is a divine writ confirming the truth [of the Torah] [In its original, unaltered form.] in the Arabic tongue, to warn those who are bent on evildoing, and [to bring] glad tidings to the doers of good: for all who say, "Our Sustainer is God," and thereafter stand firm [in their faith]—no fear need they have, and neither shall they grieve. It is they who are destined for paradise, therein to abide as a reward for all that they have done. (46:12-14)

COMMON SPIRITUAL TRUTH

And so [O man], if thou art in doubt about [the truth of] what We have [now] bestowed upon you from on high, ask those who read the divine writ [revealed] before your time. [And you will find that] indeed, the truth has now been revealed unto you from thy Sustainer. Be not, then, among the doubters, and neither be among those bent on giving a lie to God's messages, lest you find yourself among the lost. They against whom thy Sustainer's word [of judgment] has come true will not attain to faith—even though every sign [of the truth] should exist within their ken—until they behold the grievous suffering [that awaits them in the life to come]. (10:94-97)

These verses address man in general and explain the reference to "what We have bestowed upon thee from on high," the guidance vouchsafed to humankind through the ultimate divine writ, the Quran. "Those who read the divine writ before your time," I.e., Jews and Christians. In its broader sense, the above verse alludes to the unbroken continuity of man's religious experience frequently stressed in the Quran. This is because all God's apostles preached the same basic truth.

ARGUE IN A MOST KINDLY MANNER

Do not argue with those who follow earlier revelations except in a most kind manner unless they are bent on evildoing. (29:46) Call thou [all humanity] unto thy Sustainer's path with wisdom and goodly exhortation and argue with them in the kindest manner – for, behold, thy Sustainer knows best who strays from His path, and surely knows who is rightly-guided. Hence, if you must respond to an attack [in argument], respond only to the extent of the attack leveled against you. However, bearing yourselves with patience is far better for [you, as God is with] those who are patient in adversity. (16:125-126)

Argue kindly with the followers of earlier revelation, except those who are evildoers and are therefore not accessible to friendly argument. The implication being that in such cases, all disputes should be avoided as far as possible. As regards religious discussions in general, see 16:125. "For it is thus," or in this spirit: a reference to the sameness of the fundamental truths in all revealed religions, to whom God has bestowed his revelation and to whom God grants the ability to understand this divine writ, except for those who deny or reject something he knows to be true.

(4) THE HOUSES OF WORSHIP

THE SACREDNESS OF MOSQUES, CHURCHES, AND SYNAGOGUES

Hence, who could be more wicked than those who bar the mention of God's name from [any of] His houses of worship? They strive for their ruin, [although] they have no right to enter them save in fear [of God]? For them, in this world, there is ignominy in store; and for them, in the life to come awesome suffering. (2:114)

It is a fundamental principle of Islam that every religion with God as its focal point deserves full respect, even if one disagrees with many of its tenets. Muslims are obligated to honor and protect any house of worship dedicated to God, whether it be a mosque, a church, or a synagogue. The Quran considers sacrilegious any attempt to prevent followers of another faith from worshipping God according to their light. A striking illustration of this principle is forthcoming from the Prophet's treatment of the delegation from Christian Najran in the year 10 H. They were given free access to the Prophet's Mosque and, with his full consent, celebrated their religious rites there. However, their adoration of Jesus as "the son of God" and Mary as "the mother of God" was fundamentally at variance with Islamic beliefs.

Those who have been driven from their homelands against all rights for no other reason than their saying: "Our Sustainer is God!" For, if God had not enabled people to defend themselves against one another, [all] monasteries and churches and synagogues and mosques—in [all] which God's name is abundantly extolled—would surely have been destroyed [before now]. (22:40) And if God had not permitted people to defend themselves against one another, corruption would surely overwhelm the earth. (2:251)

Lit., "were it not that God repels some people through others": an elliptic reference to God's enabling people to defend themselves against aggression or oppression. The same phrase occurs in **22:40,** which deals with fighting in self-defense. The defense of religious freedom is the foremost cause for which arms may—and, indeed, must—be taken up (see 2:193). Otherwise, corruption would surely overwhelm the earth.

DIVERSITY OF WORSHIP: *(22:67-70)*

(See previous chapter: The divine law of diversity)

DIVERGENT VIEWS AND THE QURANIC EXPLANATION

Behold, this Quran explains to the children of Israel most [of that] whereon they hold divergent views; it is guidance and grace unto all who believe [in it]. [O believer], thy Sustainer will judge between them in His wisdom—for He alone is almighty, all-knowing. Therefore, trust in God alone-for what you believe is self-evident truth. [But], you cannot make the dead hear: and [so, too], you cannot make the deaf [of heart] hear this call when they turn their backs [on you] and go away, just as you cannot lead the blind [of heart] out of their error; none can you make hear save such as [are willing to] believe in Our messages, and thus surrender themselves unto Us. (27:76-81)

The term "children of Israel" includes Jews and Christians, as both follow the Old Testament. Because of the alteration of the Bible and the substantial influence that Jewish and Christian ideas exert over a large segment of humanity, the Quran explains certain ethical truths to both these communities. The above reference to "most" (and not all) of the problems alluded to in this context shows that the present passage bears only on man's moral outlook and social life in this world and not on ultimate, metaphysical questions which—as the Quran so often repeats—will be answered only in the hereafter. The passage above corresponds to the often-repeated Quranic statement that God guides him who wills to be guided.

CHAPTER 24
EVIL OF SECTARIANISM

DEFINITIONS OF SECTARIANISM

Narrow-minded adherence to a particular sect (political, ethnic, or religious) often leads to conflict with those of different sects or possessing different beliefs. At a conceptual level, sectarianism includes bigotry, prejudice, and discrimination. In the real world, sectarian conflicts are common breeding grounds for acts of violence and persecution against other sects, denominations, or groups. The breach of unity is often due to worldly greed and power.

MUTUAL JEALOUSY

And be not like those who have drawn apart from one another and have taken to conflicting views after all evidence of the truth has come unto them: for these, tremendous suffering is in store. (3:105) Yet the same people who were granted this [revelation] began, out of mutual jealousy, to disagree about its meaning after all evidence of the truth had come unto them. But God guided the believers to the truth about which, by His leave, they disagreed. God guides those who wish to be guided on the right path. (2:213)

The Quran refers to Jews, Christians, and Muslims who have departed from the fundamental religious principles they originally shared. They have adopted different ways of interpreting doctrine and ethics. Examples include Sunni versus Shia within Islam, Orthodox and Reform within Judaism, and Protestants and Catholics within Christianity. The Quran condemns all sectarianism arising out of intolerant, mutually exclusive claims to the only true followers, while everyone else is on the wrong side. The phrase "out of mutual jealousy" refers to the various religious groups of followers of the earlier revelations who, over time, consolidated themselves into different denominations. Each of them was jealously guarding its own set of tenets, dogma, and rituals and becoming intensely intolerant of all other ways of worship.

ONE GOD, ONE COMMUNITY

FORMATION OF SECTS AND DENOMINATIONS

They [who claim to follow you] have torn their unity wide asunder, piece-by-piece, each group delighting in [but] what they possess [by way of tenets]. (23:53) And be not among those who ascribe divinity to others besides Him, [or] among those who have broken the unity of their faith and have become sects, each group delighting in but what they hold dear [in terms of tenets]. (30:31-32)

The above verses are directed at all who believe in God and the prophets' followers, regardless of their historical denomination. The various religious groups, over time, divided themselves into different "denominations," each jealously guarding its own set of tenets, dogmas, and rituals. They are intensely intolerant of all other ways of worship. The above condemnation applies to followers of Muhammad as well. Thus, it constitutes a prediction and condemnation of Islam's doctrinal disunity in our time.

SUFFERING ON THE DAY OF JUDGMENT

But men have torn their unity wide asunder, [forgetting that] unto Us they are all bound to return. (21:93) [As for those who have torn the unity of faith asunder], their hearts are lost in ignorance of all this! But apart from that [breach of unity], they have [on their consciences] more heinous deeds. They will [continue to] commit them until—after We shall have taken to task, through suffering, those who [now] are lost in the pursuit of pleasures—they cry out in [belated] supplication. [But they will be told]: "Cry not in supplication today for you shall not be helped by Us!" (23:56-65)

The worst deeds are actions and dogmatic assertions, which utterly contradict the very apostles' teachings whom they claim to follow, like ascribing divine qualities to beings other than God, worshipping saints, or rejecting divine revelations, which do not accord with their likes and dislikes or with their customary mode of thinking. People at present, lost in pursuing pleasures, will be taken to task on Judgment Day's suffering. It is a major sin to break faith unity. Sectarianism can also have negative consequences in life, such as social ruin. The purveyors of hate among religious leaders of various sects, who divide and deceive the vulnerable masses into pursuing their pleasures, will be taken to task on Judgment Day. They will cry out in belated supplication but will not be helped.

The above passages refer to the Bible's followers and all communities that base their views on revealed scripture. These communities initially subscribed to the doctrine of God's oneness and held that man's self-surrender to Him is the essence of all true religions. Jews, Christians, and Muslims, however, have departed from fundamental religious principles. They have taken different approaches to doctrine and ethics. The followers of earlier revelation and the Quran did not break up their unity until after knowledge came to them—i.e., the knowledge that God is one and that the teachings of all His prophets were essentially the same. Their subsequent divergence was caused by sectarian pride and mutual exclusivity.

SECTARIANISM AMONG BIBLE FOLLOWERS

And [as for the followers of earlier revelations], they broke up their unity, out of mutual jealousy, only after they knew [the truth]. And had it not been for a decree already gone forth from thy Sustainer, [postponing all decisions] until a term set [by Him], all would indeed have been decided between them [from the outset]. As it is, behold, they who have inherited their divine writ from those who preceded them are [now] in grave doubt, amounting to suspicion, concerning it. (42:14)

Those who were vouchsafed revelations aforetime took, out of mutual jealousy, to divergent views [on this point] only after knowledge [thereof] had been revealed unto them. But as for him who denies the truth of God's messages—behold, God is swift in reckoning! (3:19) Now those who have been vouchsafed revelations aforetime did break up their unity [of faith] after such evidence of the truth came to them. (98:4)

The above passages refer not only to Bible followers but to all communities that base their views on revealed Scripture. All these communities initially subscribed to the doctrine of God's oneness. They held that man's self-surrender to Him (Islam in its original connotation) is the essence of all true religions. Those who refer to the Bible and its followers in later times are doubtful as to whether God revealed the relevant scripture. In addition, they are doubtful whether divine revelation can be believed.

SHUN ALL THE DIVIDERS

Shun those who have broken the unity of faith—As for those who have broken the unity of their faith and have become sects—you have nothing to do with them. Their case rests with God, and in time He will make them understand what they were doing. (6:159)

GUIDANCE FOR THOSE GUILTY OF SECTARIANISM

It is not [conceivable] that such as are bent on denying the truth - [be they] from among the followers of earlier revelation or from among those who ascribe divinity to aught beside God - should ever be abandoned [by Him]. Before conclusive evidence of truth is offered: a revelation from God accompanied by ordinances of ever-true soundness and clarity conveyed [unto them] by an apostle from God]. (98:1-3) And had it not been for a decree already issued from thy Sustainer, [postponing all decisions] until a term set [by Him], all would indeed have been decided between them [from the outset]. (42:14)

WHAT IS TRUE RELIGION?

The only [true] religion in the sight of God is [man's] self-surrender unto Him. (3:19)

FOLLOW THE BASIC MORAL LAW

Furthermore, they were commanded to worship God, be sincere in their belief in Him alone, and turn away from all that is false. They should be constant in prayer and spend in charity, for this is a moral law endowed with ever-true soundness and clarity. (98:5)

The above definition of moral law outlines, in a condensed form, all the basic demands of true religion: a cognition of God's oneness and uniqueness and man's responsibility to Him; and, finally, kindness and charity toward all of God's creatures. The seven Noahide laws come close to the fundamental moral law of the Quran. Those who deny the self-evident principles formulated as the beginning and the end of all moral law will suffer in the afterlife.

THE SEVEN NOAHIDE LAWS

God communicated the Noahide Laws to Adam and Noah, ancestors of all human beings. That makes these rules universal for all times, places, and people. Without these rules, it would be impossible for humanity to live together in harmony. The following is a slightly modified version of Noahide laws:

1. **Do not profane God's Oneness**: Acknowledge that there is a single God who cares about what we are doing and desires that we take care of His world. Do not ever curse your Creator.

2. **Do not murder**: The value of human life cannot be measured. To destroy a single human life is to destroy the entire world—because, for that person, the world has ceased to exist.

3. **Do not steal**: Never steal, give short measures, or take bribes or kickbacks. Whatever benefits you receive in this world, make sure that none of them are at the unfair expense of someone else.

4. **Give charity** and be kind toward all of God's creatures. (Added to Noahide laws)

5. **Do not be cruel to animals**

6. **Keep your base desires in check**: Incest, adultery, rape, and homosexual relations are forbidden. These sinful acts destroy the family unit, the foundation of human society. Sexuality is sacred, being the fountain of life. When abused, nothing can be more debasing and destructive to human beings.

7. **Establish the rule of law**: With every small act of justice, we restore harmony to our world, synchronizing it with a supernal order. That is why we must keep the laws for stability and peace of the society.

CHAPTER 25
ANTI-SEMITISM

There is not a single verse in the Quran that can be labeled anti-Semitic. The word "antisemitism" means prejudice against Jews generally, often rooted in hatred of their ethnic background, culture, and/or religion. Antisemitism is a deadly combination of racism and sectarianism. The role Jews played in Jesus' supposed crucifixion is one of the main reasons for antisemitism among Christians. The hatred of Jews in Western civilization is also heavily influenced biracial and economic reasons. Jews had the misfortune of being crucial to Christian theology. Once Christianity decided, in the second century, to supersede Judaism, it required Jews to disappear. The Christian religion could fulfill a new covenant that invalidated the old one. Jews' persistence, however small their numbers, reminded them of this failure. The response was, historically, to destroy the Jews. However, with every massacre, the survivors also reminded Christians of the hypocrisy just beneath their message of peace. Christian eschatology is antisemitic. According to a literal reading of Revelation, when the rapture comes, Christians will be taken to heaven. Jews will be left behind to deal with the Antichrist, plagues, sores, boils, frogs, and other torments.

ANTISEMITISM AMONG MUSLIMS

Originally a Christian vice, antisemitism has found roots among some Muslims. Anti-Semitism among Muslims is mostly political. Muslim hatred of Jews became marked after creating the state of Israel in 1948. The massacre, ethnic cleansing, and continuous persecution of Palestinian Arabs by Israel's Jews have laid the foundation of hatred for Jews in the Islamic world. Desperation spawned the cult of death in some parts of the Islamic world. In our times, fundamentalist Christians, and Jews, despite their two thousand years of enmity, have found a common enemy, "Islam."

For a large part, the Christian world has supported Israel's occupation and ethnic cleansing of Palestinians. It is the collective failure of Jews, Christians, and Muslims that results in terrorism.

ANTI-SEMITISM IS ANTI-ISLAMIC

Islam has no antisemitism tradition. Muhammad's struggle against Jewish tribes in Medina was political. Theologically, Islam and Judaism have much in common. The fundamental egalitarian message of Islam is the universal form of Judaism. The narrow ethnocentric emphasis of Judaism and strong racial overtones in the form of "chosen people" created a barrier, thus restricting Judaism's growth.

Muslims were compelled to import anti-Jewish myths from Europe and translate into Arabic such virulent anti-Semitic texts as the Protocols of the Elders of Zion because they had no such traditions. Because of this new hostility toward the Jewish people, some Muslims now quote selective Quranic passages that refer to Prophet Muhammad's struggle with the three rebellious Jewish tribes. These Muslims with an anti-Jewish agenda will only quote passages of the Quran that are critical of Jews but conveniently ignore those passages that honor them. By taking these verses out of context, they have distorted both the Quran's message and the Prophet's attitude. This is because the Prophet himself felt no such hatred for Judaism. Five times a day, every Muslim ends the prayer by saying, "You are the most praised, the most glorious. O God, bestow Your grace on Muhammad and his family as You bestowed it on Abraham and his family. You are the most praised, the most glorious." Muslims bless Abraham's family, which includes the Jews and Arabs, in their five daily prayers.

GOD'S BLESSINGS FOR THE JEWS

Read the chapter on Moses and how God empowered the Jews and liberated them from the clutches of Pharaoh in the second volume. The Quran describes Pharaoh as God's enemy for his antisemitism.

FORERUNNER OF MONOTHEISM

I favored you above all other people—O children of Israel! Remember those blessings of mine with which I graced you, and fulfill your promise to Me, [whereupon] I shall fulfill My promise unto you; and of Me, of Me stand in awe! (2:40) It was Our will to bestow Our favor upon those [very people] who were deemed [so] utterly low in the land, and to make them forerunners in faith. We also wanted to make them heirs [to Pharaoh's glory]. (28:5)

Jews were the first to adopt a monotheistic creed in an unequivocal formulation. They became the forerunners of Christianity and Islam. The Torah inaugurated a new phase in mankind's religious history as the first divinely inspired law.

THE CONCLUSION

The revolutionary new order brought by the Prophet was viewed by many as a threat to the old tribal alliance system, as it certainly proved to be. Yet the Prophet did not confuse clan relations with Judaism's religious message. The Quran's warning to Muslims not to make pacts with Arabia's Jews emerged from these specific wartime situations. A larger spirit of respect, acceptance, and comradeship prevailed, as recorded in a later Quran chapter (5:44).

A few Medinan Jews, including at least one rabbi, became Muslims. But generally, Medina's Jews remained true to their faith. In keeping with Jewish belief, they were waiting for a prophet to emerge from their "chosen" tribe. Since the Prophet's genealogy was linked to Ishmael, who was not chosen, theologically, they could not accept Muhammad as a messenger of God.

The exiled Banu Nadir, who moved to the prosperous northern oasis of Khaybar, pledged political loyalty to the Prophet. Other Jewish clans honored the pact they signed and continued to live in peace in Medina long after becoming the Muslim capital of Arabia.

David J. Wasserstein, Professor of History and Jewish Studies, stated in a seminar: "In the early seventh century C.E., Judaism was in crisis. In the Mediterranean basin, it was battered by legal, social, and religious pressure, weak in numbers, and culturally almost non-existent. It was also largely cut off from the Persian Empire's Jewry in Babylon, present-day Iraq. The future seemed clear: extinction in the West, decline to obscurity in the East. Salvation came from Arabia. Islam conquered the entire Persian Empire and most of the Mediterranean world. Uniting virtually all Jews in a single state it gave them legal and religious respectability, economic and social freedoms, and linguistic and cultural conditions. This made possible a major renaissance of Judaism and the Jews."

In his discussion of "Muslim Spain," Uri Avnery, Israeli author, former Knesset member, and founder of the Gush Shalom Peace Movement, called it a "paradise for the Jews." He wrote: "there has never been a Jewish Holocaust in Muslim countries." Even pogroms were extremely rare. Muhammad decreed that 'the Peoples of the Book' be treated equally, subject to conditions more liberal than in contemporary Europe."

However, Jews were inferior legally. There were occasional violent outbursts in the Islamic lands, but never sanctioned by the state. This was a clear violation of the spirit of the Medina Constitution, in which the Prophet gave equal rights to Jews. Yet, there is a lot of truth that Jews fared much better in Islamic lands than in Christian Northern Europe and Spain. This is because of more frequent and severe oppression in Europe, frequently sanctioned by the Church and the state, including the Holocaust.

A CASE FOR JEWISH HOMELAND

Jews have suffered for two thousand years, mostly at Christian hands and rarely in Muslim lands. The latest catastrophe happened in the second world war, called the Holocaust. According to Jewish sources, six million Jews were exterminated. Today, the worldwide Jewish population is about 15 million and roughly 7 million live in Israel. Historically, during persecution waves in medieval Europe, many Jews found refuge in Muslim lands. Following the same tradition of egalitarianism and humanitarian grounds, Jews have the right to live in peace and security.

The Quran unequivocally supports Jews' right to live in the holy land, and any attempt to destroy Israel will defy its teachings. Muslims are not against Israel. It is its policies of apartheid, subjugation, and ethnic cleansing of indigenous populations they are against. There will be peace in the holy land if Jews abandon the evil concept of chosen people and join the human family as equals.

CHAPTER 26
SECTARIANISM AMONG MUSLIMS

[For, you are the bearer of a divine writ] such as We have bestowed from on high upon those who [afterward] broke it up into parts, [and] who [now] declare this Quran to be [a tissue of] falsehoods! But, by thy Sustainer! [On the Day of Judgment] We shall call them to account, one and all, for whatever they have done! (15:90-93)

The same is true for many Muslim sects, who cherry-pick specific parts of the Quran to their liking and ignore the rest.

THE RIVAL MOSQUE IN QUBA

And [there are hypocrites] who have established a [separate] house of worship to create mischief, and to promote apostasy and disunity among the believers, and to provide an outpost for all who from the outset have been warring against God and His Apostle. And they will surely swear [to you, O believers], "We had but the best of intentions!" While God [Himself] bears witness that they are lying. Never set foot in such a place! [To pray therein] (9:107-8)

The historical occasion to which the verses below refer may be thus summarized: Ever since his exodus from Mecca to Medina, the Prophet was violently opposed by one Abu Amir (The Monk), a prominent member of the Khazraj tribe, who had embraced Christianity many years earlier and enjoyed a considerable reputation among his compatriots and among the Christians of Syria. From the very outset, he allied with the Prophet's enemies, the Meccan Quraysh, and took part on their side in the battle of Uhud. Shortly thereafter, he migrated to Syria and did all he could to induce the Emperor of Byzantium, Heraclius, to invade Medina and crush the Muslim community once and for all. In Medina itself,

Abu Amir had some secret followers among his tribe, with whom he remained in constant correspondence. In the year 9 H., he informed them that Heraclius had agreed to send out an army against Medina and that large-scale preparations were being made to this effect (which was apparently the reason for the Prophet's preventive expedition to Tabuk). In order that his followers should have a rallying place in the event of the expected invasion of Medina, Abu Amir suggested to his friends that they should build a mosque of their own in the village of Quba, in the immediate vicinity of Medina (which they did). Thus preventing the necessity of congregating in the mosque that the Prophet himself had built in the same village at the time of his arrival at Medina. It is this "rival" mosque to which the above verse refers. It was demolished at the Prophet's orders immediately after his return from the Tabuk expedition. Abu Amir died in Syria shortly afterward. Although the whole of this verse relates primarily to the historical occasion explained in the preceding note, it has a definite bearing on all attempts at creating sectarian divisions among Muslims and is thus a clear amplification of an earlier injunction to this effect (see 6:159).

THE HOUSE OF WORSHIP FOUNDED ON GOD-CONSCIOUSNESS

Only a house of worship founded, from the very first day, upon God-consciousness is worthy of your setting foot there in—[a house of worship] wherein there are men desirous of growing in purity: for God loves all who purify themselves. Which, then, is better: he who has founded his building on God-consciousness and [a desire for] His goodly acceptance—or he who has built his building on the edge of a water-worn, crumbling riverbank, so that it [is bound to] tumble down with him into hell's fire? For God does not grace with His guidance people who[deliberately] do wrong. The building they have built will never cease to be a source of deep disquiet in their hearts until their hearts crumble to pieces. And God is all-knowing and wise. (9:108-110)

"Indeed, a house of worship founded upon God-consciousness is most deserving" refers to the mosque erected by the Prophet at Quba, a village close to Medina, on his arrival there in the month of Rabi al-Awwal in the year 1 H. It was the first mosque built by him or his followers. However, the Prophet applied the designation of "a house of worship founded on God-consciousness" to his (later-built) mosque at Medina as well. It is, therefore, reasonable to assume that it applies to every mosque sincerely dedicated to God's worship.

THE PROPHET'S DEATH

Muhammad, in full Abu al-Qassim Muhammad ibn Abd Allah ibn Abd al-Muttalib ibn Hashim, was the founder of Islam and the proclaimer of the Quran. Prophet Muhammad is traditionally said to have been born in 570 in Mecca and died on June 8, 632, in Medina. He was forced to emigrate with his followers in 622. The cause of death is not recorded, but it is assumed it was a fever. The symptoms were consistent with meningitis, a common ailment from bacterial infection of the delicate brain coverings.

POLITICAL DISPUTE OVER SUCCESSION

The origin of the significant difference between Shiah and Sunni was political: who had the right to succeed after Prophet Muhammad's death? The Sunni party believed Abu Bakr should be the Caliph, while the Shiah party supported Ali ibn Talib. Since no arrangements for his succession had been made, his death provoked a major dispute over the future leadership of the community he founded. Because of the very strong prohibition against sectarianism in the Quran, either party could not use the Quran to advocate factional interests. Instead, they resort to Hadith to support their position. Over time, both Sunni and Shiah have their own sets of fabricated Ahadith to support their claim.

COMMUNITY'S DECISION: THE GOLD STANDARD FOR STATECRAFT

Muslims, whether Sunni or Shiah, believe that the Quran is the infallible word of God. Its statement takes precedence over the hadith literature. The Quran contains legislation about statecraft:

And take counsel with them in all matters of public concern. When thou hast decided upon a course of action, place thy trust in God, for, verily, God loves those who place their trust in Him. (3:159) And [remember that] whatever you are given [now] is but for the [passing] enjoyment of life in this world. While that which is with God is far better and more enduring. [It shall be given] to all who attain faith, and in their Sustainer place their trust. They shun the more heinous sins and abominations and readily forgive whenever they are moved to anger. And who respond to [the call of] their Sustainer and are constant in prayer, and whose [in all matters of common concern] is consultation among themselves. (42:36-38)

Consultation: This qualification of true believers was regarded by the Prophet's Companions as so vital that they always referred to this surah by the keyword "consultation" (shura). Firstly, it is meant to remind all Quran followers that they must remain united within one community (ummah). Secondly, it lays down the principle that all public business must be conducted in mutual consultation.

One of the fundamental principles of Quranic statecraft law is government by consent and council. The pronoun "them" refers to believers, the whole community. The phrase *amruhum shura baynahum* in 42:38 denotes all matters of public concern, including state administration. The above ordinance is binding on all Muslims at all times. The Prophet considered himself bound by his council's decisions. When he was asked to explain the implications of the word *azm* ("deciding upon a course of action"), which occurs in the above verse, the Prophet replied, "[It means] taking counsel with knowledgeable people (*ahl ar-ray*) and following them [therein]."

THE PROPHET'S EXAMPLES

A shining example of the Prophet's leadership is the fact that he conducted important public business in mutual consultation to determine its outcome. To devise a strategy and plan for major battles, he always consulted his companions. Before the battle of Badr, a man questioned the Prophet's decision to halt the army at a particular place. He suggested stopping at the last spring nearest to the enemy and taking possession of all Badr wells. This would deprive the enemy of water. His suggestion was immediately accepted, giving Muslims a strategic advantage. Before the battle of Uhud, he accepted the majority's opinion against his own views.

DEMOCRATIC METHOD IS THE ISLAMIC WAY

The two crucial factors that played a significant role in the Shiah-Sunni split were ignoring the Quranic injunctions of: "The government by consent and council" and, secondly, the power of tribalism. The gold standard is that all public business must be conducted in mutual consultation and let the majority decision prevail. This is provided the decision does not affect others' rights. Involving the whole community in deciding whatever is under consideration will avoid power struggles and bloodshed.

THE POWER OF THE TRIBAL SYSTEM

In the 1300s, Arab historian Ibn Khaldun wrote Muqaddimah, in which he outlined that "tribal societies are defined by their social cohesion and a sense of group interconnectedness." This loyalty "brings groups together in ways crucial for creating public goods" and can be used to "build strong empires, forge strong armies, and develop effective governance structures." However, on the extreme, blind loyalty, when divorced from moral considerations, can be a very destructive force.

ADVERSE EFFECTS OF THE TRIBAL SYSTEM

To truly understand the significant factors behind the power struggle throughout Islamic history, one must acknowledge the power of tribalism, always lurking behind various conflicts. Tribalism is behaviors and attitudes that stem from blind loyalty to one's tribe or social group.

The Prophet described a negative side of tribalism: He said: *"He is not of us who proclaims the cause of tribal partisanship, and he is not of us who fights in the cause of tribal partisanship, and he is not of us who dies for the cause of tribal partisanship."* When asked to explain the meaning of "tribal partisanship," the Prophet answered, *"It means helping your people in an unjust cause."* The prejudice based on tribal partisanship runs deep across many cultures. With the wrong leader, tribalism can lead to major tragedies.

Tribalism excludes others' rights, status, and independence. If people are loyal to their social group above all else, that can lead to discrimination. Nepotism becomes the order of the day. Merit is replaced by average to incompetent people, and society suffers the consequences. When tribes demand blind loyalty, and in return, they confer the security of belonging. It can make critical thinking unnecessary, the basis for progress. The psychology of "us versus them" can lead to brutal wars based on mutual suspicion, racism, and ethnocentrism.

TRIBAL PARTISANSHIP

The contentious selection process for the Prophet's successor was a rivalry between the two major Quraysh clans: Banu Hashim and Banu Umayyah. Their feud existed before Islam. Although the

Prophet succeeded in breaking Arab tribalism and uniting them, the tribal spirit did not die entirely. It reared its ugly head after his death.

Muslim victories in battles against Meccan polytheists kindled new fierce fires of hatred and hostility among the Banu Umayyah. These fires were against the Prophet and Ali ibn Abi Talib. In the battle of Badr, Ali alone killed 22 Meccans, twelve of them being the leading members of Banu Umayyah. After the battle of Badr, their hostility focused on Ali and his children.

LEADING CANDIDATES: ABU BAKR, ALI AND UBAYDAH

There were three leading candidates, Abu Bakr, Ali ibn Talib, from the Quraysh tribe, and Saad ibn Ubaydah, the leader of the Ansar.

ABU BAKR (632-634).

Abu Bakr was Muhammad's closest companion, known for his piety. He was also called al-Siddiq (Arabic: "the Upright," born 573—died August 23, 634). His supporters claimed he was Muhammad's first male convert. Although not from the Banu Hashim, he belonged to a minor clan of the ruling merchant tribe. His prominence was clearly marked by being an early convert, Muhammad's marriage to Abu Bakr's daughter Aishah; Muhammad chose Abu Bakr as his companion on the journey to Medina (the Hijrah, 622). In Medina, he was Muhammad's chief adviser (622–632). He led the pilgrimage to Mecca in 631. Above all, he led public prayers during the Prophet's last illness. This was a function performed by the Prophet as head of the Ummah.

ALI IBN TALIB

Ali's partisans pretended that Ali looked to the Caliphate himself. But nothing in his previous life or the Prophet's attitude towards him warrants such a surmise. He showed no interest in becoming a caliph. When the leaders of Medina urged him to become the fourth caliph after Uthman's death, Ali initially refused. However, Ali and his party should have been included in Abu Bakr's election.

Ali was a member of Banu Hashim, the Prophet's clan, and his cousin. Ali's father, Muhammad's uncle Abu Talib, was the clan head. He protected the Prophet even when other Quraysh tribe members pressured him to muzzle the new Prophet. Ali grew up in the Prophet's house from childhood. He was one of the Prophet's first converts and the husband of his daughter Fatima. Ali ibn Abi Talib was remembered as one of early Islam's greatest warriors. He never lost in one-to-one combat. His battlefield conquests were legendary, and his contribution to Islam cannot be overstated. Ali was not only an exceptional warrior but also an intellectual and a man of the utmost honesty and piety.

SAAD IBN UBAYDAH

Saad ibn Ubaydah, the leader of the Khazraj tribe of Medina, was also a candidate for Caliph. The Ansar had two leaders, Saad ibn Ubaydah and Saad ibn Muadh, who died from a wound he received in the battle of Trench. After his death, Saad ibn Ubaydah was the sole Ansar leader. The Khazraj and the Aus, the two tribes of the Ansar, distinguished themselves by their services to Islam. There was a time when the Prophet was homeless, and the Ansar offered sanctuary and hospitality. They invited Muhammad to be their guest, and they made him the king of their city – Yathrib (Medina). The city of Ansar won the honor and glory of being the cradle and capital of Islam.

In battles, the Ansar were always at the forefront. They fought against the combined might of all Arabian pagans. No tribe in Arabia produced more martyrs for Islam than the Ansars. In the battle of Uhud, when everyone fled except the 14 companions, Saad was one of these 14 heroes who fought against the enemy. He defended God's apostle. Saad was appointed governor of Medina many times in the Prophet's absence.

DID THE PROPHET CHOOSE HIS SUCCESSOR?

ALI AS HIS SUCCESSOR? (SHIAH INTERPRETATION)

Let's examine Shiah's claim that the Prophet pronounced a significant declaration favoring Ali b. Abi Talib. His announcement took place on 18 Dhul Hijjah at Ghadir Khumm as he returned from his farewell pilgrimage. This is three miles from al-Juhfa on the way from Mecca to Medina. It was a strategic meeting area from which travelers dispersed to their respective routes.

The Prophet said, "man kuntu mawlahu fa 'Ali mawlahu" (he whose mawla I am, Ali is his mawla). The Shiahs believe that Muhammad's declaration at the Ghadir Khumm designated Ali to lead the Muslims after the Prophet.

THE SUNNI INTERPRETATION

According to both traditions, the Prophet said that Ali was his inheritor and brother since the Prophet had no male inheritor of his own. Those who later formed the Sunni community concur on the historicity of the Prophet's statement: "He whose mawla I am, Ali is his mawla." The operative word is "mawla," and what does it mean? The word mawla is derived from the root w-l-y, meaning to be close to, friends with, or have power over. Mawla can have reciprocal meanings, depending on whether it is used in the active or passive voice: master or slave/freedman, patron or client, uncle or nephew, or merely a friend.

Like many Arabic words, Mawla has many meanings. The Sunnis, by contrast, take them only as an expression of the Prophet's closeness to Ali. He also wished Ali, his cousin and son-in-law, would inherit his family responsibilities upon his death. This was a call for Ali to be held in affection and esteem rather than a confirmation of his succession.

DID THE PROPHET DECLARE ALI IBN TALIB HIS SUCCESSOR?

Why did the Prophet use the ambiguous word "mawla?" He could have made an unequivocal statement that Ali would be his successor after his death, but he chose not to. This is analogous to Christians' bold claim that Jesus was God, but Jesus never made such a statement. Extraordinary claims require extraordinary proof. There is a major leap from being a friend to becoming the state head, not supported by this statement. The Prophet never publicly named Ali to succeed him.

DID THE PROPHET DECLARE ABU BAKR HIS SUCCESSOR?

The most substantial evidence supporting Abu Bakr's candidacy was that the Prophet appointed him to lead prayer just before his death. This was done by the Prophet or the community head. Sunnis claimed that the Prophet did not designate a successor. However, he indicated his preference for Abu Bakr by asking him to lead the prayer. So, Abu Bakr's supporters took that as the Prophet's approval as his successor. It is again a major leap from being a prayer leader to a state head. The Prophet never named Abu Bakr as his successor.

Sunni and Shiah partisans' categorical statements in favor of their candidates are based on sectarianism and tribal partisanship, not solid evidence.

WHY DID THE PROPHET NOT CHOOSE HIS SUCCESSOR?

- Electing the next caliph was the community's collective duty and not the Prophet's responsibility. Under the Prophet's leadership, the Muslim community was expected to mature to be able to elect their leader.

- Even if the Prophet chose his successor, that might have avoided all confusion temporarily. However, the same problem will reoccur in the next succession.

- Hypothetically speaking, if the Prophet had chosen his successor, he would have violated the Quranic rule that all public business must be conducted in mutual consultation.

- Prophet Muhammad's lack of a living male heir meant one option, choosing a direct male descendant, was nonexistent. It was divine will that the Prophet's successor should be chosen rather than appointed.

In hindsight, the Muslim community never matured to handle differences peacefully. This contrasts with the Prophet's profound saying, *"The differences of opinion among the learned men of my community are an outcome of divine grace."* It implies that critical thinking and differences of opinion are the basis of all progress in human thought and, therefore, the most potent factor in man's acquisition of wisdom.

The Muslim community quickly returned to tribal partisanship and sectarianism before Islam. They could not overcome those biases after fourteen hundred years.

CHAPTER 27
THE RIGHTLY GUIDED CALIPHS

CLASSIFICATION OF ISLAMIC HISTORY

Islamic history had two periods: the Caliphate and the Sultanate period. The Caliphate was traditionally divided into three periods:

1. The Rightly Guided Caliphate (632-661)

Abu Bakr (632-634),

Umar ibn al-Khattab (634-644)

Uthman ibn Affan (644-656)

Ali ibn Abi Talib (656-661)

2. The Umayyad Empire (661-750)

3. The Abbasid Empire (750-1258).

ELECTION OF THE FIRST CALIPH, ABU BAKR

Why should the First Caliph come from Medina? After the Prophet's death, the Ansar clans met in a roofed enclosure called a saqifa to decide what should be done. The men of Medina were determined to pursue an independent course. They had already favored Sad ibn Ubaydah, leader of the Khazraj, who was sick with a fever and lay covered up at the farthest end of the Hall.

Umar and Abu Bakr heard about it and rushed to the spot. They were just in time, for had the citizens elected Sad and pledged their allegiance to him, Medina might have been irretrievably compromised. A divided power would fall to pieces, and all might be lost. The Prophet's mantle must fall on one successor and him alone. The meeting was tense, and one Ansar announced, "We are God's Helpers and the squadron of Islam. We have sheltered this nest of strangers, and the Ruler of Medina shall be from amongst ourselves."

Why should the First Caliph come from the Quraysh? Abu Bakr, calm and firm, answered, "What ye, men of Medina, have uttered in your praise is true and more than true. However, the Quraysh held a preeminent position among the Arabians because of being the custodian of Kabah, the holiest site for all. Moreover, the noble birth and influence of the Quraysh are paramount, and to none but them will Arabia yield obedience." Therefore, it was more likely that adjacent tribes and Bedouins would accept their leadership. Abu Bakr's recommendation of electing a Quraysh as the next leader was based on the region's politics. Since he belonged to the Quraysh tribe, it is unknown if his personal bias played a role in the outcome.

Option of Two Caliphs: The Ansar replied: "Let there be one Chief among you and one from us." "Away with you!" exclaimed 'Umar, "two cannot stand together," and even Sad from beneath his covering muttered that splitting the power would only weaken it.

UMAR PLEDGED ALLEGIANCE TO ABU BAKR

At this critical moment, Umar intervened: "Stretch forth thine hand," said Umar to Abu Bakr; he did so, and they struck their hands on his (as is the Arab custom) in a token of allegiance. The Aus, jealous of the rival tribe, spoke among themselves. The Khazraj will rule forever if Sad ibn Ubaydah is chosen. Let us salute Abu Bakr as our chief." (Note the tribal partisanship at play.) The example was set. Group after group advanced to strike their hand on Abu Bakr's till none was left but Sad, who still lay covered in the corner.

Acknowledged thus by the men of Medina, there could be no doubt of Abu Bakr's acceptance by the Meccan "Refugees." And so, homage was done on all sides to Abu Bakr. He was saluted as the Caliph (Khalifa in Arabic) or Successor of the Prophet. Abu Bakr was elected through partial consent and came close to satisfying the Quranic standard of consultation among themselves in selecting the caliph. Ali and his party were absent, and their views were not considered.

It became the privilege of the leading figures in the community to have the right to choose, and the populace usually ratified their decision. Abu Bakr was selected during a shura, or consultative council meeting likely made primarily of Medinans. Sad ibn Ubaydah lost the election process.

ABSENCE OF ALI AND THE ORIGIN OF THE SHIAH-SUNNI DIVIDE

Ali's party has been excluded for various reasons. After the Prophet's death, his relatives, including his cousin and son-in-law Ali, kept vigil over the body. They were busy preparing for the Prophet's burial. Meanwhile, an emergency meeting of the Ansaris was held elsewhere. The saqifa diplomacy was not a planned affair, and it represented confusion in the aftermath of the Prophet's death.

THE POLITICAL REASONS

It may also have reflected the preference of other clans that Banu Hashim was not to be seen as the locus of both spiritual (prophethood) and political (caliphal) power. Abu Bakr, who was in his sixties, was known for his counsel as the Prophet's advisor. Ali was still young, in his early thirties, and will have future chances to become Caliph. Ignoring Ali's input in electing the Caliph was a far-reaching mistake, and the seeds of the eventual Sunni-Shia split were sown. The word **Sunni** comes from Sunnah, which means Prophet Muhammad's words, actions, or examples. Sunnis are traditionalists and orthodox Muslims. The term **Shia** denotes a distinct group of people with the same behavior principles in common. It also means a sect.

FATIMAH'S GRIEVANCE AGAINST ABU BAKR

Under Abu Bakr's rule, the Quraysh acquired special status, while the Banu Hashim lost their former privileges. The Banu Hashim protested this turn of events by refusing to pledge allegiance to Abu Bakr. Fatima claimed her share in Khaybar's crown lands under the Prophet's custody the day after her father's death. Abu Bakr disallowed the claim, holding that the revenues were destined for the state, as the Prophet desired. Fatima took the denial so personally that she held herself entirely aloof from the Caliph for the remainder of her life. Hence, it was only after her death that Ali recognized the title of Abu Bakr as the Caliphate with any cordiality. Ali refrained from paying homage until after Fatima's death.

THE CONTRIBUTIONS OF ABU BAKR

ABU BAKR'S INAUGURAL ADDRESS

When the Prophet's funeral was over, and the Grand Mosque was still crowded with mourners, Abu Bakr ascended the pulpit and said: "Oh people! Now, I am a ruler over you, albeit not the best among you. If I do well, support me; if I am not doing well, set me right. True, wherein is faithfulness; eschew the False, wherein is treachery. The weaker among you shall be as the stronger with me, until I shall have redressed his wrong; and the stronger shall be as the weaker until if the Lord will, I shall have taken from him that which he hath wrested. Leave not off to fight in the ways of the Lord; whosoever leaveth off, him verily shall the Lord abase. Obey me as I obey the Lord and his Prophet; wherein I disobey, obey me not. Now rise to your prayer, and God has mercy upon you!" The assembly stood up for prayer, and Abu Bakr, for the first time as a Caliph, filled Muhammad's place.

Compilation of the Quran: The first written compilation of the Quran is said to have taken place during Abu Bakr's caliphate, and

Umar ibn al-Khattab urged Abu Bakr to have the Quran written down.

Avenging the Defeat: Abu Bakr's first act as head of state was to show that the will of the Messenger of God was law. He dispatched the expedition that was organized by the Prophet to avenge the defeat at the Battle of Mutah, which the Muslims had suffered in Byzantine territory.

PRESERVING THE UNITY OF ISLAMIC STATE

The faithful were a flock of sheep without a shepherd. Their Prophet was gone, and their foes a multitude. Abu Bakr's major contribution was the preservation of Islamic state unity. The rebels were testing the new leader's resolve, and there was a grave danger that Islamic State would soon disintegrate. In four of the six rebellion centers, rebels rallied around men who claimed to be prophets. As a basic tenet of Islam, Muhammad is regarded as the last and seal of the prophets. The Arabs were on all sides rising in rebellion. Apostasy and disaffection emerged.

REBELLION AGAINST PAYING ZAKAH

A delegation of rebels offered to hold on to Islam and its rituals if only the poor tax (zakah) was excused. Medina chiefs welcomed strangers bearing this message, but the Caliph rejected their advances. He would not relax an iota of legal duties. "If ye withhold but the tether of a tithed camel," said Abu Bakr sharply, "I will fight you for it." (Zakat or poor tax is one of the five pillars of Islam, and it is mandatory upon every Muslim. (A refusal to pay Zakat will adversely affect the poor's welfare.) Abu Bakr was justified in using force against wayward Muslims.

Yet if they repent, and pray, and render their purifying dues, they become your brethren in faith. We clearly convey these messages to people of [innate] knowledge! (9:11)

There are three conditions for becoming brethren in faith. When Abu Bakr was questioned about the justification for using force, he cited this verse. He explained that their failure to pay Zakat was a deal breaker. The rebels did not satisfy all three conditions in the above verse.

REBELLION OR INSURRECTION AGAINST THE STATE

Use of force is justified against whoever incites, assists, or engages in any rebellion or insurrection against the government's authority or gives aid or comfort thereto. Abu Bakr suppressed the tribal political and religious uprisings known as the riddah ("political rebellion," sometimes translated as "apostasy"), bringing central Arabia under Muslim control. One after another, tribes were subdued by troops. Some of the bloodiest battles were fought with heavy losses much greater than the Prophet's battles. For example, in the battle of Yamama, 1200 Muslims perished, many Companions of the Prophet. Medina had hardly a house without wailing. Thousands of rebels were killed. It took a year to reclaim the Peninsula, a year of ferocious fighting and obstinate resistance in every corner of the land. Muhammad's indomitable spirit crowned the success of his faithful followers. After consolidating his rule in Arabia, Abu Bakr initiated the conquests of Iraq and Syria.

TRIBUTE TO KHALID BIN WALID

Much of the success on the battlefield was due to the brilliant commander and famous strategist Khalid bin Walid. To him, the Prophet conferred the title of 'The sword of God,' which, in subsequent operations, he deserved. Khalid was the most prominent figure in early Islam besides Abu Bakr, Umar, and Ali. A dashing soldier, even rash, tempered by calm and ready judgment. His conduct on the battlefields decided the fate of two superpowers of the day, the Persian and the Byzantine Empires. He never lost a single battle, even though he fought hundreds of battles and was often outnumbered by his enemies. He was one of the greatest generals in the world. At the battle of Uhud, Khalid was responsible for the only defeat suffered by the Prophet and his army. Over and again, always with consummate skill and heroism, he cast the dye in crises where a loss would have destroyed Islam. He was not an armchair commander and actively participated with his troops. Just as Ali and Hamza played a key role in the Prophet's battles, Khalid's military genius was indispensable during the caliphates.

As a human being Khalid had his own flaws. As a hardened soldier, he hardly cared about the loss of life. He would wed the widow of his enemy on the field, still sodden by his own soldiers' blood. His brutal massacre of an unoffending tribe led to the Prophet's harsh reprimand.

UMAR IBN AL-KHATTAB (634-644)
THE SECOND CALIPH

In 644, before his death, Abu Bakr urged the Companions to elect Umar ibn al-Khattab as his successor. It was no secret that he had many virtues, including his energy and ability to organize. The formal process of "consultation in all public matters" was completely ignored. A member of the Adi clan of the Meccan tribe of Quraysh Umar opposed Muhammad but, in about 615, became a Muslim. By 622, when he moved to Medina with Muhammad and the other Meccan Muslims, he became one of Muhammad's chief advisers. He was closely associated with Abu Bakr. His position in the state was marked by Muhammad's marriage to his daughter Hafsah in 625. On Muhammad's death in 632, Umar was largely responsible for reconciling Medinan Muslims to the acceptance of a Meccan, Abu Bakr, as head of state (caliph). As a caliph, Umar called himself "commander of the faithful" (Amir al-mu minin).

ARABIAN STATE TO WORLD POWER

Umar was one of the most brilliant administrators in Islam's history. His reign saw the Islamic state transform from an Arabian principality into a world power. Throughout this remarkable expansion, Umar strictly controlled general policy and laid down the principles for administering the conquered lands. The structure of the later Islamic empire, including legal practice, is due to him.

A strong ruler, stern toward offenders, and ascetical to the point of harshness, Umar was universally respected for his justice and authority. His role in decisively shaping the early Islamic community is widely acknowledged. The following summarizes the remarkable achievements of the second Caliph:

Economy: Establishment of the Public Treasury, state intervention to control merchandise prices and establishment of guilds for certain trades.

Legal: Created the qadi (judge) office, punished monopolists, and established and used jails.

Religious: Zakat on the produce of the sea, such as fish, lobster, shrimp, etc., inaugurated the Islamic Hijri calendar, and the salary for Imams, Muadhins (Callers to prayer) teachers, and public lectures and Punishment for drunkenness, discovered the place of Ascension of the Messenger to heaven at Jerusalem and establishment of a more exact system of calculation of inheritance.

Land Development: Establishment of the Land Revenue department, survey and assessment of lands, the construction of canals and bridges, establishment of public rest areas, hostels, and Wudu (Ablution) Stations, the establishment of the garrison cities of Al-Fusṭaṭ in Egypt and Basra and Kufah in Iraq.

Administrative: Public census, dividing the state and the conquered territories into provinces, use of secret reports and specially designated emissaries to provide first-hand reports on what was going on in different provinces, stipends for the poor among Jews and Christians who lived in conquered lands, and establishment of a postal service.

Defense: Placing the reserve army on the state's payroll, organization of the war department, establishment military bases at strategic points in the different provinces, establishing the diwan (a register of warriors' pensions)

Military Successes: Muslim armies annexed Egypt's fertile land and pushed westward along North Africa's coast. They overran Palestine and Syria and, after crushing the Persian King's armies, established Arab rule over practically the whole of the old Persian empire.

Iranian Reaction to Their Historic Defeat: The relationship between Arabs and Persians has always been controversial. This isn't just due to the current hegemony conflict in the region, but it's also a result of centuries of history. Persians will never forget their defeat by the Arabs in the Battle of Qadisiya 1,400 years ago. The Shiah religious establishment expresses their resentment of Arabs in constant attacks and curses directed at Sunnis. This is especially against Umar al Khattab, who was the caliph during the battle of Qadisiya, although he did not participate directly in it. Sunnis consider the Shiah doctrine a wayward form of Islam. The extremists on each side consider the other party non-Muslims altogether.

Forced Conversion: The Sunni Arabs' animosity towards Shiah is partly due to the forced conversion of Iran's majority Sunni population to Shiah Islam. The Safavid dynasty forced Iranians to convert to Shia Islam in the 16th through 18th centuries. It turned Iran (Persia), a Sunni majority population, into the spiritual bastion of Shia Islam.

UTHMAN IBN AFFAN (644-656)
THE THIRD CALIPH

Death of Umar: In 644, Umar fell at the hands of an assassin, a Persian Christian slave who took offense at Umar for unknown reasons. Umar, on his deathbed, appointed a committee of six men, all Quraysh of Mecca. From this committee, the next Caliph was to be chosen in 3 days. The six men were Uthman, Ali, Talha bin Ubaydullah, Zubair bin al-Awam, Abd ar-Rahman bin Awf, and Saad bin Abi Waqas. Abd al-Rahman ibn Awf asked to be trusted with choosing the next caliph, a request that was granted. Uthman and Ali were the two most favored candidates. He questioned both Uthman and Ali and decided on the former. In the end, one man chose the caliph and the entire community was ignored. Men from Medina were excluded from the decision-making process, ignoring the Quranic injunction of public business, which necessitated a transaction conducted in mutual consultation.

Once again, the Umayyad clan was preferred over the Hashim clan, and Ali was ignored. Uthman was selected as a compromise. It was that he would continue Umar's policy. Ali, as a caliph, might prejudice well-established interests.

Uthman was born into the rich and powerful Umayyad clan of Quraysh. He was a wealthy merchant, and Muhammad allowed Uthman to marry one of his daughters. Uthman also represented the Umayyad clan, which had suffered a partial eclipse during the Prophet's lifetime but was now reasserting its influence. Uthman followed the same general policies as Umar but had a less forceful personality than his predecessor.

Standardizing the Quran: The existence of total unity in the Quranic text for fourteen centuries proves Uthman's foresight and wisdom. The unparalleled success in gathering a single text of the Holy Quran was accepted by all Muslims, regardless of their sectarian leanings. Unlike the New Testament, which presents four different versions of the earthly ministry of Jesus, Uthman's timely decision prevented a theological split among Muslims. Perhaps this is one of the most outstanding achievements in Islamic history.

Continued the Conquests: He continued the conquests that had steadily increased the Islamic empire, but the victories now came at a higher cost and brought less wealth in return.

Cohesive Central Authority: He centralized caliphate administration. Uthman tried to create a cohesive central authority to replace the loose tribal alliance that emerged under the Prophet.

NEPOTISM AND THE DOWNFALL

Uthman's administration was a classic example of tribal partisanship. He was often dominated by his relatives and had difficulty imposing his authority on governors. Many provincial governors were his family members. The central government treasure was transferred to Uthman's family and other provincial governors rather than to the army. Tragically, Uthman was assassinated by the rebels. His death marked the beginning of open religious and political conflicts within the Islamic community.

ALI IBN ABI TALIB (656-661)
THE FOURTH CALIPH

ALI'S REACTION TO THE SELECTION OF ABU BAKR, UMAR, AND UTHMAN

After Abu Bakr's election, Ali retired to private life. He served as Abu Bakr's counsel and held the position of Chief Judge. Ali accepted Umar's selection as caliph and even gave one of his daughters, Umm Kulthum, to him in marriage. Ali also recognized Uthman's authority, according to Shiite sources, but remained neutral between Uthman's supporters and his opponents.

There is no proof that Ali himself ever claimed the divine right of the holy family to rule. No such claim was made for him during Abu Bakr and Umar's Caliphates. It was not till the election of a successor on Umar's death that he became a candidate, and even then, his claim was grounded on being one of the chief companions rather than on any supposed right due to his relationship to Muhammad by marriage to his daughter.

After the assassination of the third Caliph, Uthman, the Prophet's companions, approached Ali, asking him to be Caliph. Ali declined the responsibility of this great office first, suggesting being a counselor instead of a chief. But finally, he decided to put the matter before the Muslim public in the Prophet's Mosque. As a result, the overwhelming majority of the Companions in Madinah considered Ali to be the most suitable person to be Caliph. Caliph Ali fully implemented in spirit and action the Quranic rule of *"in all matters of common concern is consultation among themselves. (42:36-38) And take counsel with them in all matters of public concern." (3:159)*

The period of Ali's caliphate, which ranged from 656 until his death in 661, was the most tumultuous and mired in civil wars. Not much was achieved during his rule.

BATTLE OF CAMEL

When Ali came into power, Zubayr and Talha ibn Ubayd Allah said their reason for revolt was Ali's failure to avenge Uthman's murder. Talha and Zubayr, joined by Aishah, daughter of Abu Bakr and third wife of the Prophet, marched upon Basra and captured it. Ali assembled an army in Kufah, his capital, and met the rebels in 656 at the Battle of the Camel; the name was derived from the fierce fighting centered around the camel upon which Aishah was mounted. Ali's forces were victorious, and Aishah, being the widow of the Prophet and the mother of the believers, returned safely to Medina out of respect.

MUAWIYAH IBN ABI SUFYAN

Early Islamic leader and founder of the Umayyad dynasty, Muawiyah, was born in 602 in Mecca, Arabia and died in 680 in Damascus. He was appointed Damascus governor by the caliph Umar. He was the son of Abu Sufyan and belonged to a clan of the Umayyads, or Banu Umayyah, of the larger Quraysh tribe. They dominated Mecca in the pre-Islamic era.

The clan of Banu Umayyah rejected Prophet Muhammad and continued to oppose him on the battlefield after he emigrated to Medina. Muawiyah did not become a Muslim until Prophet Muhammad conquered Mecca and reconciled his former enemies with gifts.

BATTLE OF SIFFIN

Muawiyah, the governor of Syria and a relative of Uthman claimed the right to avenge Uthman's death. Ali was advised to keep the governors in their posts, at least until the Empire at large recognized his succession to the throne. Ibn al-Abbas also pressed the same view: "At any rate," he said, "retain Muawiyah (as governor of Syria), and it was Umar, not Uthman, who placed him there, and all Syria follows after him."

The advice, coming from a close family member, deserves consideration. In the end, tribal rivalry came into play. Ali, with family hatred against the Umayyad line, answered sharply, "Nay; I will not confirm him even for a single day." "If thou depose him," reasoned his friend, "the Syrians will question your election and, still worse, accuse you of Uthman's blood and rise up as one man against you."

After the battle of Camel, Ali turned his attention north to Muawiyah, engaging him in 657 at the Battle of Siffin. With his army on the verge of defeat, Muawiyah, on the advice of Amr ibn al-Aṣ, ordered his soldiers to put Quran pages on their lances.

Muawiyah asked Ali to resolve the dispute according to Quranic rules. Tearing the Quran pages desecrates the sacred text. Ali's army, seeing the sacred text, put down its arms, and Ali was forced to arbitrate.

ALI CONCLUDES A TREATY WITH MUAWIYAH

A truce was concluded between Ali and Muawiyah. In this truce, they agreed to lay aside their arms, respect each other's territory, and maintain, in time to come, a friendly attitude. Muawiyah, however, assumed the title of Caliph at Jerusalem in July 660 A.D. and was recognized as the Caliph throughout Syria and Egypt. With this, the Islamic State had two caliphs simultaneously: Muawiyah and Ali.

CRUSHING KHARIJITES REVOLT

A breakaway faction of Ali's army considered arbitration between Muawiyah and Ali as a violation of the Quran's teachings. Therefore, they formed a rebellion against Ali, who crushed this agitation.

THE DEATH OF ALI

Some Kharijites assassinated Ali, Muawiyah, and Amr ibn al-As. Although the latter two escaped, Ali did not. On the 19th of holy Ramadan in 661, he was assassinated and buried in Najaf. Along with Qom in Iran, Najaf became—and remains one of the most revered seats of Shiite learning and a major pilgrimage site.

ALI'S FORBEARANCE AND MAGNANIMITY

The following is the conclusion of Ali's career as a Caliph by Sir William Muir: "The Caliphate and its Rise, Decline, and Fall." In his youth, he was one of the most distinguished heroes in the early wars of Islam. But after the Prophet's death, he took no part in military expeditions. From his wife Fatima, the Prophet's daughter, he had three sons (One of these died in infancy; the other two were Al-Hasan and Al-Hussain, and two daughters, the progenitors of the Sayed race—the so-called nobility of Islam." He was the last of the four "rightly guided" Caliphs and the first of the twelve Shiite Imams.

Ali was mild mannered, kindhearted and except for Muawiyah, he conciliated with his enemies to the extreme. Ali was wise in counsel, and many an adage and a sapient proverb have been attributed to him. As with Solomon, his wisdom was for others, not for himself.

CHAPTER 28
THE KARABLA TRAGEDY AND IDEOLOGICAL DIFFERENCES BETWEEN SHIAH AND SUNNI

After Ali's death, Al-Hasan, the eldest son of Ali, commandeered the 40,000 army prepared by his father. However, he had no stomach for the war and agreed to abdicate and retire to Medina. Muawiyah became the sole and undisputed Caliph of Islam. In comparison to Ali, Muawiyah was a cunning ruler. He was a politician rather than a soldier. Ali was a soldier, not a politician. Muawiyah preferred money over force and outmaneuvered Ali politically.

He was a gifted politician and administrator. He established the Arab-Muslim government system and strengthened its foundations, and thus produced a huge empire that ruled over half of the world.

THE DEATH OF MUAWIYAH

After a long and prosperous reign, Muawiyah died in his seventies. Before his death, Muawiyah committed another abomination by nominating his son Yazid as his successor and disregarded the traditional election process based on the Quranic injunction 42:38: "Rule by consensus and consultation." He introduced the alien concept of hereditary succession and set a precedent for the appointment of dictators and despots in the Islamic world.

THE TRAGEDY OF KARBALA

Al-Kufah, house of Ali, now turned eagerly to Al-Hussein, Ali's younger son. Support was promised to him if he appeared at Al-Kufah and claimed his caliphate right. His friends in Mecca strongly advised him not to trust the fickle populace of that factious city. Al-

Hussein, heedless of his faithful friends' opposition, started from Mecca with his family and a small band of devoted followers. Al-Hussein pitched his camp on Karbala's field on the riverbank, twenty-five miles above Al-Kufah. Surrounded by enemy troops, Al-Hussein resolved to fight the battle to the bitter end. During the night, women and children wailed in terror. On the morning of the fatal 10th, Al-Hussein assembled his small band for battle. There was a conversation, and again, he offered to retire or be led to the Caliph's presence. Finding all in vain, he alighted from his camel and, surrounded by his kinsmen, who stood firm for his defense, resolved to sell his life dear. There was a moment of stillness. At length, one shot an arrow from the Kufan side, and amid the cries of the women and children, the unequal fight began. Arrows flew thick and killed Al-Kasim, Al-Hussein's nephew. He was only ten years old and died in his uncle's arms. One after another the sons and brothers, nephews and cousins of Al-Hussein fell. Some took shelter behind the camp, but it was set on fire, and the flames spreading to the tents added new horror to the scene. For long none dared to attack Al-Hussain, and it was hoped he might still surrender. Eventually, thirst drove him to the riverbank. The enemy surrounded him, and he was cut off from his people. The "cursed" Shamir led the attack. Al-Hussein, struck by an arrow, fell to the ground, and the cavalry trampled his corpse. The camp was plundered, and the survivors, mostly women and children, were carried, together with the ghastly load of seventy trunkless heads, to Governor Obaidullah's palace in Kufah. A thrill of horror ran through the crowd when the gory head of the Prophet's grandson was cast at Obaidullah's feet. The cold hearts were melted. An aged voice was heard crying: "Gently! It is the Prophet's grandson. By the Lord! I have seen these very lips kissed by Muhammad's blessed mouth."

HUSSEIN'S FAMILY SENT TO MEDINA

The sister of Al-Hussein, her little son al-Asghar, and two daughters, the sole survivors of the family, were sent, along with the head of al-Hussain, to Yazid in Damascus. The ladies and children were eventually sent to their Medina home. Medina saw a wild outburst of grief and lamentation. Thus, the most shameful chapter in Islam's history ended. The toll was on Islamic unity with a permanent schism between Shiah and Sunni.

THEOLOGICAL DIFFERENCES BETWEEN SHIAH AND SUNNI

THE DIVINE RIGHT OF THE HOLY FAMILY TO RULE

The concept of the divine right of the Prophet's family and Ali should have succeeded as a Caliph instead of Abu Bakr were latter-day contentions arising out of the tragedy of Karbala.

Traditions regarding Ali are colored and distorted by the canvass of a political and tribal faction, which, in the end, assumed the divine right of succession vested in Ali and his descendants. After Ali's death, the Shiah party demanded Ali's family's rule. From that demand developed Shiite legitimism, or the divine right of the holy family to rule.

SHIAH IMAM AND ESOTERIC KNOWLEDGE

The Shia believe that the Imam, or leader of the Muslims, who must be a male descendant of Muhammad, possesses unique qualities. He is free from error (*Masum*) and the most perfect man (*Afzal*) of his era. Muslims owe obedience to the Imam, whose decisions are inspired. Thus, for Shiahs, it is the Imam and not ijma (or community consensus) that determines whether a ruling is Islamic or not.

Imam in Shia Islam has uncanny similarities with a Zoroastrian priest called Magi. They belong to a special class of priests endowed with occult knowledge, magical powers, and divination power. As in Shia Islam, the Zoroastrian priesthood is also hereditary, and the priestly class was superior in society.

Shiah Imams are a Manifestation of God: The old Iranian (dualistic) influences, the figure of the political ruler, the Imam (exemplary leader), was transformed into a metaphysical being, a manifestation of God. Through the imam alone, the hidden and true meaning of the Quranic revelation can be known because the imam alone is infallible. The Shiah thus developed a doctrine of esoteric knowledge similar to the Magi's claim of occult knowledge and magical powers. The Shiah imams have been imbued with Pope-like infallibility that gives all powers to mullahs to govern ordinary people. The Orthodox Shiahs recognize twelve such imams, the last of whom disappeared in the 9th century. Since that time, the mujtahids (Shiah divines) have been able to interpret law and doctrine under the putative guidance of the last Imam Mahdi who will return at the end of time to fill the world with truth and justice. The Sunnis also believe in Mahdi's arrival at the end of time. Much of this material is reported in the Prophet's hadiths. However, there is no mention of Mahdi in the Quran.

No Central Authority: On the contrary, Sunni Islam has no central religious authority. There is no intermediary between God and the believer in Sunni Islam. On Judgment Day, every human being will stand alone to be judged by God. There will be no sages or Imams to save us. Therefore, each of us is responsible for our actions.

PERFECTION BELONGS TO GOD ALONE

All such claims of Shiah imams as infallible, esoteric knowledge etc., are innovations derived from Zoroastrianism and alien to Quranic teachings. Perfectionism belongs to God alone. Even the Prophets were not infallible, as the following verses indicate:

Verily [O Muhammad,] we have laid open before thee a manifest victory so that God might show his mercy on all thy sins, past as well as future. (48:1-2)

Thus indicating that freedom from faults is an exclusive prerogative of God. In the Quran, God rebuked the Prophet many times and corrected him when he was wrong.

SUMMARY

1. Abu Bakr united Arabia under Islam , and Umar elevated the Arabian state to a world power. During Abu Bakr's election process, Ali and his party were not included in the consultation process. This may have led to the Shiah-Sunni schism.

2. The party of Shiah rejected the first three caliphs and only recognized Ali as the legitimate successor of the Prophet. Ali himself recognized all three previous caliphs. After Ali's death, the Shiah party demanded the restoration of rule to Ali's family in favor of the hereditary monarchy. Aristocracy or monarchy is against the Quran's teachings, which advocate community decision-making.

3. The Shiah party regarded Ali and his descendants as "chosen people." The Quran repeatedly criticizes the Jews for the concept of "chosen people" due to their descent from Abraham.

He (God) said: "I shall make you a leader of men." Abraham asked: "and [wilt thou make leaders] of my offspring as well?" [God] answered: "My covenant does not embrace evildoers." (2:124)

The above verse rejects the notion that hereditary alone should determine a leader of men and, by implication, that all human beings are equal. Abraham's exalted status did not automatically confer equal status on his physical descendants and certainly not on the sinners among them. History is full of examples where prophets' sons turned out to be evil men, for example, the sons of Noah or the sons of Jacob, who tried to kill Joseph, and so on.

4. Ironically, Muawiyah ibn Abi Sufyan also believed in hereditary monarchy and appointed his son Yazid to be caliph after him. Yazid was the most hated figure responsible for the Karbala massacre.

5. Only the election of Abu Bakr and Ali satisfied the Quranic command of government by consent. Umar and Uthman's election falls short of Quranic standards.

6. One of the defining tragedies was the assassination of three famous Caliphs—Umar, Uthman, and Ali—and countless civil wars since there was no process to replace rulers peacefully. Government by consent provides a peaceful mechanism for power transfer, resulting in more stable and peaceful societies in the long run.

7. The basis of the rule should be a meritocracy rather than an aristocracy, monarchy, or theocracy. Any Muslim, irrespective of race, color, and sex, is eligible to be a ruler—provided he or she has the qualifications. In the last sermon, the Prophet said: "All humanity is from Adam and Eve. An Arab has no superiority over a non-Arab, nor a non-Arab has any superiority over an Arab; also, a white has no superiority over a black, nor a black has any superiority over a white except through piety and virtuous actions."

8. Muslims, regardless of their sectarian leanings, believe in the exalted status of the four rightly guided caliphs. These were giants in Islam's history, and their contribution to Islam is invaluable. However, they were still human and fallible. To critically analyze their performance is not disrespecting their exalted status. One can only learn from history through

objective analyses of past events. Those who cannot remember the past or fail to learn from history are condemned to repeat it. This is precisely what has happened for the past fourteen hundred years. Sunnis and Shiahs play negative roles against each other. Many unfriendly entities have taken advantage of Muslim disunity. Sectarianism among Muslims is one of the significant factors in Islamic civilization's downfall.

9. Besides facing humiliation at the hands of Islam's enemies in this world, sectarianism can adversely affect its practitioners' fate in the afterlife.

And be not like those who have drawn apart from one another and have taken to conflicting views after all evidence of the truth has come unto them. For these, severe suffering is in store. (3:105) They [who claim to follow you] have torn their unity wide asunder, piece-by-piece, each group delighting in [but] what they possess [by way of tenets]. (23:53) No, but they do not perceive [their error]! [as for those who have torn the unity of faith asunder], their hearts are lost in ignorance of all this! (23:56-65)

10. All Muslims are followers of the Prophet Muhammad, who was neither Sunni nor Shiah; these labels should be relegated to the dustbin of history. The diversity of opinions among Muslims should not only be tolerated, but respected if it does not contradict the Quran. Imagine if all 1.8 billion Muslims united morally. No world power can humiliate the ummah.

CHAPTER 27
DOCTRINE OF SALVATION AND CALL FOR UNITY

RIGHTEOUS AMONG JEWS AND CHRISTIANS

However, they are not all alike. Among the followers of earlier revelation, some upright people recite God's messages throughout the night and prostrate themselves [before Him]. They believe in God and the Last Day and enjoin the doing of what is right and forbid what is wrong. They vie with one another in doing good works, and these are among the righteous. And whatever good they do, they shall never be denied the reward, for God has full knowledge of those who are conscious of Him. (3:113-115)

And behold, among the followers of earlier revelation, there are indeed such as [truly] believe in God, and in that which has been bestowed from on high upon you. In addition, they believe in what has been bestowed upon them. Standing in awe of God, they do not exchange His messages for a trifling gain. They shall have their reward with their sustainer-for, behold, God is swift in reckoning! O you who have attained faith! Be patient in adversity, remain patient with one another, and be prepared [to do what is right] at all times. Remain conscious of God so that you might attain a happy state! (3:199-200)

Islam is the only major religion that categorically states that followers of other faiths can also attain salvation in the afterlife. This is the ultimate example of religious pluralism. The verses below clearly state that righteous Jews and Christians will enter the "Kingdom of God," borrowing Jesus' famous words.

THE TIMELESS DOCTRINE OF SALVATION

Verily, those who have attained to faith [in this divine writ] [Muslims], *as well as those who follow the Jewish faith, and the Christians, and the Sabians-all who believe in God and the Last Day and do righteous deeds—shall have their reward with their Sustainer, and no fear they should have, and neither shall they grieve. (2:62) For, verily, those who have attained to faith [in this divine writ], as well as those who follow the Jewish faith, and the Sabians, and the Christians—all who believe in God and the Last Day and do righteous deeds—no fear need they have, and neither shall they grieve. (5:69) But as for those from among them* [Jews] *who are deeply rooted in knowledge, and the believers* [Muslims] *who believe in that which has been bestowed upon thee from on high as well as that which was bestowed from on high before thee, and those who are [especially] constant in prayer, and spend in charity, and all who believe in God and the Last Day-to these We will grant a mighty reward. (4:162)*

The Quranic passages teach a fundamental doctrine of salvation, which transcends all religious affiliations. It is of timeless import, as it applies to Adam down to the last human on this earth. With a breadth of vision unparalleled in any other religious faith, salvation is granted by God's grace for having faith. This includes belief in Judgment Day and doing good works while avoiding major sins. If good deeds exceed sins, salvation will be granted through God's grace regardless of denomination. Jews and Christians have the wishful belief that only followers of their denominations will share God'sgrace in the hereafter.

MONOTHEISTS AS ONE SINGLE COMMUNITY

[O you, who believe in Me], this community of yours is one single community since I am the Sustainer of you all. Worship, then, Me [alone]! But men have torn their unity wide asunder, [forgetting that] unto Us they are all bound to return. And yet, whoever does

[the least] of righteous deeds and is a true believer in God, his endeavor shall not be disowned. We shall record it in his favor. (21:92-94)

The principle of oneness should be reflected in the unity of all who believe in Him. The sudden change of the discourse from the second person plural to the third person indicates God's severe disapproval of those who break believers' unity.

And this community of yours is one single community since I am the Sustainer of you all: remain, then, conscious of Me! (23:52)

The above verse is addressed to all who truly believe in God, whatever their historical denomination. It applies to all prophets' followers. Prophets always preached the same essential truth—namely, the existence and oneness of God—and the same ethical principles. It is imperative that all believers in the one God, whatever their historical denomination, regard themselves as "one community" (see verses 42:13 and 15 below).

Steadfastly uphold the [true] faith, and do not break your unity. [And even though] that [unity of faith] to which thou callest them appears oppressive to those who ascribe to other beings or force a share in His divinity. God draws unto Himself who is willing and guides everyone who turns unto Him. (42:13)

"Do not break up your unity" is an unmistakable reference to the ecumenical unity in all religions based on the belief in one God. This is notwithstanding all the diversity of statutes and practices enjoined for the benefit of the various communities. See 3:19— "The only true religion in the sight of God is man's self-surrender unto Him," and 3:85— "If one seeks in search of a religion other than self-surrender unto God, it will never be accepted from him." Parallel with this principle, enunciated by all of God's apostles, is the categorical statement in 21:92 and 23:52— "Verily, O you who believe in Me, this community of yours is one single community since I am the Sustainer of you all."

SUMMON ALL MANKIND TO UNITY AND EQUALITY

Summon [all mankind], and pursue the right course, as you have been bidden [by God]; and do not follow their likes and dislikes but say: "I believe in whatever revelation God has bestowed from on high, and I am bidden to bring about equity in your mutual views. God is our and your Sustainer. To us shall be accounted for our deeds, and to you, your deeds. Let there be no contention between us and you: God will bring us all together—for with Him is all journeys' end." (42:15)

This breach of the original unity of man's faith in the one God summons all humanity and induces them to be more tolerant of one another. This is an allusion to the bitterness that stands in the way of understanding between the various sects and schools of thought in all revealed religions.

ATTRIBUTES OF AN IDEAL COMMUNITY

And hold fast, all together, to the bond with God, and do not break apart from one another. And remember the blessings God has bestowed upon you: how, when you were enemies, He brought your hearts together so that through His blessing, you became brethren. And [when] you were on the brink of a fiery abyss, He saved you from it. In this way, God makes clear His message to you so that you might find guidance. There might grow out of you a community [of people] who invite unto all that is good and enjoin the doing of what is right and forbid the doing of what is wrong, and it is they, they, who shall attain a happy state! (3:103-104)

The Quran condemns all sects among Muslims, Jews, and Christians. The saying of the Prophet: *"The Jews have been split up into seventy-one sects, the Christians into seventy-two sects, whereas my community will be split up into seventy-three sects."* In classical Arabic usage, the number "seventy" often stands for "many"—just as "seven" stands for "several" or "various"— and does not necessarily denote an actual figure. Hence, the Prophet meant to say that Muslim sects would become even more numerous than Jews and Christians.

PART 2
THE PROPHET'S MARRIAGES
AND
THE TRIBUTE TO THE PROPHET

CHAPTER 28
THE PROPHET PATTERN OF MARRIAGES

The Prophet was among those great men who have the good fortune to win and retain the energetic support and wholehearted devotion of some able and loving women. This contributed largely to their success. All his marriages except the first with Khadijah occurred during the Medina period.

POLITICAL AND TRIBAL ALLIANCES

In 622 CE, the Prophet left Mecca for Medina to form the first ideological-based society. As the chief of the Ummah, it was his responsibility to forge links within and beyond his community through the only means at his disposal: marriage. According to the old Arabian practice, marriages cemented the relationships between tribes and were a sure way to win the hearts of your enemies. This gesture almost always won a defeated adversary on the battlefield. Not only in Arabia but also within the Roman and Persian Empires, marriages served as political and dynastic alliances. Most of the Prophet's later marriages were more socio-political than sexual. He married to support widows or form political alliances.

- Thus, his union with **Aishah** and **Hafsah** linked him to the two most influential leaders of the early Muslim community, Abu Bakr and Umar.

- Umm **Salamah** became a widow after Abu Salamah was martyred in the Battle of Uhud. Besides being a deserving widow, she was a close relative of the patriarch of the Meccan clan of Makhzum, the archenemy of the Prophet.

- His union with **Sawdah**—by all accounts, an unattractive widow long past the age of marriage—served as an example to the Ummah to marry those women in need of financial support. Her husband died from wounds suffered in the battle of Badr. Sawdah's husband was the brother of a man Muhammad wanted to keep from becoming an extreme opponent.

- Juwayriyah was the daughter of the chief of the al-Mustaliq tribe, with whom Muhammad had trouble.

- Zaynab **bint Khuzaimah married** Abdullah bin Jahash, who was martyred in the battle of Uhud. The Prophet married Zaynab bint Khuzaimah to provide for her. Zaynab's husband belonged to the al-Muttalib clan, for which Muhammad had special responsibility.

- Umm **Habibah**, daughter of Abu Sufyan, married Zaynab bint Jahash's brother. When her husband died in Abyssinia, Muhammad sent a representative to arrange a marriage for her. At that time, Abu Sufyan was an archenemy of the Prophet.

- The marriage to **Maymunah** would similarly help cement relations with her brother-in-law, Muhammad's uncle, al-Abbas.

- The Union with the Jewess, **Rayhanah,** was a political announcement that the Apostle had closed the chapter of bitterness. He was making another attempt to win the friendship of B. Qurayzah through marriage to a lady of their clan. The gesture would have been meaningless and empty if all male adults were slain, and their women and children were sold as slaves.

- The marriage to **Mariyah**, a Christian and a Copt, created a significant political alliance with Egypt's ruler.

- Through the same act of goodwill, the Apostle strengthened his negotiated peace with Khaybar. He married **Safiyah**, also Jewish, and thus sealed his alliance with the most powerful Jewish group in Arabia.

Muhammad's marriages are notable for using his and his closest companions to further political ends. The other two important companions, Ali and Uthman b Affan, were bound to Muhammad by marriages to his daughters.

- Fatimah was married to **Ali**.

- Ruqayyah **was married** to Uthman. After Ruqayyah's death, Uthman was a widower. He married Umm **Kulthum**, Muhammad's third daughter.

Thus, it was not only Muhammad's political marriage, though in his case, as head of the community, there were special reasons for political considerations. It is noteworthy that Muhammad had no Medinan wife. He could only succeed in Medina if he were impartial, and such marriages would seriously infringe on his impartiality. However, there was very hardly any inter-marriage at Medina between the Meccans and the Medinans, perhaps because of social differences.

PROHIBITION OF ACQUIRING CONCUBINES

And as for those who, owing to circumstances, are unable to marry free believing women, [let them marry] believing maidens from among those whom you rightfully possess. And God knows your faith. Each one of you is an issue of the other. Marry them, then, with their people's leave, and give them their dowers in an equitable manner: these women who give themselves in honest wedlock, not in fornication, nor as secret love companions. (4:25) And [you ought to] marry the single from among you as well as such of your male and female slaves as are fit [for marriage]. If they [the person you intend to marry] are poor, [let this not deter you]. God will grant them sufficiency out of His bounty - for God is infinite [in His mercy], all-knowing. (24:32) And as for those who are unable to marry, [I.e., because of poverty or cannot find a suitable mate, or for any other personal reason.] *let them live in continence until God grants them sufficiency out of His bounty. Do not gain some of the fleeting pleasures of this worldly life, coerce your [slave] maidens into whoredom if they are desirous of marriage. If anyone should coerce them, then, verily, after they have been compelled [to submit to their helplessness], God will be much-forgiving, a dispenser of grace! (24:33)*

These passages establish unequivocally that sexual relations with female slaves are permitted only through marriage. In this respect, there is no difference between them and free women; therefore, concubinage is ruled out. Many misogynistic commentators postulate that the Prophet kept concubines. The above Quran verses should dispel such misleading assertions.

SEX AND MARRIAGE

Prophet Muhammad's numerous wives have aroused prurient interest in the West. Thomas Carlyle's essay "The Hero as Prophet" was a rare objective analysis of Muhammad's life. In Carlyle's words, all his supposed irregularities date from after his fiftieth year when the good Khadijah died. All his 'ambition,' seemingly, had been, hitherto, to live an honest life; his' fame,' the mere good opinion of neighbors that knew him, had been sufficient hitherto. Not until he was already getting old, the prurient heat of his life all burnt out, and peace growing to be the chief thing this world could give him, did he start on the 'career of ambition;' and belying all his past character and existence, set-up as a wretched empty charlatan to acquire what he could now no longer enjoy! For my share, I have no faith whatsoever in that."

It would be a mistake to imagine the Prophet basking decadently in sensual delights, as some later Islamic rulers did. He led a monogamous life during his youth, and his first marriage was with a twice-widowed senior. He remained true and loyal to Khadijah for twenty-five years until he was more than fifty years old and when Khadijah died in 619 CE. Aishah once said of Khadijah, "I never felt so jealous of any woman as I did of Khadijah, though she had died three years before the Prophet married me, and that was because his Lord had ordered him to give her the glad tidings that she would have a place in paradise."

ISLAMIC VIEW OF MARRIAGE AND SEXUALITY

W. Montgomery Watts observes that all of the Apostle's marriages "could be seen to tend to promote friendly relations in the political sphere." Of all his later wives, he only had a son with Mariyah. He spent most of his days focusing on government and security. He participated in many battles. Most nights, he meditated and prayed. He often fasted for days. There was hardly any time for conjugal luxury. This is not to say that the Prophet Muhammad was uninterested in sex. On the contrary, traditions present him as a man with a robust and healthy libido. Regardless of motives, the Prophet's marriages should not obscure the fact that he enjoyed his wives' company. To deny this would contradict the Islamic view of marriage and sexuality. This view emphasizes the importance of family and views sex as a gift from God to be enjoyed within the marriage bond.

IN SUMMARY

Most of the Prophet's wives were widows or divorced and needed help. Of the Prophet's wives, Aishah was a virgin, Zaynab bint Jahsh was divorced, and the others were widows.

Some of the women he married were related to other tribe chiefs, who became his allies.

He also broke the barrier to inter-tribal, interracial, and interreligious marriages. Prophet Muhammad had two Jewish wives, a Christian and a black wife.

He overcame the age barrier by marrying Khadijah, 15 years older than him, and Aishah, the youngest of all wives.

The two wives of the Prophet, who played a significant role in his life, were Khadijah and Aishah.

CHAPTER 29
THE MARRIAGE TO AISHAH

Prophet Muhammad's marriages to Aishah and Zaynab bint Jahsh are perhaps the most misunderstood and maligned of all marriages. Therefore, these two marriages are discussed in some detail, highlighting their social and political underpinnings.

WHY DID THE PROPHET MARRY AISHAH?

The Prophet was married to Khadijah, an influential businesswoman fifteen years his senior, for twenty-five years. When she died, he was devastated because of his deep love and respect for her. Tradition generally credits a maternal aunt of the Prophet, Khawlah bint Hakim with putting the idea into his head. She was close enough to him to suggest he marry again. "Who shall I marry, O Khawlah? You women know best in these matters," answered the Prophet. If you wish a virgin, there is the daughter of him whom you love best, Aishah bint Abi Bakr; but, if you desire a non-virgin, there is the widow Sawdah bint Zamah who believed in you and followed you." Go," said Muhammad, "bespeak to them both for me." Aishah was already engaged before her marriage to the Prophet. The boy's family broke her engagement because Abu Bakr, Aishah's father, embraced Islam. Local customs say Aishah reached marriageable age.

Political Reasons: A union with Aishah would also have cemented the Prophet's longstanding friendship with her father, Abu Bakr. As was the tradition in Arabia (and still is in some parts of the world today), marriage typically served a social and political function—uniting tribes, resolving feuds, caring for widows and orphans, and strengthening bonds in a volatile and changing social environment.

Divine command: Narrated by Aishah: The Prophet of God said: "You have been shown to me twice in my dreams. A man carried you in a silken cloth and said, 'This is your wife.' I uncovered it and realized it was you. I thought to myself, 'If this dream is from God, He will make it come true.'"

Aishah's personality: With her lively temperament and charm, Aishah brought refreshing air of romance into the closing years of the Prophet's life. She was a bright young lady, known for her assertive temperament and mischievous sense of humor, with the Prophet sometimes bearing the brunt of the jokes.

MARRIAGEABLE AGE AND MATURITY

Due to wars and the short lifespans, there were many orphans' dependent upon the surviving adults of the community. The Prophet himself was an orphan as a child. The following verse mentions marriageable age and maturity in the context of the protection of orphan girls' interests:

And do not entrust those lacking judgment with the possessions God has placed in your charge for [their] support. But let them have their sustenance from there, clothe them, and speak kindly to them. And test the orphans in your care until they reach marriage age. If you find them mentally mature, hand over their possessions. Do not consume them by wasteful spending and in haste ere they grow up. (4:5-6)

Using this verse to evaluate whether orphans can manage their inheritance and other assets, two distinct criteria must be met: marriageable age and cognitive maturity. According to the Quran, as well as the Prophets' traditions, a female must be physically and mentally mature to consent. She must also be capable of handling the responsibilities associated with a marriage. Women have the right to accept or reject marriage proposals. Her consent is a prerequisite to marriage contract validity. The whole chapter emphasizes the necessity of consent in Sahih Muslim. A six-year-old girl cannot consent to marriage.

LIMITATIONS OF THE CHRONOLOGICAL AGE

Did Aishah know her exact Age? In the pre-modern, pre-literate, and stateless society of seventh-century Arabia, Aishah would not have known her actual age. This is borne out by numerous studies of pre-literate communities today. In a society without a birth registry and where people did not celebrate birthdays, most people estimated their age and that of others. Aishah would have been no different.

Physical maturity is usually understood as the beginning of menses in girls. According to the National Institutes of Health, puberty usually begins in girls between 8 and 13 years of age. And boys between 9 and 14. Puberty onset is a range, not a specific number. It is perhaps why no specific age is mentioned in the Quran to marry. This allows believers to make their own choices.

Emotional maturity: Readiness for marriage cannot be determined by chronological age alone. There is no direct relationship between emotional maturity and chronological age. Teenage marriages generally have an increased risk of failure when the partners are not mentally mature enough to cope with heavy responsibilities. Some teenagers are excellent mothers.

DOES THE QURAN ADVOCATE CHILD MARRIAGES?

Now, as for such of your women as are beyond the age of monthly courses, as well as for such as do not have any courses, [I.e., for any physiological or pathological reasons.] *their waiting-period - if you have any doubt [about it] - shall be three [calendar] months. (65:4)*

This verse is used by child marriage proponents because they erroneously believe the mention of "do not have any courses" refers to prepubescent girls only. Amenorrhea is the medical term for women without menstrual periods. In the above Quran verse, there is no mention of pre-pubescent girls who naturally have amenorrhea. The following is a short list of adult women suffering from amenorrhea.

WHAT CAUSES AMENORRHEA?

- A family history of amenorrhea or early menopause.
- A genetic or chromosomal defect affecting ovary function and the menstrual cycle.
- Severely overweight or underweight
- Eating disorder
- An extreme exercise patterns
- A poor diet
- Stress
- Pregnancy

AGE OF AISHAH?

Few aspects of the Prophet Muhammad's life stirred as much debate and controversy as the claim that he married his third wife, Aishah, while she was a minor. It was Aishah herself who reported, according to Sahih al-Bukhari, the most authoritative but imperfect collection within the Sunni Hadith canon:

Muhammad b. Yusuf related to us: "Sufyan related to us, from Hisam, from his father, from Aishah, that the Prophet married her when she was a girl of six years, and she was taken to him when she was a girl of nine, and she lived with him for nine [years]." Technically, this report is not a hadith since it is attributed to Aishah and not the Prophet.

FALSE HADITH

- The above-stated so-called hadith violates the Quran and the Prophet's tradition, which states that marriage is only valid between two consenting adults. As the living embodiment of Islam, Prophet Muhammad's actions reflect the Quran's teachings.

To conclude, modern scientific research has answered this hadith's validity. The research was conducted by Dr. Joshua Little, a hadith specialist working under Oxford's Professor Christopher Melchert — a world-renowned Islamic studies expert.

RESEARCH METHODOLOGY

In contrast to traditional religious methods, the historical-critical approach involves using the latest techniques from the modern historian's toolkit to ascertain historical plausibility or lack thereof. Dr. Little's contribution is especially noteworthy in that he argues the case from a rigorous academic perspective. He refined a scholarly methodology known as "isnad-cum-matn analysis." The following are the findings from this study:

1) ABSENCE OF MARITAL AGE IN EARLIEST SOURCES

In the earliest sources, no marital age is reported, including some key biographical and legal works.

- Ibn Ishaq — Muhammad's best-known biographer — mentioned nothing about Aishah's age at marriage; the detail was, however, added later by the historian Ibn Hisham (d. 833 CE).

- The marital age hadith is absent from the earliest Medinan legal collections, including Imam Malik's al-Muwatta ("well-trodden path"), written in the 8th century, one of Hadith's earliest collections.

- The hadith is also absent from al-Mudawwana, a compendium of legal opinions of the Medina school, as stated by Imam Malik. It is a proto-Maliki collection of

Medinan legal transmissions. This book is called 'al Umm' or 'The Mother' of the Maliki school.

2) UNRELIABILITY OF HISHAM IBN URWA

The hadith was fabricated by a narrator named Hisham ibn Urwa, nephew of Aishah. He relocated to Iraq from Medina between 754 and 765 CE. It puts the publication of this report almost a century and a half after the events. It was fabricated in Iraq, a Shiite hotbed 1,000 miles from the Arabian city of Medina (where the marriage occurred). Ibn Urwa — the report's originator — was considered unreliable even according to traditional criteria, at least after he relocated to Iraq. He was accused of "senility" and academic deception.

3) SECTARIAN RIVALRY BETWEEN AISHAH AND ALI

Aishah, Muhammad's wife and the daughter of the first "Rightly Guided" Caliph, Abu Bakr, had a famous rivalry with the Prophet's cousin and son-in-law Ali, the first imam for Shiites and the fourth caliph for Sunnis. Not only did Aishah's father compete with Ali for the caliphate, but Aishah herself later led an insurrection against Ali.

4) MOTIVATION FOR UNDERSTATING AISHAH'S AGE

Aishah was the Prophet's favorite, and her virginal purity was implied by the extremely young age at which she was said to have been married.

Islamic belief says the Muslim community should honor Prophet Muhammad's household — and its descendants. The earlier someone entered Prophet Muhammad's house, the more honor accrued to that person (and to anyone claiming descent from them). To understate Aishah's age was meant to elevate her status (and their own lineage through her).

Sectarian sentiments were stoked by Aishah's young age. It prompted some Shiites to assert that Fatima - the Prophet's daughter and wife of Ali, revered especially in Shiite (but also Sunni) Islam - had also been married at age nine.

CONCLUSION

1. The findings of this research reveal strong indications that the fabricated hadith originated in Iraq in the middle of the 8th Century CE.

2. The proposition that Muhammad's marriage to Aishah was consummated when the latter was nine cannot be verified as a genuine historical memory from the early 7th Century CE.

3. The Aishah hadith is not a historical fact, but sectarian propaganda meant to elevate the status of the Aishah (Prophet's third wife) and her relatives. It stresses her purity and places her in the prophetic household from a young age. Khadijah's age at marriage was exaggerated to emphasize her seniority. Aishah's age was exaggerated to highlight her youth and virginity. An educated guess is that Aishah's age at her marriage was anywhere from 15-19 years.

HISTORICAL CONTEXT OF CHILD MARRIAGES

- In biblical times, people were married at a young age. It was common for girls to be betrothed before puberty - most of the time, the wedding was consummated when the girl reached puberty. This may sound abhorrent to contemporary readers, but that was life then. Before the 20th century, puberty was considered adult in most cultures/societies.

- According to the Roman legal system, girls could not marry before age 12. This age restriction derived from general observation of female pubescence; girls aged 12 were, as a rule, thought to have become physically capable of having normal sexual relations with men and of bearing children.

- In 1880, most of the United States agreed that a ten-year-old girl was considered old enough to consent to sexual relations; this was only 120 years ago. California, for instance, has no minimum age if participants have parental consent. In New Hampshire and Massachusetts, people can get married with parental permission at thirteen and twelve respectively.

- Some people with ulterior motives or out of ignorance pass judgment on social events that happened fourteen centuries ago through rose-colored glasses.

- Five centuries after the Prophet's marriage to Aishah, 33-year-old King John of England married 12-year-old Isabella of Angouleme, France. Interestingly, of the many criticisms of Muhammad made at that time by his opponents, none focused on Aishah's marriage age.

Loving relationship: The records are clear that the Prophet and Aishah had a loving and egalitarian relationship, which set the standard for reciprocity, tenderness, and respect enjoined by the Quran. Insights into their relationship, such as the fact that they liked to drink out of the same cup or race one another, are indicative of a deep connection. This belies any misrepresentation of their relationship. To paint Aishah as a victim is at odds with her persona. She was certainly no wallflower. During the Battle of the Camel, a controversial battle in Muslim history, she emerged riding a camel to lead the troops.

Authority to Consult: The Prophet established her authority during his lifetime by telling Muslims to consult her in his absence; after his death, she became one of the most prolific and distinguished scholars of her time.

The Prophet and the Muslim community highly respected Aishah because of her superior intellect and significant contribution to Islam. A considerable body of the Prophet's sayings and traditions were recorded from her first-hand account and interpretations. She lived forty-eight years after the Prophet's death and played a major role in educating later generations. A stateswoman, scholar, mufti, and judge, Aishah combined spirituality, activism, and knowledge. She remains a role model for many Muslim women today.

Aishah may have been young, but she was not younger than the norm at the time. It is impossible to know how old Aishah was when she married the Prophet. What we do know is what the Quran says about marriage: that it is valid only between consenting adults and that a woman has the right to choose her spouse.

HEALTH ISSUES DUE TO CHILD MARRIAGE

- Child marriages can cause health issues:
- Gynecological problems due to early childbirth
- A higher risk of uterine cancer
- A higher risk of suicide and other mental health problems. These include depression and anxiety. There is the issue of a child raising a child. If a young bride can hardly care for herself, how can she care for a small child?

CHAPTER 30
MARRIAGE TO ZAYNAB BINT JAHSH

The Prophet faced criticism from his contemporaries in Medina when he married Zaynab bint Jahsh because it was incestuous in their eyes. She was a divorcee of his adopted son Zayd. Prophet Muhammad faced no such criticism when he married a much younger Aishah, which was within the norms of the time. The essential reforms intended in this whole affair were:

- All men are equal regardless of their social status. A freedman is good enough to marry a freeborn woman who belongs to the Quraysh nobility.

- A divorcee of a freed slave is good enough to be the mother of believers.

- To promote the transformation from a matrilineal to a patrilineal social order. Also, this union had potential political advantages.

(1) EQUALITY BETWEEN FREEDMAN AND FREEBORN

The Prophet was inspired by the desire to break down the ancient Arabian prejudice against slaves or a freedman marrying a freeborn woman. When Muhammad married Khadijah, she made him a gift of one of her slaves, a youth named Zayd. This youth was captured by a raiding party and sold into slavery. Zayd b. Harithah was freed by the Prophet and adopted him as his 'son.' There was no formal or legal adoption procedure fifteen centuries ago. The Prophet persuaded Zayd his adopted son, to marry Zaynab.

(2) THE POLITICAL ANGLE

It is clear from the records that the Prophet used his cousins' marriages, like his daughters, for political ends. There can be no doubt that Zaynab's union with Zayd was part of this scheme of alliance. This is because Zayd was a prominent man in the community, like Abu Bakr. (In the later part of his life, Zayd led several expeditions, including the large one to Mutah, where he was martyred.) The clan of Abd Shams and Abu Sufyan b. Harb was the primary opponent of the Prophet. Zaynab's family was a confederate of the father of Abu Sufyan, who directed the Meccan campaign against Prophet Muhammad. This aspect of the match cannot escape him.

(3) FROM A MATRILINEAL TO A PATRILINEAL SOCIAL ORDER

A person's *lineage* is their *line* of ancestors. So *matrilineal* means "through the mother's line", just as *patrilineal* means "through the father's line". At the time of the Hijrah, Arabian society was in transition from a matrilineal to a patrilineal society. At Medina, matrilineal social structures were more frequent and at Mecca, the patrilineal system predominated. During this transition, unscrupulous men often took unfair advantage of weaker relatives for their benefit. The Quran's marriage reforms are understood against this background.

ORGANIZATION OF MATRILINEAL GROUPS

Matrilineal groups consist of women and their descendants. The matriarch is the family head. When she died, the head of the household would be her eldest daughter, and her next eldest sister would perhaps follow her.

SEX AND MARRIAGE

The matrilineal social system may have evolved because of a tribal desert culture where families moved from pasture to pasture. All aspects of life were transient, including relationships. Marriage for a woman did not mean leaving the family home, and the husband must 'visit' her for longer or shorter periods. The husband would have no home of his own but live in his mother's or sister's house when not visiting his wife.

Some women only have one husband at a time. In several cases, a woman seems to have had two husbands simultaneously, one from her clan and another tribe or clan. Some women had up to ten, and some had sexual relations with any man who came to them.

CHILD PATERNITY

It was not essential or sometimes impossible to know who a child's father was; it was sufficient to know the mother. The child belonged to his mother's family and lived in her family house. When a man married a chief woman, he automatically became the adoptive 'father' of any sons and daughters living with her. Such a system deprived children of their birthright to know their paternity and absolved the biological father of the responsibility of providing for his children. It promoted sexual promiscuity.

PATRILINEAL GROUP

Patrilineal groups refer to family relationships in societies by lines of descent from male ancestors through the child's father. Both male and female offspring belong to a patriline, but only male children can continue the bloodline. Patrilineality is also called agnatic kinship. It was the result of individualism growing in Mecca and other parts of Arabia.

MARRIAGE BETWEEN ZAYD AND ZAYNAB

Zaynab was the Prophet's cousin, the daughter of his father's sister. At the Hijrah, she was a widow and migrated to Medina, presumably with her brothers. The Prophet was unaware that she had been in love with him since childhood. Zaynab and her relatives rejected this marriage proposal based on her superior lineage from the noble Quraysh family.

She consented to the union with much reluctance, on insistence, and in deference to the Prophet's authority. Zayd, too, was not keen on this alliance—he was already happily married to another freed slave, Umm Ayman, the mother of his son Usamah. It was not surprising that the marriage did not bring happiness to Zaynab or Zayd.

TEMPTATION

The story that the Prophet was swept off his feet by Zaynab's physical attractiveness should be rejected for the following reasons: The Prophet had known Zaynab since her childhood, and suddenly, he discovered her beauty and was smitten by it. When she married Muhammad, Zaynab was thirty-five, or perhaps thirty-eight, advanced for an Arab woman fifteen centuries ago. The only wife older at the marriage was Khadijah. All the Prophet's other wives, except Khadijah, were younger when he married them, and most of them were much younger. It is unlikely that a man of fifty-six should have been carried away by a passion for a woman of thirty-five or more whom he had known since childhood.

The scandalous story of Muhammad's lust for Zaynab was not reported in earlier sources and was later invented to discredit the Prophet. There is a strong presumption in the Zaynab bint Jahsh case that the Prophet was not carried away by passion but looked at the political implications. Although, a social motive may have outweighed the political one in her case to demonstrate that Muhammad had broken old taboos.

RELUCTANCE TO MARRY ZAYNAB AND DIVINE REPRIMAND

And lo, [O Muhammad], you did say to the one to whom God had shown favor and to whom you had shown favor, [referring to Zayd] "Hold on to your wife and remain conscious of God!" And [thus] would you hide within yourself something that God was about to bring to light—for you did stand in awe of [what] people [might think], whereas it was God alone of whom you should have stood in awe! (33:37)

The Quran indicates that Prophet Muhammad initially refused to marry Zaynab. Instead of submitting to God's will, the Prophet was reluctant because of public opinion. The divine reprimand was a reminder that it was God alone you should have stood in awe of, not people. Referring to this divine reprimand, Aishah said, "Had the Apostle of God been inclined to suppress anything revealed to him, he would surely have suppressed this verse.

Shortly after her divorce from Zayd, the Prophet married Zaynab to redeem his moral responsibility for her past unhappiness. And to demonstrate that the divorcee of an ex-slave was worthy of being a Prophet's wife and mother of believers. The Prophet faced severe criticism from his contemporaries, who considered marrying an adopted son's divorcee akin to incest. Islam rejected this objection.

DIVINELY ORDAINED MARRIAGE TO ZAYNAB

[But] then, when Zayd ended his union with her, [and divorced Zaynab] We gave her to you in marriage. So that [in the future] no blame should be attached to believers for [marrying] the spouses of their adopted children when the latter have come to the end of their union with them. And [thus] God's will is done.

(33:37) [Hence], no blame whatsoever attaches to the Prophet for [having done] what God has ordained for him. [Indeed, such was] God's way with those who had passed away before. And [remember that] God's will be always destiny absolute; [and such will always be His way with] those who convey God's messages [to the world]. They stand in awe of Him and hold only God in awe. For none can count [man's deeds] as God does! (33:38–39)

The translations of 'adoptive son' in Arabic do not signify any legal adoption process like we have nowadays but designate a relationship automatically. It means someone known as the son of a man who is not physically his father. The Quranic verse quoted implies that adoptive sons should not be treated as real or biological sons. This is why there should be a complete break with the past in this respect.

ZIHAR

In pre-Islamic Arabia, there was a custom called zihar, where a husband could divorce his wife by simply declaring, "Thou art [henceforth as unlawful] to me as my mother's back," the term zihar ("back") being, in this case, a metonym for "body." In pagan Arab society, this mode of divorce was considered final and irrevocable; but a woman thus divorced was not allowed to remarry and had to remain forever in her former husband's custody.

ELECTIVE VS. BLOOD RELATIONSHIPS

Never has God endowed any man with two hearts in one body: and [just as] He has never made your wives whom you may declare "unlawful to you as your mothers," so, too, He never made your adopted sons your [real] sons. These are but [figures of] speech uttered by your mouths - whereas God speaks the [absolute] truth, and it is He alone who can guide you to the right path. [As for your adopted children], call them by their [real] fathers' names: this is more equitable in God's eyes. If you do not know who their fathers were, [call them] your brethren in faith and your friends. However, you will incur any sin if you err in this respect: [what matters is] what your hearts intend - for God is indeed much-forgiving, a dispenser of grace! (33:4-5)

At the time of the present Surah, this cruel pagan custom of zihar had already been abolished. It is mentioned here only as an illustration of the subsequent dictum that the "figures of speech [lit., "your sayings"] which you utter with your mouth" do not make her your real mother. Similarly, an adopted son is not your real son."Two hearts in one body" refers to assigning two mutually incompatible roles (from wife to mother) by a man who intended to divorce in Arabia's pre-Islamic society. The concept that one person can play both the roles of wife and mother within human relationships conflicts with God-ordained laws of nature and is unjust and morally objectionable.

MARRIAGE RESTRICTION DOES NOT APPLY TO ADOPTIVE RELATIONSHIPS

The divine purpose of causing the Prophet to marry his adopted son's former wife was to show that an adoptive relationship does not carry marriage restrictions. The marriage restriction applies only to biological parent and child relationships. The Prophet married Zaynab to exemplify a point of Canon law and satisfy his moral duty. After her waiting period (iddah) was observed, marriage to Muhammad was arranged.

The words, *"And if you don't know who their fathers are,"* (let them be) your brethren in religion or your friend. These may refer to a matrilineal household where the physical paternity of a woman's children was not known. However, her husband was considered their 'father' for social purposes. These social customs were features of the old matrilineal family organization that were undesirable.

TRANSFORMATION FROM MATRILINEAL TO PATRILINEAL SYSTEM

God-made biological relations will supersede man-made relations through adoption. The marriage between the Prophet and his adopted son's ex-wife was meant to reaffirm this principle. One cannot, however, marry the divorcee of his biological son.

The most significant is the simple prescription that when a woman is divorced or widowed, she must have a waiting period of three months before remarrying to ensure there is no doubt about a child's paternity. Thus, it is in line with the principle of discouraging promiscuity and making clear who a child's father was. Modern DNA technology makes this process foolproof.

The three-month waiting period implies that a woman has only one husband at a time and not multiple sexual partners. It was through the strict determination of biological paternity that the Quran transformed a matrilineal society into a patrilineal one.

The biological father would be responsible for the financial and emotional support of his children. This is not the stepfather or some stranger who married their mother. Under Islamic law, only biological children are entitled to inheritance from their parents. Adopted children cannot claim inheritance from their adopted parents.

CONCLUSION

According to W. Montgomery Watts: "In the sphere of marriage and family relations, Muhammad effected a profound and far-reaching reorganization of society's structure. Before his time, individualistic tendencies were certainly present. However, their presence led more to the breakdown of the old structure than to building a better one. Muhammad's essential work here was to use these individualistic tendencies in the raising of a brand-new structure. The customs and practices of the communal (tribal) stage of society, to vary the metaphor, had suffered a shipwreck; Muhammad salvaged what was valuable from them and carried it over to emerging individualism. In this way, he produced a family structure that, in many respects, has proved attractive and satisfactory for societies emerging from the communal stage and passing into an individualistic one. Both by European Christian standards and Islam's, many old practices were immoral, and Muhammad's reorganization was, therefore, a moral advance. The old nomadic system may have been satisfactory in desert environments so long as it remained intact. Once disintegration commenced, however, it became unsatisfactory and had to disappear. It is to Muhammad's credit that he produced a viable substitute."

CHAPTER 31
THE MARITAL LAWS EXCLUSIVE TO THE PROPHET

The discourse below describes the marital laws applied exclusively to the Prophet and not to other believers.

MARRIAGE TO RELATIVES WITH STRONG FAITH

[We have made lawful to you] the daughters of your paternal uncles and aunts, and the daughters of your maternal uncles and aunts, who have migrated with you [to Yathrib]. (33:50)

Muslims can marry their paternal or maternal cousins. The Prophet was allowed to marry only those who had proven their strong, early attachment to Islam by accompanying him on his exodus (the Hijra) from Mecca to Medina. According to ancient Arabian usage, the term "daughters of your paternal uncles and aunts" includes all women of the Quraysh tribe, to which Muhammad's father belonged. The term "daughters of your maternal tribe" includes all women of his mother's tribe, the Banu Zuhrah.

EXEMPTION FROM DOWRY

Any believing woman who offers herself freely to the Prophet and whom the Prophet might be willing to wed: [this latter being] a privilege for you, and not for other believers. [seeing that] We have already made known what We have enjoined upon them concerning their wives and those their right hands may possess. [And] so that you will not be burdened with [undue] anxiety; for God is indeed much-forgiving, a dispenser of grace. (33:50)

The relevant clause reads "if she offered herself as a gift" to the Prophet without demanding or expecting a dower. This is an essential item in a marriage agreement for ordinary Muslims.

NO NEED FOR CONJUGAL ATTENTION

[Know that] you may put off whichever of them you please for a time and take whichever pleases you. And [that] if you seek out any from whom you have kept away [for a time], you will incur no sin [thereby]: this will make it more likely that their eyes are gladdened [whenever they see you], and that they do not grieve [whenever they are overlooked]. And that all of them may find contentment in whatever you have given them. For God [alone] knows what is in your hearts— and God is indeed all-knowing, forbearing. (33:51)

The Prophet was told he did not need to observe a strict "rotation" in marital attention due to his wives. However, he was impelled by an inborn sense of fairness and always endeavored to give them a sense of equality. Whenever he turned to any of them, he did so out of genuine affection and not marital obligation. According to a hadith on Aishah's authority, the Prophet used to divide his attention equitably among his wives and then would pray, "O God! I am doing whatever is in my power. Therefore, do not blame me for failing at something in Thy power alone and not in mine!"

PROHIBITION TO DIVORCE AND PERMISSION FOR MORE THAN FOUR WIVES

No [other] women shall henceforth be lawful to you- nor shall you be [allowed] to supplant [any of] them with other wives, even though their beauty should please you greatly— [none shall be lawful to you] beyond those whom you [already] possess. And God watches over everything. (33:52)

At the time when the verse limiting wives to four was revealed, the Prophet had more than four wives. His dilemma was to decide which wife to divorce in order to keep the number of wives under four. God exempted the Prophet from the restriction of 'no more than four wives.' The above verse limited the Prophet's marriages to those already contracted ("those whom you possessed through wedlock"). The Prophet was not allowed "to supplant [any of] them with other wives" by divorcing any of his wives. The prohibition of divorce assured the Prophet's wives of God's reward in this world for their faith and fidelity. In AH 7, the Prophet conquered Khaybar and married Safiyyah—his last marriage.

RULES ONLY FOR THE PROPHET'S WIVES

STANDARD OF LIVING

O Prophet! Say unto your wives: "If you desire [but] the life of this world and its charms—well, then I shall provide for you and release you in a becoming manner. But if you desire God and His Apostle, and [thus the good of] life in the hereafter, then [know that] for the doers of good among you, God has prepared a mighty reward!" (33:28-29)

It was a lifelong principle of the Prophet that the standard of living of his family should not be higher than the poorest of believers. This was voluntary poverty because there are no Quranic injunctions to this effect. Being a supreme ruler, the Prophet continued to lead as he had in the days of his obscurity, an unpretentious life. A world away from palaces, he lived in an ordinary clay house and milked his own goats. He was constantly accessible day or night to even the humblest of his subjects. The furniture in his household consisted of a mat, an earthen jug, and a blanket. These were his furniture when he was ruler of Arabia.

By the time the above verses were revealed, the Muslims had conquered the rich agricultural region of Khaybar, and the community had grown prosperous. While life became easier for most of its members, not in the Prophet's household. He continued to allow himself and his family only the minimum for simple living. It was natural that his wives long for a share of the luxuries that other Muslim women could now enjoy. When his wives argued over money, the Prophet threatened to divorce them all unless they lived more frugally. Immediately after the revelation of verses 33:28-29, the Prophet recited these verses to his wives. Each one emphatically rejected all thoughts of separation, declaring they had chosen "God and His Apostle and the good of the hereafter."

DOUBLE THE REWARD OR PUNISHMENT

O wives of the Prophet! If any of you were to become guilty of manifestly immoral conduct, [gross sin] double [that of other sinners] would be her suffering [in the hereafter]. But if you devoutly obey God and His Apostle and do good deeds, on her shall We bestow her reward twice-over: for We shall have ready for her most excellent sustenance [in the life to come]. O wives of the Prophet! You are not like any of these [other] women, provided you remain [truly] conscious of God. (33:30–32)

DO NOT BE OVERLY SOFT IN SPEECH OR FLAUNT YOUR CHARMS

Hence, be not too soft in your speech, lest any whose heart is diseased should be moved to desire [you]: but, with all, speak kindly. And abide quietly in your homes, and do not flaunt your charms as they used to flaunt them in the old days of pagan ignorance. And be constant in prayer, and render the purifying dues, and pay heed unto God and His Apostle: for God only wants to remove from you all that might be loathsome, O you members of the [Prophet's] household, and to purify you to the utmost purity. And remember all that is recited in your homes about God's messages and [His] wisdom. For God is unfathomable [in His wisdom], all aware. (33:32–34)

The term Jahiliyyah denotes the period of moral ignorance in pre-Islamic Arabia before Muhammad's advent. This term describes the state of moral ignorance or unconsciousness in its general sense, irrespective of time or social environment. (See also 5:50.)

HIJAB FOR THE PROPHET'S WIVES ONLY

And [as for the Prophet's wives], whenever you ask them for anything you need, ask them from behind a screen (hijab); this will deepen the purity of your hearts and theirs. Moreover, it does not behove you to offend the Apostle of God, just as it would not behove you to marry his widows after he passed away: that would be an enormity in God's sight. Whether you do anything openly or secretly, [remember that], God has full knowledge of everything. [However,] it is no sin for them (wives of the Prophet) [to appear freely] before their fathers, or their sons, or their brothers, or their brothers' sons, or their sister's sons, or their womenfolk, or such [male slaves] as their right hands may possess. But [always, O wives of the Prophet] remain conscious of God—for God witnesses everything. (33:53-55)

The term "hijab" denotes anything that intervenes between two things or conceals, shelters, or protects one from the other. It may be rendered, according to the context, as a barrier, obstacle, partition, screen, curtain, veil, etc. Approaching the mothers of the faithful behind a curtain was meant to show respect. Most of the companions took it literally. The verse above was prompted by the need to separate public from private space. This verse addresses only the Prophet's wives and not women in general, so the requirement to wear a hijab was solely meant for the Prophet's wives.

SURAH 66
AT-TAHRIM (PROHIBITION)

RENUNCIATION OF MARITAL LIFE

The sixty-sixth surah, at-tahrim (prohibition), has been described as "the Surah of the Prophet," the first half of which deals with certain aspects of his personal and family life. Sometime during the second half of the Medina period, the Prophet declared on oath that he would not have marital relations with any of his wives for one month.

THE ADMONITION TO THE PROPHET

O Prophet! Why do you, out of a desire to please [one or another of] your wives, impose [on yourself] a prohibition on something God has made lawful to you? God has already enjoined upon you [O believers] the breaking and expiation of [such of] your oaths [as may run counter to what is right and just]. For God is your Lord Supreme, and He alone is all-knowing, truly wise. (66:1–2)

DIVULGING CONFIDENTIAL INFORMATION

And lo! [It so happened that] the Prophet told something in confidence to one of his wives; and when she thereupon divulged it, and God made this known to him, he acquainted [others] with some of it and passed over some of it. (66:3)

As repeatedly stressed in the Quran, the Prophet was a human being, subject to feelings and emotions. He was liable to commit an occasional mistake pointed out to him and rectified through divine revelation. The purport of the Quranic allusion to this incident is not biographical but to bring out a moral lesson applicable to all human situations—namely, the inadmissibility of regarding as forbidden (haram) anything that God has made lawful (halal). See under "oath," wherein certain circumstances an oath should be broken and atoned for—hence the above phrase, "God has enjoined upon you the breaking and expiation."

The central theme of all these stories is mutual jealousy among some of the Prophet's wives. This resulted in an emotional and temporary renunciation of marital life by the Prophet. The Prophet's contemporaries related many conflicting versions of the stories, and only two common versions are presented here.

The Apostle had a sweet tooth and loved honey at Zainab's house, spending more time with her. Aishah and Hafsa, both jealous, hatched a plan and told the Apostle: I notice you have foul breath. The Prophet replied: I have taken honey in Zainab bint Jahsh's house, and I will never do it again. The following verse was revealed: 'Why do you hold forbidden what God has made lawful for you, i.e., honey? "And when the Prophet confided this information to one of his wives" refers to his statement: "But I've taken honey."

The second version, according to some authorities, is that the Prophet made a veiled prediction that Abu Bakr and Umar ibn al-Khattab would succeed him as Muslim community leaders. The recipient of the information was Hafsah, the daughter of Umar. The one she disclosed was Aishah, Abu Bakr's daughter. If this interpretation is correct, it would explain why the Prophet "acquainted others with some of it and passed over some of it," because once his confidential prediction was divulged, he saw no point in withholding it from the community. Nevertheless, he alluded deliberately in vague terms not to give the succession of Abu Bakr and Umar the appearance of an apostolic sanction but to leave it to the free decision of the community in pursuance of the Quranic principle of consultation to choose a leader (see 42:38). The nature of confidential information in this scenario is who is the Prophet's successor after his death.

SEEK REPENTANCE

And as soon as he (the Prophet) let her know it, she asked, "Who has told you all these things?" [To which] he replied, "The All-Knowing, the All-Aware has told me." [Say, O Prophet]: "Would you both turn unto God in repentance, for your hearts have swerved [from what is right]? As you defend each other against him [who is God's message-bearer], know that God Himself is his protector. Gabriel, all the righteous among the believers, and all the [other] angels will come to his aid." (66:3-4)

The Prophet is commanded through revelation to speak to his wives regarding the divulgence of confidential information. She asked, "Who told you this?" She had broken the Prophet's confidence. "You both" in the above verse refers to Hafsah, who betrayed the Prophet's trust, and to Aishah, who, by listening, contributed to this betrayal.

THE WARNING TO THE PROPHET'S WIVES

[O wives of the Prophet!] Should he divorce any of you, God might give him spouses better than you. Women who surrender themselves unto God, who truly believe, devoutly obey His will, turn [unto Him] in repentance [whenever they have sinned]. Worship [Him alone] and go on and on [seeking His goodly acceptance] - whether they were previously married or virgins. (66:5)

The Prophet did not divorce his wives. The hypothetical formulation of this passage shows that it was an indirect admonition to the Prophet's wives, who possessed the virtues referred to above despite their occasional shortcomings. It seems to be a warning to all believers, men and women alike, on a broader plane.

WAS PROPHET MUHAMMAD INFALLIBLE?

Say: "I am not the first of [God's] apostles; and [like all of them,] I do not know what will be done with you or me, for I am nothing but a plain warner." (46:9) [O Muhammad,] We have laid open before thee a manifest victory so that God might show His forgiveness of all thy sins, past and future. And [thus] bestow upon you the full measure of His blessings, and guide you on a straight path. God will provide you with a mighty help. (48:1-3) Has He not found thee an orphan and sheltered thee? And found thee lost on thy way and guided thee? And found thee in need, and gave thee sufficiency? (93:6-8) Have we not opened your heart and lifted the burden that weighed so heavily on your back? And [have We not] raised you high in dignity? And with every hardship comes ease: with every hardship comes ease! Hence, when you are freed [from distress], remain steadfast, and turn to your Sustainer with love. (94:1-8)

The statement that I do not know what will happen to all of us, in this world or in the hereafter, implies a denial on the Prophet's part of any foreknowledge of the future and, in the broader sense, any knowledge of "that is beyond human perception" (al-ghayb).

The phrase In other words, I am nothing but a plain warner like all of God's message-bearers before me. The burden of your past sins is now forgiven. In Muhammad's case, this relates to mistakes committed before his prophethood call.

In the Quran, God took the Apostle to task many times when he erred. Prophets are infallible only in conveying divine messages and performing divine trusts. Like all men, prophets are truly fallible; however, God does not leave them in error. Only God is perfect and infallible in every way. Considering a human being "infallible" is tantamount to elevating him to godhood, an unforgivable act of shirk or idolatry.

So highly has the Prophet been regarded that his status has come close to threatening the monotheism he preached. When Muhammad died, some attempted to deify him, but his chosen successor, Abu Bakr, killed the thought with one of the most famous speeches in religious history: "If there are any among you who worship Muhammad, he is dead. But if it is God you worship, He lives forever." Similar deification happened in Jesus' case by early Christians. Muslims should learn that Prophet Muhammad was still a human being despite his miracles. The attempt to deify the Prophet will be an unforgivable sin of idolatry and damnation in the afterlife.

A MODERN HUSBAND AND A FEMINIST

The Prophet diligently helped with chores at home and mended his clothes. When the Prophet's wife, Aishah, was asked, "What did the Prophet do at home?" she answered, "He used to work for his family." He was a remarkable modern husband who truly enjoyed the company of his wives and related to them with respect and understanding, often relying on their advice. He liked to take one of them on an expedition, consult with them, and take their advice seriously.

Muhammad granted his wives a position unknown in Arabia. Some of his male companions were astonished by his leniency toward his wives, the way they stood up to him and answered him back. Umar ibn al-Khattab said, "My wife once tried to dissuade me from doing what I had planned to do. When I told her that this was none of her business, she said, 'How strange of you, Umar! You refuse to be told anything, whereas your daughter Hafsah may criticize her husband, the Prophet of God, and do so strongly that he remains upset the whole day long.'" Umar confronted his daughter, and Hafsah answered, "Indeed, other wives and I do criticize him." Umar warned his daughter that this would bring both the punishment of God and the wrath of his Prophet. He left his daughter and visited Umm Salamah, Umar's close relative and another Prophet's wife. Upon asking her the same question, Umm Salamah replied, "How strange, O ibn al-Khattab! Are you intending to interfere with everything, even the Prophet's domestic affairs?" The Prophet Muhammad never used violence against his wives. They displayed mutual jealousy and were critical of him.

CHAPTER 32
WHY MUHAMMAD, THE GREATEST MAN EVER LIVED

VISION

The Prophet's mission started as a one-man show. For the first 2-3 years, he limited his message to his family and close friends. He invited forty of his chief kin from his clan to a grand dinner. There, he stood up and told them what his pretension was: that he had this thing to promulgate abroad to all men; that it was the highest thing, the one thing: which of them would second him in that? The sight there of one unlettered elderly man deciding on such an enterprise against all mankind appeared ridiculous to them; the assembly broke up in laughter. But it was not a laughing matter. He was way ahead of his time. Against all odds and repeated rejections, he continued to spread his message. Today, 1.8 billion of his followers are spread in every corner of the world. Perhaps the greatest quality any leader can have is vision - the ability to see the big picture and what it will take to get there.

INSPIRATION AND INTERACTION

The Medinese found the Prophet to be a master whom it was difficult not to love or obey. He had, as one biographer wrote, "the gift of influencing men, and he had the nobility only to influence them for good." He conveyed his vision to others and got them excited about it.

Effective leaders must be able to interact with people in a genuine way. The Prophet made himself available to the humblest of his followers at any hour of the day. Being the head of the state and his enemies determined to harm him, he remained approachable to ordinary citizens for counseling. A level of accessibility that takes enormous security risks is unprecedented. When the prophet was trying to persuade prominent leaders in Mecca, he was interrupted by a blind Muslim who had some questions. The Prophet was annoyed at this interruption and received an immediate divine reprimand.

PATIENCE & TENACITY

From 610-622, the Prophet had only a few hundred followers. He fought three battles, and after 20 years of struggle, he finally entered his hometown of Mecca victorious.

RELIGIOUS ACHIEVEMENTS

MONOTHEISM

Belief in one God alone is absolute monotheism, a hallmark of Islam. To the pagan peoples of Western Arabia, the Prophet brought the religion of monotheism and its ethical doctrines. These stood on an incomparably higher level than the paganism it replaced. Faith received a revelation through him, which became the guide to thought for countless believers over the centuries.

FREEDOM OF RELIGION

There is a strict prohibition of coercion in faith or religion. Islamic jurists hold that forcible conversion is null and void, and any attempt at coercing a non-believer to accept Islam's faith is a grievous sin."

RELIGIOUS PLURALISM

A striking illustration of religious equality is found in the Prophet's treatment of the delegation of the Christians of Najran and St. Catherine's Monastery. The Medina Agreement gave equal rights to Jews.

THE QURAN'S CONTRIBUTION

ARABIC LANGUAGE

The Quran's literary influence has been incalculable. The Quran's classical Arabic is the enduring standard of excellence in speech. The first prose book in Arabic set the style for future products. It kept the language uniform. So, whereas today, a Moroccan uses a dialect different from an Iraqi, all write in the same style.

MORAL REVIVAL

Within a half-century, the moral climate changed near-miraculously. Muhammad, as a reformer, condemned pagan Arab practices such as female infanticide, exploitation of the poor, usury, murder, false contracts, fornication, adultery, and theft. The Prophet insisted that each person was personally accountable not to tribal customary law but to an overriding divine law that shook Arabian society's very foundations. In his book The Religions of Man, Huston Smith writes, "Looking at the difference between pre-and post-Islamic Arabia, we are forced to ask whether history has ever witnessed a comparable ethical advance among so many people in such a short time."

THE REVIVAL OF WESTERN CULTURE

Islam unveils one of history's most remarkable panoramas. By a century, his followers conquered Armenia, Persia, Syria, Palestine, Iraq, Egypt, and Spain. They crossed the Pyrenees into France.

ADVANCEMENT OF SCIENCE AND LITERATURE

Islamic civilization holds the distinction of being, from the mid-eighth century to the end of the twelfth century, unmatched in its brilliance and unsurpassed in its literary, scientific, and philosophical output.

POLITICAL

UNITING ARABIA

He established a community and a well-organized armed state, whose power and prestige made it a dominant factor in Arabia. A new nation was born from a collection of unruly Arabian tribes that had never united. No other sacred scripture has ever had such a profound impact on the lives of the people who first heard its message. This has had a profound impact on civilization. It shook Arabia and made a nation out of its perennially warring tribes.

The Constitution of Medina guaranteed equal rights for minorities. The document was drawn up to end the bitter intertribal fighting between the clans of the Aws (Banu Aws) and Banu Khazraj within Medina. To this effect, it instituted several rights and responsibilities for Medina's Muslim, Jewish, and pagan communities, bringing them into the fold of one community- the *Ummah*. The Prophet embraced religious pluralism, envisioned a civic nation, stood for anti-racism, and made seeking knowledge part of a religious obligation.

EGALITARIANISM AND HUMAN RIGHTS

ANTI-RACISM

Egalitarian doctrines say all humans are equal in fundamental worth and should be accorded equal political, economic, social, and civil rights. Humanity comes from Adam and Eve. An Arab has no superiority over a non-Arab, nor does a non-Arab have superiority over an Arab. Also, a white has no superiority over a black, nor does a black have any superiority over a white except for piety and righteous actions.

Due to its egalitarian nature, Islam rejected aristocratic privilege and hierarchy and embraced a formula for careers for all.

Muhammad proclaimed a sweeping religious and social reform program that affected religious beliefs, business contracts and practices, gender equality, and family relations. The Quran's reforms consist of regulations or moral guidance that limit or redefine rather than prohibit or replace existing practices.

SLAVERY

In Muslim lands, slaves had a certain legal status, obligations, and rights to the slave owner, an improvement over slavery in the ancient world. Due to these reforms, the practice of slavery in the Islamic Empire represented a vast improvement on that inherited from antiquity, Rome, and Byzantium."

WOMEN'S RIGHTS

In The Religions of Man, Huston Smith writes, "Chiefly because it has permitted a plurality of wives, Islam has been accused of degrading women. If we approach the question time-wise, comparing the status of Arabian women before and after Muhammad, the charge is patently false. In the pre-Islamic days of the Dark Age, women were regarded as little more than chattel to be done with as their fathers or husbands pleased. Women were considered private property. In the face of these conditions, the birth of a daughter was regarded as a calamity. Islamic reforms improved the status of women enormously, as follows:

Right to life: The Quran forbids female infanticide.

Inheritance rights: Daughters were included in an inheritance, not equally but up to half the proportion of sons. Daughters would not need to bear economic responsibility for their households.

Right to education and income.

Equal testimony under the law: There is no mention of gender when testimony is described in the Quran, except in a verse about debt (2:282) that equates the testimony of two women to that of one man. The original purpose was to secure testimony, as women usually did not engage in commercial transactions and thus were more likely to make a mistake or be deceived.

Equal partners: The Quran makes men and women partners before God, with identical duties and responsibilities.

The sanctification of marriage: Islam made its greatest contribution to women in marriage. It sanctifies marriage by making it the sole locus of sexual acts. There is no alternative to well-adjusted marriages, which provide a haven for mothers and a place to raise children in an ideal environment. Single-mother families are the major cause of poverty among children and women in the United States.

Right to divorce: The Quran gave women the legal right to divorce. Most Western women had nothing comparable until the nineteenth century. Muslim women have a long way to go before reaching full rights.

ECONOMIC CHANGES

The Quran provided a blueprint for a new order in society in which the poor would be treated more fairly than before. The Quran demands that Muslims pursue a path of social justice rooted in the recognition that the earth belongs ultimately to God. Human beings are its caretakers. One of the main points of Muslim economics is the concern that people's wealth should be widely shared. Society's health requires material goods that are widely distributed and wealth is in easy circulation. Material rewards are, therefore, subject to social responsibility toward other community members.

The Quranic method of wealth distribution is both compulsory and voluntary. Zakah is a tax to help poor people. Its purpose is twofold. First, it is meant to purify Muslim possessions from greed and selfishness. Second, the proceeds of this tax are utilized in what the

Quran describes as "the cause of God" or the welfare of the community."

THE WARRIOR PROPHET

In 10 years, the Prophet brought a revolution in Arabia and changed human history. In his book, "Islam- A Way of Life," Philip K. Hitti sums up the Prophet's career in the following words: "Judged only by achievement, Muhammad the man, the teacher, the orator, the author, the statesman, and the warrior stands out as one of the ablest men in all history. He laid the basis of a religion—Islam; initiated a state—the caliphate; prompted a culture—the Arabic-Islamic culture; and founded a nation—the Arab nation. He is still a living force in millions of men's lives."

CHAPTER 33
THE FINAL SERMON

Arabian tribal society, with its Bedouin, polytheistic ethos, provided the context for the rise of Islam. The Prophet brought a revolution to Arabian life, a reformation that sought to purify and redefine its ways of life. He introduced a new moral order in which the origin and end of all actions were not self or tribal interests but God's will. Old ways were modified, eliminated, or replaced by new regulations. Thus, Islam brought reformation to a morally corrupt and deviant society. It was the call to total surrender or submission (Islam) to Allah and the implementation of His will as revealed in its complete form one final time to Muhammad, the last or "seal" of the prophets. His dispensation sums up and supplements all the preceding ones; eventually, it supplants them all. Muhammad said repeatedly,

"No Prophet after me." Muslims look to the Prophet's example for guidance in all aspects of life: how to treat enemies and friends, what to eat and drink, and how to make love and war. Muhammad was among those great historical figures whose remarkable character and personality inspired uncommon confidence and commitment. He was a shrewd military strategist and warrior-prophet like Moses. He elicited steadfast loyalty from his followers despite persecution and oppression. He had phenomenal success in attracting followers and creating a community-state that dominated Arabia. His impact on Muslim life cannot be overestimated since he served as both the religious and political head of Medina.

THE FINAL SERMON AT THE FAREWELL PILGRIMAGE

The last sermon delivered by Prophet Muhammad at the end of his final pilgrimage to Mecca and shortly before his death to more than

100,000 early Muslims was considered the Prophet's will to his companions and teaching the Ummah.

In its historical context, it was one of the earliest declarations of human rights in written history. Almost everything he said in this sermon was almost unheard of and inconceivable before Islam's arrival. The Prophet addressed some of the core universal values in a society where they were forgotten or nonexistent. Here is his sermon.

"O People, listen well to my words, for I do not know whether, after this year, I shall ever be among you again. Therefore, listen to what I am saying to you very carefully and take these words to those who could not be present here today.

THE SACREDNESS OF LIFE AND PROPERTY

O People, just as you regard this month, this day, this city as sacred, so you regard every Muslim's life and property as a sacred trust. Return the goods entrusted to you to their rightful owners. Treat others justly so that no one is unjust to you. Remember that you will indeed meet your LORD and that HE will indeed reckon your deeds.

FORBIDDANCE OF USURY

God has forbidden you to take usury (riba); therefore, all riba obligations shall henceforth be canceled. Your capital, however, is yours to keep. You will neither inflict nor suffer injustice. God has judged that there shall be no riba and that all the riba due to Abbas ibn Abd al Muttalib shall be waived.

[Abbas ibn Abd al Muttalib was the paternal uncle of the Prophet. He was a wealthy merchant and must have loaned money with interest.]

FORBIDDANCE OF VIOLENCE

Every right arising out of homicide and blood-killing in pre-Islamic days is henceforth waived, and the first such right I waive is that arising from the murder of Rabiah ibn al Harith ibn Abd al Muttalib.

[Rabiah ibn al Harith was the Prophet's first cousin. His son Adam was a small child caught in the battle crossfire. A Hudhayl man's rock hit and crushed his head. Rabiah intended to demand blood money or a counter-killing from the Hudhayl for his son's death. The Prophet waived this right to end the circle of violence.]

TAMPERING WITH THE NATURAL CALENDAR

O people, the unbelievers manipulate the calendar to make permissible what God forbids and forbid what God has permitted. With God, the months are 12 in number. Four of them are sacred, three occur consecutively, and one occurs only between the Jumada and Shaban months.

[The pre-Islamic Arabs used to arbitrarily add the thirteenth month in the third, sixth, and eighth years to make the lunar calendar stationary, thus roughly corresponding to the solar year.]

Beware of the devil for the sake of your religion. He has lost all hope that he will ever lead you astray in big things, so beware of following him in small things.

RIGHTS OF WOMEN

O People, it is true that you have certain rights over your women, but they also have rights over you. Remember that you took them as your wives only under God's trust and with His permission. If they abide by your rights, they have the right to be fed and clothed in kindness. Treat your women well and be kind to them, for they are your partners and committed helpers. It is your right that they do not make friends with anyone you disapprove of, nor should they be unchaste.

OBSERVE THE FIVE PILLARS OF ISLAM

O People, listen to me in earnest, worship God (The One Creator of the Universe), perform your five daily prayers (Salah), fast during Ramadan, and give your financial obligation (zakah) of your wealth. Perform the Hajj if you can afford it.

ALL HUMAN BEINGS ARE EQUAL EXCEPT FOR PIETY

Humanity comes from Adam and Eve. An Arab has no superiority over a non-Arab, nor a non-Arab has any superiority over an Arab; also, a white has no superiority over a black, nor a black has any superiority over a white except through piety and virtuous actions. Learn that every Muslim is a brother to every Muslim and that Muslims constitute one brotherhood. Nothing shall be legitimate to a Muslim that belongs to a fellow Muslim unless given freely and willingly. Do not, therefore, do injustice to yourselves.

DAY OF JUDGMENT

Remember, you will appear before God (The Creator) one day, and you will answer for your deeds. So beware, do not stray from the path of righteousness after I am deceased.

THE QURAN AND THE PROPHET'S EXAMPLE AS A GUIDE

O People, no prophet or messenger will come after me, and no new faith will be born. Reason well, therefore, O People, and understand the words I convey to you. I am leaving you with the Book of God (the Quran) and my Sunnah (the lifestyle and the Prophet's behavioral mode). If you follow them, you will never go astray. All those who listen to me shall pass on my words to others and again, and may the last ones understand my words better than those who listen to me directly. Be my witness, O God, that I have conveyed your message to your people.

CHAPTER 34
FAMOUS NON-MUSLIMS TRIBUTE TO THE PROPHET

THOMAS CARLYLE

Thomas Carlyle was a Scottish historian, satirical writer, essayist, translator, philosopher, mathematician, and teacher. Born: December 4, 1795, died February 5, 1881. In his essay "The Hero as Prophet," Thomas Carlyle described Prophet Muhammad's contribution in the following words.

A VERITABLE HERO

"Muhammad himself, after all that can be said about him, was not a sensual man. We shall err widely if we consider this man as a common voluptuary, intent mainly on base enjoyments, —nay on enjoyments of any kind. His household was of the most frugal; his common diet barley, bread and water: sometimes, for months, there was not a fire once lighted on his hearth. They record with just pride that he would mend his own shoes and patch his own cloak. A poor, hard-toiling, ill-provided man, careless of what vulgar men toil for. Not a bad man, I should say; something better in him than the hunger of any sort —or these wild Arab men, fighting and jostling three-and-twenty years at his hand, in close contact with him always, would not have reverenced him so! They were wild men, bursting ever and anon into quarrel, into all kinds of fierce sincerity; without right worth and manhood, no man could have commanded them. They called him Prophet, you say? Why, he stood there face to face with them; bare, not enshrined in any mystery; visibly clouting his own cloak, cobbling his own shoes; fighting, counselling, ordering amid them: they must have seen what kind of a man he was, let him be called what you like! No emperor with his tiaras was obeyed as this man in a cloak of his own clouting, during three-and-twenty years of rough actual trial. I find something of a veritable Hero necessary for that, of itself. Generous things are recorded of him: when he lost his daughter, the thing he answers is, in his own dialect, every way sincere, and yet equivalent to that of Christians, "The Lord giveth, and the Lord taketh away; blessed be the name of the Lord."

He answered in like manner of Zayd, his emancipated, well-beloved Slave, the second of the believers. Zayd had fallen in the War of Tabuk, the first of Muhammad's fightings with the Greeks. Muhammad said, it was well; Zayd had done his master's work, Zayd had now gone to his Master: it was all well with Zayd. Yet Zayd's daughter found him weeping over the body; —the old gray-haired man melting in tears! "What do I see?" said she. — "You see a friend weeping over his friend."

His last words are a prayer, broken ejaculations of a heart struggling up, in trembling hope, towards its Maker. We cannot say that his religion made him worse; it made him better, good, not bad. He went out for the last time into the mosque, two days before his death; asked, if he had injured any man. Let his own back bear the stripes. If he owed any man? A voice answered, "Yes, me three drachms," borrowed on such an occasion. Muhammad ordered them to be paid: "Better be in shame now," said he, "than at the Day of Judgment." Traits of that kind show us the genuine man, the brother of us all, brought visible through twelve centuries —the veritable Son of our common Mother.

"To the Arab Nation, it was as a birth from darkness into light; Arabia first became alive by means of it. A poor shepherd people, roaming unnoticed in its deserts since the creation of the world: a Hero-Prophet was sent down to them with a word they could believe: see the unnoticed becomes world-notable, the small has grown world-great; within one century afterward, Arabia is at Granada on this hand, at Delhi on that: - glancing in valor and splendor and the light of genius, Arabia shines through long ages over a great section of the world. Belief is great, life-giving. The history of a nation becomes fruitful, soul-elevating, and great so soon as it believes. These Arabs, the man Muhammad, and that one century - is it not as if a spark had fallen, one spark, on a world of what seemed black unnoticeable sand; but lo, the sand proves explosive powder, blazes heaven-high from Delhi to Grenada! I said, the Great Man was always as lightning out of Heaven; the rest of men waited for him like fuel, and then they too would flame."

PHILLIP HITTI

Phillip Hitti (1886–1978) was **born** in Lebanon and taught at Princeton University from 1926 to 1954. He was renowned for his contributions to Arab studies in the West.

During all the first part of the Middle Ages, no other people made as important a contribution to human progress as did the Arabs if we take this term to mean all those whose mother tongue was Arabic, and not merely those living in the Arabian Peninsula. For centuries, Arabic was the language of learning, culture, and intellectual progress for the whole of the civilized world except for the Far East. From the 9th to the 12th century, there were more philosophical, medical, historical, religious, astronomical, and geographical works written in Arabic than in any other human tongue.

KAREN ARMSTRONG

Karen Armstrong (born November 14, 1944) is a British author and commentator of Irish Catholic descent known for her books on comparative religion. A former Roman Catholic religious sister, she transitioned from a conservative to a more liberal and mystical Christian faith. Muhammad: A Prophet for Our Time, Book by Karen Armstrong:

"Muhammad had great spiritual as well as political gifts — the two do not always go together — and he was convinced that all religious people have a responsibility to create a good and just society. He could become darkly angry and implacable, but he could also be tender, compassionate, vulnerable, and immensely kind. We never read of Jesus laughing, but we often find Muhammad smiling and teasing the people who were closest to him. We see him playing with children, having trouble with his wives, weeping bitterly when a friend dies, and showing off his new baby son like any besotted father. If we could view Muhammad as we do any other important historical figure, we would surely consider him to be one of the greatest geniuses the world has known. To create a literary masterpiece, to found a major religion and a new world power are not ordinary achievements."

JOHANN WOLFGANG VON GOETHE

Johann Wolfgang von Goethe, born August 28, 1749, Frankfurt [Germany]—died March 22, 1832, German poet, playwright, novelist, scientist, statesman, theatre director, critic, and amateur artist. He is considered the greatest German literary figure of the modern era. As early as 1773, Goethe wrote a poem comparing the Prophet to a stream, which moves forward, always increasing, carrying his brothers with him to the eternal father.

NAPOLEON BONAPARTE

Napoleon Bonaparte was a French military and political leader. He rose to prominence during the French Revolution and led several successful campaigns during the Revolutionary Wars. As Napoleon I, he was Emperor of the French from 1804 until 1814. He said: "I hope the time is not far off when I shall be able to unite all the wise and educated men of all the countries and establish a uniform regime based on the principles of the Quran, which alone are true, and which alone can lead men to happiness."

SIR GEORGE BERNARD SHAW

Sir George Bernard Shaw was an Irish playwright, critic, polemicist, and political activist. His influence on Western theatre, culture, and politics extended from the 1880s to his death and beyond.

"I have always held the religion of Muhammad in high estimation because of its wonderful vitality. It is the only religion that appears to me to possess that assimilating capacity to the changing phase of existence, which can make itself appeal to every age. I have studied him - the wonderful man, and in my opinion, far from being an anti-Christ, he must be called the Savior of Humanity. I believe that if a man like him were to assume the dictatorship of the modern world, he would succeed in solving its problems in a way that would bring it much-needed peace and happiness. I have prophesied about the faith of Muhammad that it would be acceptable to the Europe of tomorrow as it is beginning to be acceptable to the Europe of today.

KONERU RAMAKRISHNA RAO

Koneru Ramakrishna Rao is a philosopher, psychologist, parapsychologist, educator, teacher, researcher, and administrator. The Government of India awarded him Padma Shri civilian honor in 2011.

"The personality of Muhammad it is most difficult to get into the whole truth of it. There is Muhammad, the Prophet. There is Muhammad the Warrior; Muhammad the Businessman; Muhammad the Statesman; Muhammad the Orator; Muhammad the Reformer; Muhammad the Refuge of Orphans; Muhammad the Protector of Slaves; Muhammad the Emancipator of Women; Muhammad the Judge; Muhammad the Saint."

WILLIAM MONTGOMERY WATT

William Montgomery Watt was a Scottish historian, academic, and Anglican priest. From 1964 to 1979, he was a Professor of Arabic and Islamic Studies at the University of Edinburgh.

"His readiness to undergo persecution for his beliefs, the high moral character of the men who believed in him & looked up to him as a leader, & the greatness of his ultimate achievement - all argue his fundamental integrity. To suppose Muhammad, an impostor, raises more problems than it solves. None of the great figures of history is so poorly appreciated in the West as Muhammad... Thus, not merely must we credit Muhammad with essential honesty & integrity of purpose."

DIWAN CHAND SHARMA

Diwan Chand Sharma was a member of the 1st Lok Sabha from Hoshiarpur in Punjab State, India. He was elected to the Lok Sabha four times: "Muhammad was the soul of kindness, & his influence was felt & never forgotten. Muhammad, peace & blessings be upon him, was a man with a noble mission, which was to unite humanity on the worship of One and Only One God and to teach them the way to honest and upright living based on the commands of God. He always described himself as, 'A Servant and Messenger of God' and so indeed every action of his proclaimed to be."

REFERENCES

1. Ahmed, Barakat, Muhammad and the Jews, a re-examination: Vikas publishing house, new Delhi, new Delhi, India. !979

2. Ali, Ameer, *A Short History of the Saracens*, Boston: Adamant Media Corporation, 2004

3. Ali, Ameer, *The Spirit of Islam*, Whitefish Montana: Kessinger Publishing, 2003

4. Armstrong, Karen, *Islam A Short History*, New York: Random House, 2002

5. Armstrong, Karen, *A History of God*, New York: Ballantine Books, 1993

6. Buchanan, Patrick, *The Death of the West*, New York: St. Martin's Griffin, 2002

7. Carlyle, Thomas, *The Hero as Prophet*, Seattle: CreateSpace Independent Publishing, 2011

8. Esposito, John L., *Islam the Straight Path*, Oxford University Press, 2010.

9. Haykal, Husein, *The Life of Muhammad*, American Trust Publications, 2005

10. Hitti, Philip K., *Islam A Way of Life*, South Bend Indiana, 1970

11. Holt, Lambton and Lewis, *The Cambridge History of Islam*, New York, 1970

12. Lewis, Bernard, *What Went Wrong?* New York: Harper Perennial, 2003

13. Parrinder, Geoffrey, *World's Religions*, New York, 1971

14. Radford, Mary F., "The Inheritance Rights of Women Under Jewish and Islamic Law," Boston College: 297 International and Comparative Law Review, volume 23, Issue 23; 2000

15. Smith, Huston, *The Religions of Man*, Chapter on Islam, pages 193–224, New York, 1964

16. Encyclopedia Britannica (2004): Islam, Shariah

17. The Reader's Digest Bible (1982)

18. The Holy Bible (authorized King James Version)

19. Allen, Jayne, Jefferson's Declaration of Independence, Origins, Philosophy and Theology, Lexington: University of Kentucky Press, 2000

20. Encyclopedia Britannica: Moses, Christianity, Jesus Christ, Synoptic Gospels, Constantine, Original Sin, Salvation, Saint Paul, Biblical literature, 2004

21. Mark D. Siljander, *A Deadly Misunderstanding-A Congressman's Quest to Bridge the Muslim-Christian Divide*, San Francisco: Harper One, 2008

WHAT IS DIFFERENT ABOUT THIS BOOK SERIES

TRADITIONAL ARRANGEMENT

The Quran is a unique book, and unlike most other books, it does not have a beginning, middle, or end. Topics or subject matter are not divided into categories. The traditional Quran is arranged according to the inner requirements of its message and not in the chronological order in which the individual passages were revealed.

The seemingly abrupt transition from subject to subject is also in accordance with the Quranic principle of deliberately interweaving moral exhortation with practical legislation. This is in accordance with the teaching that man's life—spiritual, physical, individual, and social—is one integral whole. Therefore, it requires simultaneous consideration of all its aspects if the concept of a good life is to be realized. The Quran, in its traditional form, was meant for common people to read daily in small installments and ponder. The role of **Tafsir**, or exegesis of the Quran, is verse-by-verse and sometimes word-by-word explanation or interpretation of the text.

The Quran, in its original format, is difficult to understand. Discussion of varying subjects within the same chapter, which seems disconnected and may cause confusion and misunderstanding. This is particularly relevant to those unfamiliar with the Quran's uniqueness. Due to the randomness of the subject matter, the Quran is vulnerable to misinterpretation. The Quran's core message is very consistent despite the randomness of the topics covered.

THE QURAN IN AN EASY-TO-UNDERSTAND FORMAT

(according to subject matter)

The author of this seven-volume series has rearranged *The Message of the Qur'an* by Muhammad Asad according to specific topics and subject matter. This approach to organize Quranic verses according to different topics is based on the central idea that the conclusions should not be drawn from isolated verses. This is a first-ever attempt to present the Quran in an easy-to-understand format—a revolutionary paradigm in understanding the Quran. For example, divorce is discussed in the Quran in Chapters 2, 33, 58, 60, and 65. Compiling all divorce verses in one place gives the reader a quick reference and comprehensive understanding. For scholars, lawyers, and anyone who needs to study a particular issue, it would be handy to have it arranged by subject matter.

www.ingramcontent.com/pod-product-compliance
Lightning Source LLC
Chambersburg PA
CBHW032039200426
43209CB00049B/48